Where Have All Our Cubs Gone?

Where Have All Our Cubs Gone?

GEORGE CASTLE

TAYLOR TRADE PUBLISHING
Dallas • Lanham • Boulder • New York • Toronto • Oxford

Published by Taylor Trade Publishing
An imprint of The Rowman & Littlefield Publishing Group, Inc.
4501 Forbes Boulevard, Suite 200
Lanham, MD 20706

Distributed by NATIONAL BOOK NETWORK

Library of Congress Cataloging-in-Publication Data

Castle, George.
   Where have all our Cubs gone? / George Castle.—1st Taylor Trade Publishing
ed.
      p. cm.
   Includes index.
   ISBN 1-58979-198-3 (cloth : alk. paper)
   1. Chicago Cubs (Baseball team)—Interviews.   2. Baseball players—United
States—Interviews.   I. Title. GV875.C6C295 2005
796.357′64′0977311—dc22

                                                                    2004022456

∞ ™ The paper used in this publication meets the minimum requirements of
American National Standard for Information Sciences—Permanence of Paper for
Printed Library Materials, ANSI/NISO Z39.48-1992.

Manufactured in the United States of America.

Contents

Foreword
John McDonough, Cubs Senior Vice President of Marketing and Broadcasting

A ny player who plays for the Chicago Cubs soon realizes he is part of a worldwide cultural phenomenon.

Here they are, on a team that hasn't won a World Series since 1908, and the home games are played primarily during the day. Many of our games are seen on TV by a national audience. Because they play for the Cubs, they are part of this one-of-a-kind love affair that our fans display every day.

I've talked to many players, and there's a wonderment that when you come to Wrigley Field, there's a strong chance you're going to be playing in front of capacity crowds. There's incredible acceptance. Very seldom do they boo a player. Many players who leave the Cubs organization by and large think of themselves as Cubs, first and foremost.

We want our players to come back here frequently, to have many back at Wrigley Field to sing in the seventh inning. We made a decision that we think that's a fun way to go. Even players such as Doug Dascenzo, who might not have had the most celebrated career of all time, feel good that they've played for the Cubs.

Since the early 1980s, we've tried to make that distinctive Cubs logo into a special brand, a twelve-months-a-year brand. It's more than just the team's playing for seven months, from the first of March to the end of October—hopefully—and then turning out the lights and giving way to the Bears, Bulls, and Blackhawks. We built that bridge through the Cubs Convention, which will be marking its twentieth anniversary in 2006, and which has given the fans the first chance in their lives to be around all of their childhood heroes. They have seen them in a social setting, giving them an opportu-

John McDonough (right) with Wrigley Field organist Gary Pressy. Author photo.

nity to celebrate their allegiance. I'm amazed to see the extreme reverence afforded Andy Pafko, Don Cardwell, and all the other players who come back for two or three days to the convention. They're treated like rock stars.

Players who performed for the Cubs in the 1980s and retired in the early 1990s realize that the spotlight hadn't been very warm for that many years. When they come back to Chicago for three days in the dead of winter, it makes them feel very much alive as a baseball figure again. Their profiles are heightened and so is their love affair for the Cubs. When they continue to get invited back to Wrigley Field during the season, it makes them feel like their career is dedicated to the Cubs. It's like a homecoming.

The common theme from those players, even though they're coming in during the cold weather, many from the Sunbelt, is that they've stepped into a collegiate atmosphere. We don't pay them to appear at the convention. They come back because they want to see their old teammates and they want to see what's happening with the organization.

The Yankees and Dodgers have been viewed as the traditional gold standard in recognizing the impact of their former players. But I feel the Cubs are in the same class with their relationship with their player alumni. Andy MacPhail, Jim Hendry, and Dusty Baker have moved mountains to improve the organization. Many players certainly want to come here and play for this regime, in

Wrigley Field. This is one of the elite franchises, not only in base-ball, but in all of professional sports. Wrigley Field is a big part of that, of course.

The current players observe the phenomenal fan adoration, and they realize they'll be branded the rest of their lives as Chicago Cubs. No matter how they perform, almost all players depart here in good stead and eventually want to return as alumni.

Being a Cub is a positive state of mind, and we're all better for that.

Acknowledgments

No book about the whereabouts of former Cubs could be accomplished without the help of the crew from the team's publications department, publishers of the monthly *Vine Line* magazine and the quarterly program magazine, on sale at Wrigley Field.

Editor Jim McArdle dropped his deadline dash on several occasions to help me look up many of my old columns and articles on former Cubs in publications going back to the mid-1980s. Jim also helped in supplementing my own phone list of old-time players with several numbers he obtained. Michael Huang and publications chief Lena McDonagh also are thanked for their assistance.

The very idea of the book originated in my trips through history that were midwived by McArdle predecessors Ed McGregor, Ernie Roth, and Jay Rand. Through all the changes of format and design that are inevitable with any publication, Roth and Rand kept my look back at ex-Cubs and their present-day lives going every month since 1992.

In gathering information and conducting some of the interviews, thanks must go out for everyday access at Wrigley Field and at the Cubs Convention to Sharon Pannozzo and her Cubs media relations staff: Samantha Newby, B. R. Koehnemann, and a bevy of energetic interns.

And an unexpected assist in helping arrange a photograph goes to, of all people, all-time former Cub Ryne Sandberg. When interviewee Shawon Dunston was slow to come out of the team lunchroom at HoHoKam Park in spring training 2004 for an agreed-to photo with old double-play partner Sandberg (and with game time fast approaching), Ryno fetched Dunston and the photo was completed.

The very concept of the Cubs Convention, at which former Cubs gather together to greet fans and relive old times, has been built up since its inception in 1986 by team-marketing maven John McDonough and staff. They have to be commended for concocting a program in which so many players can be interviewed in one place and at one time.

Of course, it took a great Cubs fan in the book publishing industry to understand the significance of access to the team's former players. That person was Jill Langford. She not only had shepherded my previous book, *The Million-to-One Team*—focusing on why the Cubs had not won a pennant since 1945—but also remembered my decade-long look at former players in the team's publications. Jill approached me in the spring of 2003 with the idea of *Where Have All Our Cubs Gone?* It may have been the easiest sell she ever made as an acquisitions editor. Jill should be justifiably proud of her idea come to fruition in these pages.

Finally, thanks must be given to photographer Chip Zellet, along with Paula Blaine and Lisa Levine of Profile Network for access to several of the former Cubs here, through published work in the past and Profile Network's annual Fans Choice Awards program in Chicago.

Introduction:
Once a Cub, Always a Cub

Y ou're marked for life.

But being an ex-Cub is no stigma. It's a badge of honor. It's more than likely that you put up with a lot while playing in Wrigley Field. And the fans will never forget you.

If you're a star, the fans will treat you like you never retired. If you were a slacker or scrubeenie, well, they'll still remember you, want your autograph, desire to talk about the good ol' days that may not have seemed such at the time. But the memory of those days grows more fond with each passing year.

In the end, there's no such thing as a lovable loser. The Cubs may have won less than any other team in existence in 1945, the date of their last pennant until the twenty-first century. And yet the hold the franchise has on their fans is unlike that of almost every other pro sports franchise in the country. Only followers of the Yankees, Dodgers, and perhaps the Red Sox have such an affinity for those who have worn their uniforms.

Not long after the start of my sports journalism career, I became fascinated with tracking down former Cubs. I'd revel in assignments that directed me to Glenn Beckert and George Altman as they worked in the trading pits in the Chicago Board of Trade, or Dick Selma, coaching out in Fresno, California, and remembering the tight hold on many fans of the 1969 Cubs for which he served as left-field bleacher-bums cheerleader.

Of course, you had to write about Mr. Cub if you were on the sports beat. The very first column I penned for Lerner Newspapers, a network of Chicago-neighborhood newspapers, in May 1980 took me to the Bank of Ravenswood's main office, about two miles northwest of Wrigley Field. In one of his many postbaseball incarnations, Ernie Banks was at this point a customer service trainee for the bank when he wasn't glad-handing on behalf of the Cubs.

I sat down with Banks at his desk in the middle of the bank lobby and talked of the good ol' days, then just a decade or so in the past. I began playing some vintage Cubs audio highlights on a cassette player. Banks called a colleague over to his desk, and he busied himself listening to Jack Brickhouse and Jim West call games. It was apparent that Banks set his own schedule and pace of work on one of many jobs he held, before he started working full-time as, well, Ernie Banks, by 1990 drawing a flat $15,000 fee per appearance. When Banks headlined a reunion of the 1969 Cubs twenty-three years later at Chicago's McCormick Place, he was the only one to get his full appearance fee. His ol' teammates all were stiffed by the suddenly cash-strapped promoter.

Banks often verbally dances around like Muhammad Ali in the ring when you want to talk to him, but he could be pinned down occasionally. On one occasion, I called the toll-free contact number connected with him, not too hopeful of a response about the Cubs–Cardinals rivalry. But about a week later, an incoming call with the voice on the other end serenaded me with "Meet Me in St. Louis." At first I couldn't figure out the identity of the crooner. "Don't you know who this is?" he protested. I then figured out it was Mr. Cub, goofing around on my time.

I got some "A" material another time from Banks about the place he called the "Friendly Confines," in which he always suggested, "Let's play two."

"I used to try to figure it out when I played," he said of the special bond between Cubs players and fans. "What is it about playing in Wrigley Field that's different than most parks? If you do love the game, fans can see that. If you do not love it, fans can see it, too.

"If you're into it, they're all behind you. It's a remarkable place to play baseball."

Banks was gracious about Sammy Sosa's passing up all his Cubs career offensive records.

"I have no problem with that," he said. "I really like to see people reach goals, move on, go to high levels and high standards. That's what Sammy has done here. There will be standards that he will set throughout his career."

But he set them in a more pressurized atmosphere than Banks did.

"For me, Hank [Aaron], Willie [Mays] and the guys who played at that time, if we were out of the race, you didn't have that extra incentive to play hard. You played hard but not hard enough. Now, everything counts, everything means a lot and they rise to the occasion."

Banks is also the quintessential eternal Cub, but I discovered many others weren't all that far behind him when I began writing regularly in 1987 for the Cubs' publications department, putting out the monthly newspaper *Vine Line* and the team program magazine. A succession of editors allowed me to develop a specialty in catching up with former Cubs. I would truly begin a journey through the history of a storied franchise.

At first it was the occasional feature. One of the early efforts tracked down a real character. Bill Faul was a right-handed pitcher in 1965–1966, usually working the second game of doubleheaders, who used to hypnotize himself before his starts. Faul would put on a record while he reclined on the trainer's table. The record would implore the listener to throw the pitch "low-w-w and away . . . low-w-w and away." Faul, of course, delved into hypnosis well before his time in the game and eventually wound up on one of Leo Durocher's trucks, backing up to Triple-A Tacoma.

In 1988, I found Faul still teaching hypnosis in Pleasant Plain, Ohio, not far from Cincinnati. He was still avant-garde, for baseball or any other walk of life. Faul claimed each of us had a little "sun" in the middle of our bodies, radiating joy and positive energy. Even as hypnosis found legitimacy in the budding sports psychology field in the 1990s, Faul was never hired by any big-league organization. He died at sixty-two in 2002.

The appeal of former Cubs led to the debut of an "alumni club"–style column at the beginning of 1992. I quickly proceeded to contact some obvious names. My favorites became the old old-timers of the Cubs' every-three-years pennant winners of the 1930s.

As I scoured the country and beyond for former Cubs, I was able to track down second baseman Billy Herman, shortstop Billy Jurges, and third baseman Woody English, all of whom at their defensive positions had the best view in the house of Babe Ruth's supposedly pointing to the bleachers to call his shot in the 1932

World Series at Wrigley Field. To a man, Herman, Jurges, and English insisted Ruth was merely pointing and jabbering at the Cubs' third-base dugout, the inhabitants of which were taunting the Bambino. To prove their point, in 1993, a home movie surfaced showing Ruth most likely pointed at the dugout, not the crowd. The existence of the film came too late, though, to back up Herman's assertion. He died in 1992, while Jurges passed away in 1997.

English quickly became my favorite old-timer. In addition to print interviews, I invited him on my weekly baseball radio show, now called *Diamond Gems,* to link up via phone from his Newark, Ohio, home with fellow all-time Cubs Billy Williams and Glenn Beckert, both of whom were in the studio. English was thrilled to talk to the 1960s Cubs. The stories English told could have filled four or five hours of live radio.

He lived like a king on a $15,000 annual Cubs salary in the Depression, paying off his parents' home and driving around a luxury car. English was no fan of some special music Cubs owner Phil Wrigley commissioned to waft over Catalina Island, where the team held spring training. English did not believe Wrigley knew anything about baseball.

In the years after he left the Cubs in 1936, English—a shortstop and leadoff man in front of slugger Hack Wilson in 1930, when the latter drove in a record 191 runs—would manage in the women's professional baseball league in Michigan and run a little nightspot in Chicago's Edgewater neighborhood, twenty blocks north of Wrigley Field.

English had two favorite contemporary players. One was master bunter Brett Butler, whom English liked because he played the little man's game in which English himself had specialized. The other became a close and cherished friend—utility player Rex Hudler.

Now an Anaheim Angels announcer, Hudler met English in 1984 at a local department store in Newark, also the hometown of Hudler's wife.

"Here was a gentleman with a hat and coat on, looking real respectful," he said. "He was a little guy. I was very attracted to his humbleness. I fell in love with Woody English, the human being and the ex-baseball player, the way he exuded humility.

"Finally he invited me to come over to his house. He lived in a small, small place. He drove a Pinto. He had all this memorabilia on the wall. He told me stories about each picture. I asked him, 'Do you mind if I bring my video camera over here? I want this for my children.' "

Whenever Hudler came to Newark, he'd seek out English, buying him groceries and other necessities. One day he told English he wanted to buy him a new car. "What do you like, a Ford?" Hudler asked him. But the proud English declined, insisting he loved his Pinto. Hudler still would slip him $100 here or there without telling him about it.

"Then I brought these batting gloves I wore with the Cardinals," Hudler said "He said, 'Rex, wow, what are these, how do these work?' I said we wear them to hit and run bases so we don't cut our fingers up. We compared [fielding] gloves. I was like a little kid."

English was proud he could still drive at age ninety in 1997. But Hudler got some tough news on the last Friday of the regular season that year. English had died.

"The final game of the season was on Sunday," Hudler said. "I'm with the Phillies. Woody's family asked me when I could make it to the funeral. I said 'Monday, the season's over. Can you possibly wait 'til Monday?' They said they would, and could I possibly eulogize him? Monday I showed up in the best suit I ever owned. I extolled everything Woody ever did—love, joy, passing the game on.

"I asked the family if it was all right if I put one of my baseball cards in his casket. It was a tremendous honor for me."

English would have figured Hudler's image was only a calling card.

"He told me one of the greatest compliments: 'Rex, when we get to heaven, we're going to have twenty-one-year-old bodies, and I'll let you in with Rogers Hornsby. You and him can alternate, and we'll turn double plays together.' He was talking about some of the greatest players of all time. I'll always cherish that."

English willed Hudler his permanent big-league pass, which former players received after eight years' service in the majors.

The radio show, done live in its first year on the air in 1994, provided an opportunity to reunite teammates or otherwise link them up with longtime fans. One such grouping had 1945 pennant-winning mainstays Phil Cavarretta from Villa Rica, Georgia, and

Andy Pafko from Mount Prospect, Illinois, on the phone with then Buffalo Bills coach Marv Levy. Why? Native Chicagoan Levy was a lifelong Cubs fan and was a young serviceman who waited in line to get into the '45 World Series to see Cavvy and Handy Andy. The mutual admiration between two old warriors and one of their fans, fresh from four straight Super Bowls, lightened up the darkening clouds of the coming strike.

Later interviews with Cavarretta revealed how much he felt for Cubs fans, waiting since '45.

"The fans in Chicago are the best," he said in 1999. "They deserve a winner. They lose, and lose, and the ballpark is still packed."

Also reunited on the air was the 1953–1954 outfield of left fielder Ralph Kiner, center fielder Frankie Baumholtz, and right fielder Hank Sauer. The legend had been embellished through the years that the slow Kiner and Sauer (whose natural position was left until he had to accommodate Kiner's arrival) always would call to the speedy Baumholtz on a fly ball in the gap, "Frankie you take it." Baumholtz had a good laugh but insisted his outfield mates never made that plea. Baumholtz died in 1997, while Sauer, the onetime "Mayor of Wrigley Field" and longtime scout with the Giants, dropped dead in 2001 on the golf course enjoying a favorite pastime. Senior citizen Kiner soldiered on as a Mets broadcaster.

One more *Diamond Gems* took place in the wake of Ken Burns's *Baseball* series on PBS in the fall of 1994. Longtime Cubs scout and coach Buck O'Neil, a prominent interviewee on the Burns programs, talked with former Cubs second baseman Gene Baker live. Baker had played for O'Neil on the Negro League Kansas City Monarchs, then was the first African American to be signed by the Cubs organization in 1950. But Baker, a shortstop, languished at Triple-A Los Angeles for the better part of four seasons. The Cubs refused to bring him up, while lesser lights manned shortstop at Wrigley Field.

Baker finally came up when another O'Neil Monarchs protégé, Ernie Banks, was signed in September 1953. Baker moved to second while he and shortstop Banks served as road roommates, a requirement for the Cubs in having any African Americans on the roster.

"The whole thing was they were just not ready at the top," Baker theorized on the radio. "There were a lot of clubs at the time that didn't have any black ballplayers. They were waiting and waiting as long as they could.

"I think the frustration was not so much as to who was playing for the Cubs. It was, fine, if they didn't want me, there were other teams that did. But they wouldn't sell me, either. They just kept me there."

After leaving the Monarchs in 1955, O'Neil scouted African American players for the Cubs, eventually signing the likes of George Altman, Lou Brock, Lou Johnson, Lee Smith, Oscar Gamble, and Joe Carter. He became the first African American coach in the majors in 1962, but management ensured he would not run the Cubs as part of the wacky rotating-coaches system of the day. O'Neil was probably more qualified to manage the Cubs than head coach Charlie Metro or any of the other coaches.

"I knew I was capable of managing in the major leagues, especially with the Cubs," O'Neil said. "I knew the Cubs system as well as anyone there. How could I have been too soon when I helped Gene Baker, Ernie Banks, and so many ballplayers that made good in the majors and in life? It was just a way of life and we changed it quite a bit. I can't be bitter or say I was too soon. I was just on time."

Baker went on to coach and manage in the Pittsburgh Pirates organization. He died in 1999. O'Neil parlayed his national TV exposure into elder-statesman's status, even into his 90s, for baseball, becoming the living symbol of the Negro League museum in Kansas City.

Brock, one of O'Neil's prize signees, is of course the centerpiece of the worst trade in Cubs history. O'Neil did not realize that Brock had another talent not shown on the diamond: elusiveness. The Hall of Fame base stealer is as pleasant a man as exists in the game when you meet him one on one. But he's phone-ophobic. Brock simply will not pick up a phone to return a call.

Attempts to reach him in early 2004, even with the St. Louis Cardinals' help, were unsuccessful. Brock would not punch up a number even when he was twenty feet away from the phone at the Cards' spring camp in Jupiter, Florida. The Cards themselves— George Altman, his best friend with the Cubs in 1962, who now lives one suburb away in the St. Louis area; and Bing Devine, the

St. Louis GM who traded for him in 1964—all have had difficulty getting Brock to respond to calls.

The one time Brock did call back was through the intercession of his son, Lou Jr., in 1992. Once captured, though, the "base burglar," as a Cards official euphemistically calls him, can give you an earful.

Brock originally came up with the Cubs at the end of the 1961 season. A Richard Dozer story in the *Chicago Tribune* at the time queried Cubs officials, who projected Brock and fellow rookie Kenny Hubbs would spend one more year in the minors and come up in 1963. But Brock and Hubbs played their way onto the Cubs in spring training 1962. Almost immediately, Brock was jerked in and out of the lineup, the raw rookie vulnerable to good left-handed pitching. But the real problem for his stumbling around in a Cubs uniform did not take hold 'til 1963.

"I had started in center [as a rookie], but the next year I was in right field," Brock said in '92. "I was ready to play center, and all of a sudden I had to learn to play right, which is the difficult sun field at Wrigley Field. . . . I was not trained on how to flip the sunglasses at the right time. We had played practically all night games in the minors, and it wasn't an issue there. Then I was in the greatest sun field in the majors. It was trial and error."

Indeed, in one April 1963 game, Brock messed up two seventh-inning fly balls against the Phillies, drawing the Wrigley Field fans' boos. After the game, head coach Bob Kennedy took Brock back out to right field, hitting him fungoes—and Brock still lost the balls in the late-afternoon sun.

Brock's "heavy swing," in the words of Devine, also threw off the rotating coaches of the time. In his first at bat during the Cubs' home opener in 1962, he belted a Ray Washburn pitch all the way onto Sheffield Avenue. Several other bombs, including a near five-hundred-footer in '62 in center, showed he had tremendous power potential, yet his true calling was with his legs. All throughout his Cardinals career, according to Devine, Brock swung like a power hitter. Fortunately, he connected enough, for 3,023 hits.

"I didn't swing like a leadoff hitter," Brock said.

Brock, who attended Southern University, also worked a long time outside baseball. In the off-season of 1962–1963, he sold heating oil "cold turkey," door to door, in Chicago for the Humble Oil

Company. But Brock said he made lifelong friends from those sales pitches, which preceded a number of business ventures outside baseball.

He opened a florist shop in St. Louis in 1968, had a short-term interest in an auto dealership, and then tried to market the Broccabrella, an umbrella worn atop the head, in the 1970s. I saw Brock promoting the headgear at a Walgreen's in Norridge, Illinois, on a Saturday night after a Cubs–Cardinals game at Wrigley Field in 1978.

The Cubs' left-field bleacher bums inspired the Broccabrella.

"The fans threw stuff at opposing players," he said. "One of the things that tempered them was some guy walking into the stadium with an umbrella on his head. I wanted one for pregame practice to wear in front of the fans to disarm them. I had to buy twelve hundred of them. So Al Hrabosky and I put those things on and walked out to left field. Mission accomplished, but I still had 1,198 of those umbrellas."

Brock made a few bucks on the Broccabrellas after Dave Kingman and Manny Trillo promoted them as Cubs and the University of Wisconsin cheerleaders wore them on TV. He also dabbled in distribution of other retail products. Each spring, Brock does some instruction for the Cardinals in camp. In 1998, he bemoaned the onset of newer but smaller ballparks that cut down on his old art of stealing bases. Such a skill, though, can still be taught if the player is open-minded.

"If [a player] can run, you can teach him the fundamentals," Brock said. "You can teach him how to read the pitchers, then teach him the jump, teach him the lead and then the run. Those are the four primary areas."

Brock now helps his wife in her ministry. During a Cubs–Cardinals game in 2004, the Brocks were spotted in the Wrigley Field box seats. No word if they had any cell phones handy.

At least Brock is spotted at public events now and then. The truly elusive former Cub is Don Young, the controversial 1969 center fielder. Rick Talley could not track down Young when he contacted all the players for his 1989 book *The Cubs of '69*.

But three years after Talley's book was published, Young was there in the flesh in a reunion of the '69 Cubs in Chicago. Choosing not to say much even then, Young revealed that he was a kind of roustabout in Colorado, working in the construction of the new Denver airport. Young and Ron Santo had long put their midseason '69 conflict behind them. Santo was never as warmly welcomed at Wrigley Field in his playing career afterward, following comments perceived as critical of Young, who goofed up two ninth-inning fly balls to lose a game to the Mets at Shea Stadium. Young wasn't even well-paid for being in the eye of the storm then. He was paid $12,000 in '69.

Young could make some money that he didn't earn in the majors if he decided to attend card shows. Several memorabilia experts said his autograph would be highly in demand due to his near-hermit status.

If the trade of Brock robbed the Cubs of their speed later in the 1960s, a deal that dispatched Andre Thornton cut down on their power production in the latter half of the 1970s. Even though he impressed at first base in 1974 and 1975, Thornton was foolishly dealt away to Montreal in early 1976 for pitcher Steve Renko and outfielder–first baseman Larry Biittner. Thornton landed in Cleveland, where he found a home on and off the field.

By the 1990's, Thornton had established his own consulting firm, helping companies improve their images. "Treat others with uncompromising truth" and "mentor unselfishly" were some of Thornton's corporate words to live by.

"For years, we thought that all business needed was the management-by-objective philosophy," Thornton said. "It doesn't matter how things get done—just get it done. But it *does* matter." If only Enron and a slew of other companies had listened to him.

He applied his management analysis to his Cubs days.

"The Cubs were an organization going through restructuring and changes," Thornton said. "We did have some good young players, some good young pitchers included, but it might not have been the best atmosphere for them to develop. There was no vision at that point as to where the Cubs were going."

Thornton had been traded to the Cubs from the Atlanta Braves for Joe Pepitone in 1973. "Pepi" seemed the same old character at a sports memorabilia show in 2002. He stepped right out of the 1970s with modishly long hair, probably purchased, and a charcoal grey suit and turtleneck shirt. The Brooklyn boy worked as a glad-hander for Yankees owner George Steinbrenner with sponsors and VIPs at Yankee Stadium.

As a Cub, Pepitone was the first player to bring a hair dryer to the clubhouse. He'd arrive at the ballpark on a big hog of a motorcycle, rubbing sleep out of his eyes after some enthusiastic night-crawling and socializing.

"I had three years [in Chicago] and loved every minute of it," he said. "We loosened the ballclub up a little bit."

Pepitone probably did not frequent the kind of neighborhood pubs where you would have found several ex-Cubs in recent years in eastern Pennsylvania and New Jersey. Ol' outfielder Johnny Callison and Mitch "Wild Thing" Williams took turns as bartenders at different establishments. Williams also had a multiyear run as manager of an independent minor-league team in Atlantic City.

Vying with Pepitone as a clothes fiend was outfielder Dwight Smith. Smitty still lights it up in the sartorial league when he attends the Cubs Convention each January. He even tried minor-league hitting instruction with the Tampa Bay Devil Rays, a stint that ended after the 2003 season. He could be a professional national anthem singer, a talent he once displayed before a 1989 game at Wrigley Field.

Enjoying a longer tenure in the minors is Leon "Bull" Durham, closer to his native Cincinnati now as a coach for the Triple-A Toledo Mud Hens, the Detroit Tigers' top farm club. Durham formerly had to go cross-continent to work as a coach at Triple-A Vancouver. The former slugging first baseman still has a goal of coming back to coach in the majors.

Durham was part of a close-knit team in 1984. But two ex-Cubs took the definition of a team as a "family" literally about a decade back. Ace sinker-baller Rick Reuschel and outfielder Scot Thompson became fast friends on the 1979 Cubs. Years later, after Reuschel had moved to Pittsburgh, he began dating Thompson's sister, Barbara. The two later married. Now in-laws Reuschel and Thompson live near each other in a Pittsburgh suburb.

Reuschel and brother Paul were among three sets of brothers to play for the Cubs in the 1970s. First baseman Hal Breeden and catcher Danny Breeden played cameo roles in 1971. The Tyrone brothers, Jim and Wayne, had stints in the outfield from 1972 to 1976, although they never played on the Cubs together. The Ty-

Dwight Smith. Author photo.

rones held a number of jobs, such as selling cars, delivering for FedEx and working for a veterinarian after their careers before settling on baseball instruction in their native Texas.

You can easily reach Bill Hands, the baseball writers' choice as Chicago Player of the Year in 1969 for his 20–14 season, at his home at the eastern end of Long Island. Hands operated a fuel-oil company when he wasn't taking advantage of the locally fine fishing before he retired. But you won't find him stalking his old team when they come through Shea Stadium; it's a one-hundred-mile drive through heavy traffic.

Down in the Caribbean, ol' lefty reliever Willie Hernandez ran a construction business in his native Puerto Rico for years until selling it in 2002. He wanted to get back into baseball. And in his hometown of Nassau, the Bahamas, former shortstop Andre Rodgers ran a sporting goods store and dabbled in real estate before retiring to the golf course.

Hernandez bullpen mate Bruce Sutter baffled hitters with devilish split-fingered fastball that made him perhaps the trickiest relief pitcher of modern times starting out in 1976. He won the Cy Young Award in 1979. But more recently, Sutter shies away from most interviews. A resident of suburban Kennesaw near Atlanta, he prefers to go on long hunting expeditions, in both the nearby piney woods and overseas. But when he was around town, he had a positive effect on the Cubs' present. Sutter's son, Ben, and Cubs center fielder Corey Patterson were best friends. Patterson was able to get extra hitting in at Sutter's batting cage.

Patterson and the younger Sutter played baseball together, helping capture the 1998 Georgia state title for Harrison High School in Kennesaw. Pops Sutter helped spearhead fund-raising for a new baseball field at the school, making it one of the best in the state.

"It was all privately funded, and we had to raise a lot of money doing a lot of golf tournaments and other events," Sutter said back in early 2000.

Sutter's scouting report on Patterson, then just a first-year minor-leaguer at the time: "He's got the right attitude. If he strikes out four times or hits four homers, he's going to be the same when he walks off the field. He's going to be a special player." .

Sutter was a special reliever who still possessed the best split-fingered fastball of modern times. He was let go through Greg Maddux–style management bungling, but he harbored no ill feelings toward his old team. And he was not upset that his logical induction to the Hall of Fame was dragging out over the years.

Ex-Cubs relievers maintained the faith of their convictions long after retirement. One-time closer Lindy McDaniel, who had a 13–7 record with twenty-two saves in 1963, maintained the ministry that he began as a pitcher. When he wasn't serving as a Church of Christ preacher, he was behind the plow at his farm near Hollis, Oklahoma.

"I have a whole series [of sermons] based on sports," McDaniel said. "I deal with the emotions of a Christian that relate a lot to my background in baseball. I preach that unless people are emotionally involved in what they're doing, they won't live up to their potential. In baseball, when you cross the white line, you're emotionally involved.

"I'm not a yeller and a shouter," he said of his sermonizing style. "I preach what will do the most good [for the congregation] at a particular time. The Bible is so full of sermon ideas."

McDaniel had to possess a lot of faith in his greatest Cubs moment on June 7, 1963. Executing a cleverly rehearsed play, McDaniel picked off Willie Mays at second with the bases loaded and one out in a 2–2 game in the top of the tenth at Wrigley Field. Then McDaniel struck out Ed Bailey on three pitches. When he led off the bottom of the inning, McDaniel slugged a game-winning homer, one of only three in his twenty-year career.

Unlike many former big leaguers whose memories of their feats can be inaccurate or foggy, McDaniel had a steel-trap mind. He recalled that in his downer 1–7 season in 1964, two losses stemmed from broken-bat hits while two others were caused by bad hops over infielders' heads.

Randy Myers also could handle a heavy workload in relief. Still holder of the Cubs record for saves with fifty-three in 1993, Myers suddenly showed up in the Wrigley Field press box ten years later, on a side trip from a family gathering in the area. Hobnobbing with the media seemed unusual for Myers, not unfriendly but slow in talking after games due to his rigorous workout schedule. Myers, a longtime resident of Vancouver, Washington, still claimed he could throw up to ninety miles per hour, but shoulder surgery finally ended his career.

Former lefty reliever Bill Henry, who teamed with the late Don Elston to make up an effective bullpen in 1958–1959, landed as a dispatcher for two mooring companies that handled huge cargo ships in the Houston Ship Channel. The work of Henry and Elston was so impressive that baseball writer Jerome Holtzman began a campaign to make the save an official statistic, which finally took place in 1969. Baseball was changed as a result.

Phil Regan had seventeen saves for the Cubs in 1969. But through a number of gigs—Cubs pitching coach (1997–1998), Baltimore Orioles manager when Cal Ripken Jr. set the new iron man record in 1995, minor-league manager in his native Grand Rapids—Regan never admitted he threw the spitter. "I don't talk off the record," he said. So what was that pitch that broke so sharply and caused the umpires to practically strip-search him on the mound one day in 1968? "Sinkers," Regan replied with a straight face.

Regan's 1969 submarining bullpen teammate was Ted Abernathy, who settled into a landscaping business in Gastonia, North Carolina. In an earlier Cubs stint in 1965, Abernathy set the games-pitched record of eighty-four. "I warmed up in thirty-seven more that I didn't get in," he said. "But I had the arm where I could pitch every day. I could pitch three, four days in a row, rest a day and come right back."

Abernathy pitched before and after the brief flowering of reliever Chuck "Twiggy" Hartenstein in 1967. After working as an advance scout for the Anaheim Angels, Hartenstein retired to Austin, Texas.

Footnote Cubs kind of stayed that way—low profile. Jimmy Qualls, one of nine center fielders in 1969 along with the elusive Young, moved to a western part of Illinois nicknamed "Forgottonia" for its rural, remote status in relation to Chicago. Qualls managed Hancock Service, a fertilizer, chemical, and seed company in West Point, Illinois, twenty-five miles northeast of Quincy and the home stomping grounds of the Reuschel brothers, Rick and Paul.

Living on a twelve-acre lot "right out in the middle of the boonies," Qualls and his family raised a few chickens. The quietude enabled him to time-trip back to July 9, 1969, at Shea Stadium, when he broke up Tom Seaver's perfect game with a one-out single in the ninth.

"It was a fastball right down the middle," Qualls said. "He laid it right in there. I was nervous. When I got to first, I was shaking so much. Everyone was booing me."

A month earlier, Qualls did the most famous somersault in Cubs history. At Cincinnati's Crosley Field, he tried to score by doing a flip over Reds catcher Pat Corralaes. Qualls missed the plate while Corrales missed the tag. Both reversed course in a mad scramble back to the plate, with Qualls winning by putting his hand in before the tag.

"I landed on my back," Qualls said. "As I went up, he [Corrales] caught my leg and flipped me on my back. I just turned over and got to the plate, bam-bam, ahead of him."

Another footnote Cub with a distinctive name and parentage was Pete LaCock. A backup outfielder–first baseman from 1972 to 1976, LaCock was the son of *Hollywood Squares* host Peter Marshall. He did not follow Dad into show business, though.

"I'm kind of a 'homebody,'" LaCock said. "I want some place to call home. My dad was gone the whole time. He did all sorts of things. At first I resented it, but then I realized that was his job. I'm so proud of him. Because of him, I could have [pursued an entertainment career], but it didn't interest me. I liked the challenge of sports."

And he still liked athletic challenges after his baseball career ended. An Overland Park, Kansas, resident, LaCock ran triathlons, the endurance test combining a ten-mile run, a fifty-six-mile bike ride, and a 1.5-mile swim. Otherwise, he dialed down to run marathons to raise money for leukemia research as executive director of the Leukemia Society of America's Mid-America Chapter. And he found time to help run a hitting academy.

LaCock was always a freer spirit than most. As a rookie in 1972, walking down Michigan Avenue, he spotted the Wrigley Building and decided to call upon Cubs owner Phil Wrigley. Admitted to his office, LaCock learned that Wrigley slipped into the left-field bleachers disguised as a senior citizen fan to surreptitiously watch games. Also desiring to practice yoga on the field with teammates Bob Locker and Bill Bonham, LaCock was told by Wrigley's lieutenants to perform what they thought were radical exercises out of sight from the fans.

Meanwhile, Steve Lake, a backup catcher in two stints (1983–1986 and 1993), went to the birds, literally, after his playing days ended. Lake and wife Patti maintained forty breeding pairs of large parrots in a nineteen-hundred-square-foot bird shed near Phoenix. Included in the menagerie were several pairs of giant hyacinth macaws; hand-fed babies sold for $6,500 and up. The Lakes had a five-person waiting list for the hyacinths.

"You can't explain it," Lake said when he doubled as a Phillies minor-league instructor. "One thing leads to another." He even produced a baseball card with himself and one of his cockatoos.

The parrots supervised an additional Lake animal collection of ten head of cattle, six horses, five exotic tortoises, four dogs, and a goat.

The Cubs had their own Frank Thomas, and he was almost as strong as the South Sider's Big Hurt. The elder Frank Thomas spent a season-plus shuttling in and out of the lineup in 1960 and into 1961. In retirement in Pittsburgh after working as a classroom rep for the ICM School of Business, Thomas found himself fielding autograph requests for the other Thomas.

"I get fifteen to twenty cards a week for Frank Thomas to sign," he said of his White Sox namesake. "His address isn't in the book [used by autograph seekers]; I write back and say it's not me."

Another distinctive Cubs name was "Handsome Ransom" Jackson. Randy Jackson was a pretty fair third baseman from 1950 to 1955 and then again in 1959. Going into the insurance business after his last Cubs season, Jackson retired to his longtime home in Athens, Georgia.

Jackson confirmed that Cubs players of his day got signals of upcoming pitches from an operative in the famed Wrigley Field center-field scoreboard.

"One of the guys would stick a foot out [of an open numbers slot]," he said. "One foot was for a curveball, two feet was a fastball. It just was for a few months. Milwaukee claimed we cheated, so they sent someone up into the scoreboard."

Authoring the most famous manager's tirade of modern times, Lee Elia did not lose out on his baseball career long term. Although the classy baseball lifer was fired four months after his expletive-deleted rant about Cubs fans early in 1983, the one-time Cubs utility infielder went on to manage the Phillies and later was a trusted top coach for Lou Piniella in both Seattle and Tampa Bay.

"I want to stay in the game until the Lord takes me," Elia said. "Baseball's my life."

That passion came out in the most memorable way when, in between profanities, Elia bellowed into Les Grobstein's whirring tape recorder, "Eighty-five percent of the world is working, but the 15 percent who come out here to Wrigley Field have nothing better to do than heap abuse and criticism on the team. Why don't they go out and look for jobs?"

For the record, Elia said those comments were never directed at Cubs fans in general—just a drunken few who were physically and verbally abusing his players after another tough loss.

"My sadness is, the tirade was something that made the papers and the airwaves and should have stayed in the locker room," Elia said. "It wasn't the way it came out, if that makes sense. . . . That's the inexperience of my first [managerial] job at the major-league level. I was too aggressive, too young in my first tenure."

Still another former manager, Jim Lefebvre, returned to coaching hitters before and after a short stint as Milwaukee Brewers manager at the end of the 1998 season. Most recently, Lefebvre was trying to establish links to the nascent baseball program in mainland China, which was thought by some to be a potential source of future talent.

Jim Marshall, manager from 1974 to 1976 (and a Cubs player in 1958–1959), landed as U.S. scout for the Orix Blue Wave of the Japanese Pacific League. Marshall had played in Japan, so he knew the lay of the land. But he also had some unfinished business from 1976. He disagreed with the remembrance of former Cubs GM Salty Saltwell that he orchestrated the trade of budding slugger Andre Thornton to the Montreal Expos, a year before Thornton became a first-base star with the Cleveland Indians.

Completing a trifecta of former Cubs with strong connections to the Far East, former pitcher Jim Colborn served a spell as Pacific Rim coordinator for the Seattle Mariners before he landed as Los Angeles Dodgers' pitching coach. Colborn's memory of how Leo Durocher handled young Cubs pitchers like himself in 1969–1971? "We were like puppies who were being whipped," he said.

Sometimes you don't give up the ghost of playing too easily. Catcher Rick Wilkins, who slugged thirty homers and batted .303 for the 1993 Cubs, hung on through injuries to still play in the Northern League with the Joliet (Illinois) Jackhammers in 2003. "The simple fact is I love to play baseball," Wilkins said then. "I still have skills, bat speed, foot speed, and arm strength to help a club out."

Even older was former outfielder Mel Hall, helping out Ray Burris with hitting instruction at his Fort Worth sports academy in 2001. Hall thought he could still hit. Like Wilkins, he turned to the independent minor leagues as a last-chance outlet. Hall was last spotted as the designated hitter for manager Les Lancaster, another former Cub, for the Corpus Christi (Texas) team in 2003.

Being a center fielder must breed a desire for privacy. Joining Don Young on the elusiveness beat were the likes of Adolfo Phillips, "Tarzan Joe" Wallis, Brock Davis, and Cleo James. The last started in left field in place of Billy Williams when the iron man Cub ended his streak of 1,117 consecutive games played.

But no matter where you end up, no matter how low or high your profile is, you remain a Cub forever. There are far worse things to be called. And when the Cubs finally put together their dynasty, you'll be the toast of your town because you once wore the blue pinstripes. It's a lifetime appointment.

Dawson's Still Awesome at Fifty

Whenever Andre Dawson steps onto Wrigley Field, you're automatically drawn to him. Nothing's changed since the days he was "Awesome Dawson," a player of utterly regal bearing who was enveloped in a city's love simply by doing what he was paid to do.

If there was a rating on character, Dawson would have been eleven on a ten scale. He was old old-school. His word—and he rationed his verbiage like few other big leaguers—was his bond. Longtime Cubs-clubhouse generalissimo Yosh Kawano worked for half a century in the locker room, rating Dawson the best man he ever had over the hundreds and hundreds of Cubs he shepherded.

Now Dawson, still lean but physically imposing at fifty, makes sure he comes into Chicago on the annual visit of the Florida Marlins, for whom he works as a special assistant to president David Samson. He'll invent other reasons to come back to a city he adopted—and which adopted him. And whenever he alights in Chicago, whether at the ballpark or some special off-the-field event, he's swarmed. The city has never forgotten Dawson, and vice versa.

"Chicago is like a second home for me," said Dawson as he laid down his fungo bat and sat in the visitor's dugout. Seeing him there seems doubly strange, beyond the fact that he's not wearing a Cubs uniform. You just can't get used to the idea of Dawson the coach or instructor, lobbing balls into the air instead of swinging his bat like a lethal toothpick. Time stops for nobody, so Dawson is nearly a decade past his last swing in anger.

But the erstwhile Second City is timeless for him.

"I do have a lot of ties, a lot of friends here," he said. "I always look for a lot of situations to get back to the city. I can't really just sit here and say what this city did for me. It was phenomenal. Had

*Andre Dawson and long-time clubhouse man Yosh Kawano at Wrigley
Field, September 10, 2004. Author photo.*

it been anywhere else, I don't think I would have had the same
reaction. This city did a lot for me in transforming me not as a
player but my whole life. I'm forever going to be grateful for that."

The fans "salaamed" en masse for Dawson's slugging feats in
1987, when he signed a blank contract the Cubs filled in for a
$500,000 base. His forty-nine-homer, 137-RBI output was just about
the outer limits by the standards of the day, thrilling the Wrigley
Field masses so much that the fans roared for him to belt a homer
in his last home at bat of the season. He obliged, of course, a la
The Natural. Dawson went on to capture the Most Valuable Player
honors, along with the fans' hearts, overcoming aching knees for
another five memorable seasons 'til he was let go as a free agent,
signing with the Boston Red Sox.

Now he has split loyalties. The lifelong Miami resident keeps a
sane family life by working for his hometown Marlins instructing
kids at both the big-league and minor-league levels. He'll skip
most road trips, except the Chicago swing. Of course, that included
a 2003 postseason that will never be forgotten in either Chicago or
Miami.

Dawson walked out onto Wrigley Field late in the afternoon of October 15, 2003, figuring he might see his old team clinch a World Series berth. Instead, the Marlins would go on to shockingly punch their own Fall Classic ticket, earning Dawson his first-ever World Series ring.

"The good thing was, one of the teams had to win," he said. "If the Marlins had lost, I would have been very excited for Chicago, for Dusty [Baker], Sammy [Sosa], and the fact it happened for someone I could be happy. From a personal standpoint, this [Marlins] team opened some eyes for a lot of people.

"I had to look at it with the perspective that I had a lot of ties here, my heart was here with the city and these fans, but I was the opposition, not from a player perspective, but just as an executive."

If the Cubs rudely allowed Dawson to leave after the 1992 season, the Marlins were bursting with class in allowing him to continue in baseball at home. General manager Dave Dombrowski brought him on as a part-time player to finish out his final two seasons in 1995–1996. Several years later, after fishing became repetitive, Dombrowski arranged for Dawson to wear the uniform again on a part-time basis as a special assistant.

Life after baseball couldn't have worked out any better for where Dawson expected to be.

"I'm enjoying retirement," he said. "I didn't know what I would do outside baseball. It took me a little while to get situated, settle down, get it out of my system, and enjoy my family and get on with the rest of my life.

"After three years, I made a determination that I wanted to get involved in the game in some aspects. Maybe not put the uniform on full-time, but get close to the players again. Be on that side of the game more so than upper management. I had a unique opportunity to do both. I made the decision that it would be worth my while, stay home, make my own schedule, do some of the things that I'd like to do with my involvement in the game. It's worked out really well."

Dawson's children, Darius and Amber, were born in 1989 and 1990, respectively. So they didn't bear the full brunt of Pops leaving while they were in school, of being away for so many summers during their formative years. As a result, he feels blessed.

"The kids were still at a young age, and I didn't want to miss my kids' growing up," he said. "I may have retired a little bit sooner when I think about it. But the Marlins' giving me a chance to come home made it easier to stick around a couple more years. I was a role player, a clubhouse influence, a mentor. I didn't mind that at all. I was able to sleep in my own bed."

Now he can coach Darius, an outfielder who was shifted to second base in high school baseball in 2004. But if you think Dawson is running a baseball school for his son, think again.

"I make sure I put my time in with him," Dawson said. "But I also realize someone else is supervising him. I sit back a little bit and let the other coaches do their thing. I just talk to him more on a basic and fundamental way about certain things you expect for yourself.

"I'm the type of individual who stresses academics more than recreation. I try to keep the game fun for him. I don't think expectations have to be made. It's a form of recreation, and you have to get your academics in order to be out there for recreation. I have to be more of a father figure than a coach. The true mentors are your parents, not your coaches. That's what I try to do as a parent."

That Dawson glare is so powerful that words need not accompany it. So Darius and Amber ensure that when report cards are brought home, they won't bring a reaction from Dad.

"Their mom [Vanessa] is the first one to see it," he said. "They work very hard, especially my daughter. She absolutely has to be at the top of her class, in the top five. It makes me feel good as a parent; she asks those expectations of herself.

"For Darius there was a point of time where he felt as long as he did enough to get by, it would be satisfactory. He saw me starting to put the hammer down a little bit because I stressed education more than anything else. Now he's in a unique situation where he can possibly get a scholarship to go to college, but the grades and the SAT scores have to be up. All of this stuff has to sink in, and it's made him a better student."

The expectations that Dawson hopes his children possess for their own lives can hardly even match the ones he always has had for himself.

"What a lot of people miss with me is that outward image of being a very serious person," he said. "I'm a very sensitive person. I'm a perfectionist. If you put forth your best effort all the time, you'll come close or meet all your goals. The youngsters, whether my kids or guys in the game, I try to stress the most that you're in a unique position to have an opportunity to be one of the elite at what you do. You have to know how to make adjustments to situations.

"You can't be satisfied with mediocrity. Maybe this was a thing or two that was instilled in me in my upbringing. But I just feel if I can share that with people who look up to me, it makes everything worth my while."

Fifteen years ago, while slugging away as a Cub, Dawson projected that he would never manage because young players even then did not have the same kind of dedication that propelled him forward. In 2004, he also lifted his eyebrows at the play of some veterans.

"If you don't work on your fundamentals once you do get to the major-league level, it's a learning process all over again. Kids at the minor-league level do work a lot harder than once they get here to the major leagues. You have to put the work in down there. The game can be easy up here if you allow it to be. If you don't have the proper preparation, it won't be tolerated up here.

"That's an absolute no-no [fundamental mistakes by veterans]. You've been in those situations before. The experience should say a lot about the lessons learned. You don't want to come here and make the same mistakes over and over. You lapse a little bit, get a little lackadaisical. Not that they take for granted they're here, but their comfort level is a little different when you're going to be out there every day."

Dawson never ended up managing. But he ended up softening his view to a modest degree as he's worked with the Marlins' youngsters.

"There are many individuals that I have come across the last few years it's been a true pleasure and joy to work with," he said. "Miguel Cabrera made the jump from Double-A and opened the eyes of people the way he performed for the organization. When you have an opportunity to work with a kid like that and they're willing to work, you really want to go that extra mile. You want to see that progress on a continuous basis.

"The unique thing about the job I have is to go around to minor-league affiliates while this team is on the road. I work with the youngsters, evaluate them, and talk to them about the game. It's a joy and a pleasure. You can see the look on a lot of their faces. They're intent; they're willing to listen. For some reason, they'll put forth the effort, that extra effort during the time you're there."

The Marlins are glad Dawson has desired to continue to work in baseball, even if he's not with the parent club full-time.

"Just having Hawk around has a tremendous influence on these players," manager Jack McKeon said. "Here's a guy who's been MVP, has had a tremendous career. He spends a lot of time with our outfielders like Cabrera and giving our young hitters some advice. Sometimes I can pick his brain on what looks good in the minor leagues. Any guy who has his background has their respect.

"He's a great guy. I think he's helped us out a lot. He's helped a lot of the young guys mature and become established big leaguers."

Dawson's presence especially impresses a fellow Miami native such as third baseman Mike Lowell.

"I followed him because he was an All-Star," Lowell said. "He went to one of the rival district high schools, on Andre Dawson Field. We always talked where he put some of the balls where he hit. You followed him as much as anyone."

Younger players could take inspiration from Dawson's ability to overcome twelve knee operations. A gifted high school player in football-crazed Florida, Dawson first injured a knee while a prep star. Since arthroscopic surgery had not been perfected in the early 1970s, the knee was carved up in the surgery. More surgeries on both knees would follow through the next two decades, even as he starred for the Montreal Expos, then the Cubs.

But Dawson's dedication to preparing himself to play was legendary. He'd get to the ballpark early for treatment and workouts. In 1989, he came back to the Cubs lineup early after one May surgery, barely functioning at 60 percent, in order to be an on-field role model for Cubs youngsters like Jerome Walton and Dwight Smith.

Now, well into middle age, he's eventually going to have to pay the piper. With his knees going bone on bone after the removal of most cartilage, Dawson will face knee replacements.

"I'll have the knee problems for life," he said. "It's basically left up to me. The best-case scenario is to bite the bullet, bide your time, and hold off as long as you possibly can. The other thing is to get them done and have a different lifestyle. I played with the injuries so long, it's just a way of life. What I do now is see how long I can hold off. I need the replacements."

Dawson's knees ached throughout his MVP season in Chicago in 1987. But the pain was more than counterbalanced by the affection showered upon him by the fans.

He had thought about playing for the Cubs two years earlier. A conversation in the same Wrigley Field visitor's dugout one September afternoon in 1985 revealed that Dawson would consider coming to Chicago if he could not re-sign a long-term deal with Montreal. The fans sensed Dawson could be one of their heroes over the next season, exhorting him to come to the Cubs from their perches in the bleachers. And when Montreal predictably went the cheapest route in not electing to re-sign one of their greatest-ever players after the 1986 season, Dawson headed on a southwestern course.

But his path was at first blocked by the owners' collusion on salaries that prevailed at the time. Dawson and agent Dick Moss practically camped outside the Cubs' spring training headquarters in Mesa, Arizona, campaigning along with the fans to be let into the place. Finally, Cubs general manager Dallas Green relented to Dawson's request to be signed to a blank contract. Green filled in a base salary of $500,000, added incentives for winning major awards and so forth, and Dawson was put to work as the starting right fielder.

Dawson began hammering the ball from Day One. During one game in St. Louis in which Cardinals announcer Jack Buck filled in for a stroke-recovering Harry Caray on the Cubs' telecast, Dawson came to bat against reliever Todd Worrell with the bases loaded. Respecting Dawson immensely, Cards manager Whitey Herzog counseled Worrell that whatever he did, he was not to walk the slugger. Worrell obliged, grooving a grand-slam homer to Dawson while a chagrined Buck had to call the play against his own team for Chicago viewers.

On July 6, Dawson belted two homers at Wrigley Field against the San Diego Padres. The next day, he slammed another homer against Padres starter Eric Show in the first inning. Angered by Dawson's spree, Show hit him in the face with a pitch in his next at bat. Still stunned and in pain, Dawson charged Show and had to be restrained by a gaggle of Cubs. The donnybrook ranged all over the infield before Dawson and Show were escorted to their respective clubhouses. Soon afterward, Show had to leave the ballpark under police escort.

Even a stitched-up face couldn't slow Dawson. He shifted into an even higher gear on August 1, slamming three homers against the Philadelphia Phillies at Wrigley Field. For the remainder of August, Dawson had twelve more homers and twenty-four RBIs. He single-handedly kept the Cubs above .500 through Labor Day, before the wear and tear of talent holes dropped them to 76–86 with a horrible September.

"It was storybook," he said of the 1987 season. "I could never write that sort of script, honestly. Things just happened for me on a daily basis. It was a dream-type season. You couldn't ask for anything more. I said it all along—I owed that season to the fans because they allowed me to relax here. They embraced me from Day One, and the only thing I had to do was play baseball."

A two-way tribute between Dawson and the fans took place in his final home at bat on September 27, 1987. With forty-six homers—an enormous total at the time—already to his credit, a capacity Wrigley Field throng rose en masse for a thunderous ovation. They pleaded with Dawson to hit one more for them. Cardinals reliever Bill Dawley, who had given up Dawson's first Wrigley Field hit and home run as a Cub the previous April 9, was on the mound.

"In all honesty, all I swung at was one pitch—3-and-1," he said. "I was so comfortable in that at bat. I knew what his pitch repertoire was. I knew basically how he was going to pitch me. It was just a matter of being patient and getting the right pitch and then letting the bat head fly. You'd figure I'd get a fastball. On 3-and-1, I got a change-up. I had gotten my comfort level with him so down pat that it didn't matter what he threw. If it was out over the plate, I was going to hit the ball hard somewhere."

The crowd went berserk as Dawson powered number forty-seven. The odds against belting a homer that the assembled demanded were astronomical. But nothing was impossible in Dawson's special season.

"I heard the fans from my approach in the on-deck circle," he said. "From that point, you're locked in. After I hit the home run, you hear the crowd noise, but then it seems it goes away. At the point you hit home plate, it gets magnified again. You're not blocking it out; you hear it some more. At that particular instance, it all kind of dawns on you that, 'Hey, I did something that the fans really called and asked for.'"

Dawson finished with forty-nine homers and 137 RBIs. The Cubs finished last in the National League East due to the collapse-ridden final month. Dawson clearly was the NL's most outstanding player. Some criticism was levied at the baseball writers' choice of Dawson as Most Valuable Player on a cellar dweller. But through the years, his MVP honor is as legitimate as anyone else's.

Dawson's home-run numbers dropped to twenty-four in 1988, when the ball was apparently "dejuiced" after the lively 1987 power production. They fell further in 1989 when he was hobbled by the aftereffects of knee surgery. Dawson was a flop at the plate in the National League Championship Series against the San Francisco Giants. Giants batting coach Dusty Baker tried a psych job on ol' pal Dawson, vowing that manager Roger Craig and his pitchers would not let Dawson beat them. Challenged, he became overanxious at the plate, swinging at bad pitches. Years later, Dawson was his own worst critic, lamenting that he should have been more patient, taken his walks and provided the Cubs an extra base runner each time he took his base.

Even with the playoff failure, Dawson thought a young Cubs team full of home-grown players and led by veterans such as himself and second baseman Ryne Sandberg was set for the next few years. He turned out to be wrong. The Cubs were about to go through a tailspin in their front-office management, not to really recover for another decade.

"I always felt after we won it in '89 and lost to the Giants, we set certain things in motion and hopefully management could take that extra step," he said. "But [as the 1990s progressed], I saw that wasn't going to be the case. We had a young ball club, and they were just content with what we had.

"You could see my days would be numbered with this organization because of your veteran status. That dream being fulfilled to play in a World Series [with the Cubs] was starting to slip away from you."

Dawson felt estranged from the regime of GM Larry Himes after he was allowed to walk away as a free agent following the 1992 season. But time started to heal the wounds. During Dawson's last visit to Wrigley Field as a player in August 1996, Himes successor Ed Lynch, a 1987 Cubs teammate, approved a special ceremony. In his Marlins uniform, Dawson toured the outfield and saluted the right-field fans who "salaamed" for him. Three years later, he would return to right field, this time in a business suit, accompanying Sammy Sosa in another ceremony. The fans had voted for Dawson and Sosa as their right fielders on the Cubs' All-Century Team.

All along, Dawson believed his old team should be a consistent winner as a wealthy franchise playing in a big market. Finally, in 2003–2004, he saw evidence of the necessary moves to build a powerhouse.

"They've stepped it up," he said." They've finally started to go that extra step. Bringing Dusty [Baker] in was a sign. Then going out and signing players. They've definitely tried to make a statement. You've just got to find the little things that will get you over the hump where you want to be. I think they're still kind of searching for that."

Make no mistake about it, the Hawk doesn't have to search for his home away from home. He knows the way to 1060 West Addison Street.

Fergie's Anthem

When Fergie and Lydia Jenkins wake up each morning, they still have a lot to get used to. Their home furnishings, outside grounds, and surrounding landscape are Arizona modern rather than Oklahoma rustic.

The Jenkinses walk out their back door to a vista of a mountain straight ahead and a golf course to the right, rather than endless miles of flat ranchland and farms. One house after another marches down their winding street instead of the wide gaps between dwellings back on the southern Plains. Not one home in Anthem, Arizona, a Del Webb–run community carved out of high desert thirty miles north of Phoenix, was built before the turn of the millennium.

And if the tall couple, Fergie at six feet five and Lydia crowding six feet, believe they had room to roam on their former Sooner-state ranch, they hadn't seen homes with the spaciousness of their present abode. The ceilings must be twenty feet high in the living room and family room. The master bedroom is big enough to contain a couch and a big-screen TV. Adjoining is the number-one bathroom, as large as many folks' living rooms, with "his" and "her" sinks. The builders must have had a sense of humor here. For all the square footage of the powder room, the toilet itself is tucked away in a tiny closetlike enclosure.

Always quick to laugh, Fergie cackled when some of the luxuriousness of his new digs was marveled at by a visitor. The Hall of Famer made good money for his time in baseball. Along with Billy Williams, he was the first Cub to make more than $100,000 in a season, by today's standards a staggeringly modest reward for his string of six consecutive twenty-victory seasons at Wrigley Field, the major part of his 167 Cubs wins. The greatest pitcher of modern Cubs history drove a Caddy, maintained a ranch in his native Ontario, had nice homes, and yet never possessed anything quite like the home in Anthem, bought for the Arizona market-rate price of $440,000. Try to get something this size back in a tony Chicago suburb, and the cost at least doubles.

Jenkins used the equity from the sale of his ranch to snare his new home in the late autumn of 2003. It's money well spent because it represents a change of life that was probably years in coming for the still-rangy former Cy Young Award winner. He left some good and, if the truth be known, too many truly horrible memories behind on that ranch forty miles north of Oklahoma City. His new routine is whatever he and Lydia, now closer to her Phoenix roots, want to make it.

Always an outdoorsman, Jenkins's living on a ranch was a given for the better part of three decades, dating back to his prime Cubs years. Moving into his sixties, he probably needed to ease up on the rugged daily schedule of running a ranch with cattle, Appaloosa horses, and assorted farm equipment. Even more so, he changed for love, for Lydia, the woman who brought light into his life hard on the heels of the darkest years of his existence.

The former Lydia Farrington, whom Jenkins first met in 1969, became his third wife, in 1993. She immediately moved into the Oklahoma ranch Jenkins had bought in 1988, when he was a minor-league pitching coach for the Texas Rangers. The Southwestern urban girl tried to like it and did so for awhile. But as the 1990s progressed, she started feeling a sense of isolation and creeping depression on the ranch, made worse when her husband traveled to one of his frequent personal appearances across the country.

"Probably six years and a lot of determination and patience," the blonde Lydia said, responding to a question of how long she worked on Fergie to move. The couple and their visitor left the new home to converse over some munchies at a nearby sports bar in the local mini-mall. Once again, hardly a structure dates back to the first Clinton administration.

Fergie listened intently as Lydia spoke. He sported a new look, seemingly appropriate for his new residence. The sprouting Afro of the early 1970s, a hairstyle that may have privately disquieted the conservative John Holland, his general manager, had been long wiped out by male pattern baldness. For years, Jenkins hid his enforced new hairline with a ten-gallon Western hat that he wore indoors and outdoors. Now both the hat and the remaining wisps of hair are gone. Jenkins has adopted a Michael Jordan–Charles Barkley hairstyle, shaving his scalp clean daily.

He let Lydia continue her story without interruption. His parents taught him well. For, whatever other personal shortcomings Fergie ever had, rudeness was never part of the equation.

"I've always loved horses and always ridden horses," Lydia said. "I loved that aspect of it. I'm a huge animal lover. It was different. I'd always kind of wanted to live on a ranch.

"I think it was mostly the distance (twenty minutes) we were from town. We lived on two miles of dirt road, terrible road. When it would rain, it was just a nightmare. It's red clay dirt that would stain your clothes and wouldn't come out. For the first three or four years I enjoyed it. As time went on, the isolation was starting to get to me. I didn't have any family out there, no friends."

Fergie admitted that unless one made friends with the townsfolk in Guthrie, the nearest community, the ranch dweller was left with other farming families for relationships. But other circumstances contributed to Lydia's declining mood.

"He's always had the best of both worlds; he could always go as he pleases," she said of Fergie. "We had a foreman that worked for us. He was great. I could leave at a moment's notice. He'd rather stay at our place than go home. I wouldn't have to worry about the animals. When he passed away, the whole picture changed."

The presence of the ranch foreman enabled Jenkins to take the Cubs' pitching coach's job in the 1995–1996 season, with Lydia staying up in Chicago much of the time. But without their trusted helper's presence, rural life became that much harder for Lydia.

"We did have another fellow working for us for awhile but on a part-time basis," she said. "I was stuck there, felt myself more and more withdrawn. I was becoming depressed. I think he finally realized my state of mind was no good and not getting any better. For my sake, it was time to get me out of there.

"Also taken into consideration was that it was not my house to begin with. Fergie's second wife lived there, and there were all the tragedies that happened. Those circumstances fell into the equation. I wanted to pick out my own house, feel it was mine, how to fix it up. There were already things from previous people. I was between a rock and a hard place."

Making matters worse was a 1999 tornado blasting the outer edges of the ranch property and causing minor damage to the ranch house while Lydia was home and Jenkins was away on business. Soon, Fergie realized he had to make a move for the sake of his marriage.

"I thought long and hard about it," he said. "I just thought we should look around. We looked in Colorado Springs and the Denver area. Also Jackson Hole, Wyoming, where we had gone on a fishing trip. We probably wouldn't have a ranch and would get a home."

Jenkins soon saw an ad touting the new Anthem community. The couple looked at five model homes. They put the ranch on the market, and it sold in 2003 in time for the Jenkinses to close on the Anthem home.

The majority of the ranch animals were sold. But a few months after moving to Arizona, the Jenkinses still boarded four horses back in Oklahoma.

"It's tough, because I get attached to animals easily," Lydia said.

Fergie wasn't so sentimental. On the ranch, Lydia wanted her dogs to live inside, which they do in Anthem. But Fergie's place for a dog was in the good outdoors, with a barn or doghouse for shelter.

"I've bought and sold animals—dogs, horses, cattle," he said. "It's a bargain. You sell them for money. You don't get too attached to them, although there are horses I like. Some horses I have for ten, twelve, fourteen years, then sell them."

Once he moved to Anthem, Jenkins realized he liked the change of atmosphere.

"You can only do a certain thing for a length of time, and then you have to change," he said. "Right now, we're here by the country club. I enjoy it, Lydia enjoys it, her mother's very close, her family's very close, she's a lot happier individual, and that's what I want. She adopted the house, put the things she wanted in it. It's your house, put the things you want in it."

"I want to thank my husband," Lydia said. "Deep down inside beneath that hard-crusted baseball life, he did have some compassion for me, moved me into civilization. That means a lot to me."

Moving away from Oklahoma also helped cement the long-term healing process to deal with the deaths of Mary-Anne, his second wife, from complications of injuries in an auto accident, and their three-year-old daughter, Samantha, in an apparent murder–suicide a year later at the hands of Jenkins's fiancee Cindy.

A year after his 1987 divorce from first wife, Kathy, Jenkins married Mary-Anne Miller, whom he met in Chicago. She brought Raymond, her son from her previous marriage, to live with them on the Oklahoma ranch. Fergie and Mary-Anne then had their own daughter, Samantha. One day late in 1990 on her way home from work in Oklahoma City, Mary-Anne lost control of her car and was thrown through the windshield. Although she seemed to start recovering from a variety of severe injuries while Jenkins jetted off to fulfill media obligations with his election to the Hall of Fame, Mary-Anne eventually developed pneumonia and died.

Left alone on the ranch to care for Raymond and Samantha, Jenkins soon welcomed Cindy Takieddine into his life. Another acquaintance from his baseball days, Takieddine came to the ranch with a friend to help out. Eventually, she stayed on. Jenkins and Takieddine apparently became engaged. But Takieddine became possessive, opening Jenkins's fan mail and getting upset that he agreed to take a Cincinnati Reds minor-league coaching job. She was showing classic signs of depression.

On December 15, 1992, two days after his fiftieth birthday, Jenkins was running errands in Guthrie when Takieddine, who had become close to Samantha, told her they would be going to a Christmas party at the child's day care center. Takieddine bundled Samantha into the Bronco and drove off to an isolated country road. She attached a hose from the vehicle's exhaust pipe into the car, sealed the windows with tape, and cuddled with Samantha in the back seat with the engine running. Carbon monoxide poisoning killed them before they were discovered by an oil-field worker.

Anger mixed with Jenkins's overwhelming grief. An uncle suggested he burn the ranch house and exorcise whatever curse it contained. But he refused. Taking care of Raymond, Jenkins soldiered on as best he could on the ranch. But soon he ran into Lydia, whom he had vaguely remembered from their first meeting more than twenty years previously. They were married, and the healing process began ever so slowly.

"You don't want to be faced alone with some things," Fergie said. "Lydia's been my companion, my friend."

"He suffered a long time," Lydia said. "I made him change. There were certain times of the year when it brought back bad memories. He was tough to live with."

Jenkins admitted he "wasn't a real nice individual to live with" in December, on the anniversaries of the tragedies. "It always came up" around the dual celebratory times of his birthday (December 13) and Christmas.

"Decembers are now a lot better," he said. "I can think about them and get into a bad mood. But I try not to. I've gotten past it with counseling, a support group, and Lydia's help. If I wasn't really positive, I'd probably be an evil individual, break a lot of things. I've really not taken out a lot of the frustrations on material things.

"I'll sit and think. I think with any tragedy or tough situation, it takes time to get over it. I think now I've gotten past it to the point where I can deal with it. Losing a young daughter, losing a wife, losing a close friend, losing my mother [back in 1970]—I just think that everybody has bumps in the road. I've had my share. I had a clergyman tell me that God won't put more on you than you can handle."

Jenkins certainly has not sat around and brooded since 1992. He's gotten involved, or attempted to, in a number of baseball-related gigs.

Foremost was the coveted role as Cubs pitching coach. Jenkins was hired at the start of the new Andy MacPhail–Ed Lynch front office administration late in 1994. Some promising performances by the hurlers in 1995 backslid the following season, and a scapegoat had to be found. Upper management at the time also believed Jenkins was not as hands-on a pitching coach as they desired. His strength was actually in a role for which he should have been hired—community relations. Jenkins never turned down an autograph. As a resident Hall of Famer at Wrigley Field, he was always in demand. The honchos' feeling was that he was spending a little too much time on the public relations end of his role and not enough on coaching.

Lydia was furious when she learned on the final day of the 1996 season that Fergie was relieved of his coaching duties. But Jenkins shook off the hurt and resumed his life as a baseball elder.

The '96 firing from the Cubs did not prevent Dusty Baker from bringing Jenkins back as a spring-training instructor in 2003–2004. He also tried different projects related to the game. Jenkins attempted to run baseball clinics both at the ranch and in different cities. He tried to represent other Hall of Famers for appearances and endorsements. In 2003, Jenkins served as commissioner of the short-lived Canadian Baseball League, which featured ex-Cubs such as Jody Davis, Pete LaCock, and Willie Wilson as managers. He also set up his own foundation, which produced a biography, *The Game is Easy . . . Life Is Hard*, the second book on his life after the 1973 tome *Like Nobody Else*, authored with Chicago sportswriter George Vass. Lydia kept nodding when Fergie was asked if he simply liked to dabble in a variety of baseball ventures.

"I'd like her to work; I don't want to work," Fergie mused. "Right now, we just want to relax and enjoy setting up the new home."

A constant throughout the entire period were paid appearances at card and memorabilia shows and awards dinners. Throughout the industry, Jenkins is known as one of the more moderately priced Hall of Famers. His appearance fee is in the $5,000 to $6,000 range plus round-trip air fare and hotel if necessary. That's in contrast with former teammate Ernie Banks, who in the early 1990s was charging a flat $15,000 for an appearance in an attempt to make a living as, well, Ernie Banks.

"I didn't try to break the bank," Jenkins said. "I was always reliable showing up. Standard fee, I'd get work. If you don't want to work, you overprice yourself. A lot of them do, and they don't get work. Overpricing is probably $8,000 to $10,000.

"If they want you to meet and greet for $1,000, fly from the West Coast, no, I won't do that. I will do charity events. I enjoy doing that. People love to see you come out, spend some time."

Jenkins actually finds the travel from Phoenix more time-consuming than from Oklahoma City. "There were nonstops to Chicago and the East Coast," he said. "Two hours or less. Now it's a longer flight from Phoenix to the East Coast. But I don't mind the travel. You take an extra day and you do it."

He would have traveled halfway around the world to have played in a World Series during his nineteen-season career. Remember, Jenkins spent ten seasons in two tours of duty as a Cub that ended with his release in spring training 1984. The rest of his

284-victory career was divided between two stints on the Texas Rangers, never a contender in his day, and a Boston Red Sox club that underachieved.

By now the Jenkinses had returned to their house. Lydia plopped down in the family room to watch a TV special on Princess Diana. Fergie and the visitor talked about the good ol' days in the living room.

"In some cases I'm a little envious," he said of former Cubs teammates who went on to play in World Series. "Kenny Holtzman got in four; Billy North, who once was my roommate, was in three. You have to be extremely lucky. You have to be an opportunist, be on the right ball club that plays well for six months. I played on teams that played well for five months. We just didn't get there. I did what I could with my ability to get there, but it just didn't happen."

So why didn't the talent-rich Cubs of the late 1960s and early 1970s reach the Fall Classic?

"I don't think it was the players," Jenkins said. "The front office could have helped us shore up our bullpen better. If we'd have had a little stronger bullpen, a bullpen this ball club's got now . . ."

The man has a point. Though Jenkins had endurance like few other starters of modern times, he was forced to finish what he started on some occasions when use of a reliever might have been better advised. Jenkins completed an astounding thirty games in 1971, when manager Leo Durocher almost abhorred using his bullpen. Six of the route-going jobs came in defeats. Jenkins still won twenty-four and his only Cy Young Award. Mention the thirty complete games to pitchers today, and the very thought does not compute. Jenkins totaled 140 complete games during his string of six straight twenty-win campaigns from 1967 to 1972. He almost always got a decision, with the 24–13 record coming in thirty-nine starts in '71. He had at least fifteen losses in each season from 1968 to 1970.

Though like most of Durocher's veterans, Jenkins had at least some conflicts with the "Lip," he tilts toward the positive in praising the controversial manager, who died in 1991. After all, it was Durocher who had the light bulb go on in his head late in 1966 that Jenkins should be a starter. After some success at that lost season's

Lydia and Fergie Jenkins at their Anthem, Arizona, home, standing beside a poster of the 1969 Cubs. Author photo.

end, Durocher reconfirmed his faith in Jenkins before the following season.

"He made a statement in the spring of '67 that he was going to give me an opportunity to be a starting pitcher," Jenkins recalled. "I worked real hard in the spring to get the opportunity. I got the opening day start against the Phillies and Jim Bunning, and I won."

Once in the rotation full-time, Jenkins did not stop winning until 1973, when the aftereffects of arm tendinitis that cropped up at the end of the 1972 season, and no doubt the cumulative wear and tear of his workload, dropped his record to 14–16. But by that season, the string of twenty-victory seasons was a feat no other modern-day pitcher has been able to match—and no one likely will anytime soon.

"The way the game is handled today, they're not going to get enough starts to get enough wins to win twenty over and over again," Jenkins said. "You've got to go to the mound every fourth day ready to pitch. During that time, I missed only a couple of starts. I wouldn't let little nagging things bother me. You're not going to go without something nagging you. Your neck, your shoulder is stiff, but you still go out there."

Pitchers today also are on short leashes with their managers. The strict adherence to pitch counts shortens many hurlers' outings. Jenkins believes the pitch-count system is counterproductive to many pitchers' careers.

"That grates on me, the pitch count," he said. "A lot of times the pitcher knows if he gets into the one hundred range, he's gone. He stays behind in the count late in the game because he knows the bullpen will save him. You don't see any five-to-six-pitch innings anymore. A lot of guys are throwers—that's how your pitch count gets high, they don't throw strikes."

Jenkins might have won even more than the twenty he posted in 1968. He lost five games by a 1–0 score, a victim of a sputtering Cubs offense in '68. But more often than not, when matched against the opponent's ace, he prevailed. Jenkins was 5–3 head-to-head against rival Bob Gibson of the St. Louis Cardinals. He went ten innings to beat Gibson 2–1 on opening day 1971 at Wrigley Field as fishing buddy Billy Williams slugged a game-ending homer off the Redbirds' Hall of Famer.

Jenkins was able to rack up the victory totals not only because he was usually left in to win or lose his own game but also because he worked on three days' rest, getting up to forty starts a season. Durocher sometimes wanted too much of a good thing. Citing the innings he already had piled up, Jenkins refused Durocher's request to start a late August 1969 game against the Reds on one day's rest after being chased in the third inning of his previous start. But Fergie finally relented, starting on just two days' rest in the infamous "black cat" series against the New York Mets at Shea Stadium two weeks later. He was ineffective and lost 7–1. He totaled a career-high forty-two starts in '69.

But when Jenkins got his proper rest, he usually did not beat himself with poor control. The top strike machine in Cubs history, even better than Greg Maddux, Jenkins walked just thirty-seven batters in 325 innings in 1971. He thus became the first pitcher in history to strike out at least 250 (263 in '71) and walk fewer than 50. The only drawback to the constant strikes were a large number of homers he served up. During the twenty-win string, he served up at least twenty-six homers each season. When he was less effective in 1973, he gave up thirty-five homers. His career-high yield was forty with the Rangers in 1979. Jenkins recalled that some of his fastballs caught too much of the plate in his attempt to keep in control.

"I used that pitch to stay in the count," he said. "I wasn't going to walk somebody. I challenged people. Give credit to the hitters. You've got seven capable fellows behind you. Make the hitter put the ball in play. These guys need to play, too. You can't get everybody out by yourself."

Such a philosophy was adopted by Maddux to carve out a career in which he exceeded Jenkins in victories despite working on four days' rest. In spring training 2004, the two number 31s got together in a Cubs uniform for the first time. They had a chance to compare notes.

"We've talked a few times," Jenkins said. "I threw a little harder. But the art of pitching is pitching ninety-five or seventy-five miles per hour. He very easily could have been a big winner in the '60s."

Other than the bout with tendinitis and a ruptured Achilles tendon in 1976, Jenkins maintained his health wire to wire in his career. He did not undergo surgery on his shoulder until he was long retired in the mid-1990s.

Two all-time-Cub number 31s—Greg Maddux (left) and Fergie Jenkins—get together for the first time in uniform at spring training in 2004. Author photo.

"One aspect was the pride [in] going out there every fourth day [not injured]," he said. "The workload was there, the mechanics were there and didn't change halfway through the season. We did things correctly. Johnny Sain said if you threw ten minutes every day, kept your arm in good shape, you should never have a problem. I used to throw batting practice in between starts, which is a lost art. We did that in the '60s. We'd warm up and throw X amount of pitches, throw to the extra men. We'd work on our breaking pitch, changeup and pitch location, instead of throwing a 'side' as they do now."

His strong opinions aren't limited to the care and feeding of pitchers. Playing the game the right way, Jenkins did not like to see Pete Rose, a once-fierce competitor, appeal to commissioner Bud Selig to reinstate him after being banned for life after being accused of gambling on baseball. He wrote a letter to Rose on January 14, 2004, that was publicized nationwide. Jenkins was particularly irked that Rose released his confessional book so close to the Hall of Fame voting announcement for 2004.

"After you were caught betting, where was your conscience all these years?" Jenkins wrote. "Why didn't you come forward with your admission of guilt soon after your lifetime ban? The time for that was the following year or the year after, before your denial became a way of life for you. Why did you let the lie get bigger and bigger?

"You have been taking advantage of all the hard work those of us have put into the sport of baseball to attain a place in the Hall of Fame. You have denied yourself a place along with us because you didn't confess early on.

"You are going to profit personally from your book's sales. Many states have passed laws that prevent convicted felons from profiting from the sale of books they write about their crimes. Why should you be any different?

"Knowing what I know now, I will never support your reinstatement to the game or your bid for the Hall."

But life isn't about getting into such heavy issues every day. He's survived his family tragedies, a drug arrest, firings, and implications he was washed up after his 1973 downturn.

It was getting late. Fergie got up from his chair and used those familiar long, loping strides to tell Lydia the visitor was driving back to Phoenix. The night would get more quiet and peaceful in Anthem. Just the way he likes it. Like nobody else in Cubs pitching annals, the man has earned the right to live on accolades and enjoy the aura of Cooperstown enshrinement.

The Sports Guru at the "J"

Putting in backbreaking hours and investing his own sweat equity into sculpting a sports and instructional program wasn't a problem for Ken Holtzman, even well into his fifties.

Remember, Holtzman used to go nine innings without complaint in the heat of day games at Wrigley Field and with Leo Durocher second-guessing his choice of pitches. And he survived the pressure of getting through the ninth inning of a pair of no-hitters, the only pitcher in Cubs history to accomplish that feat twice.

Holtzman would do some impromptu landscaping in and around the Marilyn Fox Jewish Community Center, nicknamed the "J," in Chesterfield, Missouri, amid one of that area's typically tropical summer days. No problem. It was all a part of the job to which he has devoted as much passion as his former pitching persona.

"He puts in incredible hours," JCC official Jeb Margolis said a few years back. "He's working his tail off to make this center work. During the hot weather this past summer, he'd be out on the field, picking up rocks and sweating his butt off."

The effort has worked at the Chesterfield center, a half-hour drive west of downtown St. Louis. In the first half-decade after Holtzman moved back to his hometown to work as supervisor of health and physical education at the Fox center, the former left-handed ace helped dramatically expand youth and adult sports programs across the board—in basketball, baseball and soccer.

When Holtzman started, the basketball program fielded 140 kids. Now more than 850 are dribbling and shooting. "We've increased 600 percent," he said.

Holtzman threw himself into building up athletics at the Fox center the way he used to attack hitters.

"Here, there was history more of a recreational nature," he said. "But we wanted to add an element of competition, for those who wanted to do it at a competitive level."

Adults wanted to let off steam, so Holtzman expanded softball and basketball programs. "Kickball has been the latest craze," he said. The "J" also was the sponsor of St. Louis's Senior Olympics while serving as the base for several marathons. Non-Jewish sports enthusiasts as well as regular "J" members from west St. Louis County and nearby St. Charles County increasingly used the Fox facilities. Several Cardinals players who live nearby work out at the Fox center during the off-season.

"People want to come to a facility that's family friendly," Holtzman said. "Mom and dad and the kids can come as a family unit. The way this building is laid out, the pool, the gym, the youth rooms, and the fitness studios are all close and are visible to one another. Parents can keep an eye on their kids. It's been remarkably designed as a family-oriented place."

But as the sports programs and resulting administrative workload has grown, Holtzman makes sure that his primary job is teaching and coaching. And that baseball is never given short shrift.

Early on, Holtzman coached the area baseball team that competed in the national Maccabiah games—a kind of national Jewish Olympics. He attracted guest instructors such as former Cardinals Andy Van Slyke and Bob Forsch to the Fox center. As a rookie, Cardinals superstar Albert Pujols stopped by to sign autographs for an hour.

"We're lucky we have three indoor batting cages that were installed six years ago," Holtzman said. "The 'J' made the investment. I give lessons there. The cages have artificial mounds for pitchers. I teach kids from seven to high school and college. And we've managed to have a successful [Little League] team.

"You teach the right mechanics. That's probably why the parents come seek us out. But I tell parents there's no way I can somehow transform your son into a future major-league player. Ninety-nine percent of that is inborn.

"There's no substitute for practice. Some parents are hard to convince. They think that as a former ballplayer I have some kind of secret formula for success. I don't.'"

Holtzman developed his own formula for the second part of his life in the mid-1990s. A long career in insurance in Chicago's northern suburbs followed his retirement at thirty-three from the Cubs in 1979 in his second Wrigley Field tenure. But in the mid-1990s, he desired a change. He went back to college at DePaul University to obtain a certificate to teach physical education. He went to school full-time for one and a half years, taking twenty-two courses spread out over 809 hours.

"It was a normal desire to change," Holtzman said of returning to school, twenty-five years after getting a business degree from the University of Illinois. "I tell people there's a difference in [doing] what you have to do compared to what you'd like to do."

Holtzman performed his student-teaching duties at Francis Parker High School and Oscar Mayer Elementary School in Chicago.

"I enjoyed student teaching, and I even helped out with the girls' softball team at Francis Parker," he said.

After trying to get a coaching job at several Chicago-area high schools, Holtzman moved back to the St. Louis area where he had first made a name for himself, going 31–3 at University City High School in the early 1960s. The affiliation with the "J" had some sentimentality. He had played in "J"-sponsored sports programs as a youth.

"I hadn't been home in thirty years," Holtzman said. "A lot of things have changed. Many of the people here are people I grew up with in University City."

But at the same time, he also came "home" to the Cubs. Back in the mid-1990s, the highly opinionated Holtzman felt a bit estranged from the team. Part of the feelings stemmed from being an old baseball labor activist at a time of the game's greatest labor crisis—and the status of Tribune Company as an apparent labor hawk.

More recently, however, Cubs marketing chief John McDonough smoothed things over and brought Holtzman back into the fold. Accompanied by his three daughters, he took a brief break from the Fox center on several summer Sundays to lead the seventh-inning sing-along.

"The last couple of years, my relationship is very well," Holtzman said. "Everyone in front office is appreciative and respectful of ex-players. Over the years, some of the things they've done have changed, and they have made an attempt to reach out to the former players."

Holtzman would be at the top of the list of any ex-Cubs. The best left-hander in the last third of the twentieth century, he started out with great expectations and a connection with a member of baseball's Valhalla that he never really shook in his first tour of duty in Chicago.

While the Cubs passed over Johnny Bench in the first two rounds of the inaugural amateur draft in 1965, they did not miss out on Holtzman, picking him in the fourth round out of the University of Illinois. Blowing through the minors with 114 strikeouts in 86 innings, he was called up to emulate Sandy Koufax as a hard-throwing lefty in batting practice on the night of September 9, 1965, in Los Angeles. The Koufax mimicry didn't do the Cubs a bit of good as Koufax threw a perfect game against them.

Being Jewish, left-handed, and possessed of a great fastball and curve, Holtzman was of course compared to Koufax as his rookie season got underway in 1966. He pitched only part-time in the first two months while finishing classes at the University of Illinois–Chicago. The most effective starter on a dreadful 103-loss team, Holtzman linked up head-to-head against Koufax on September 26, the final Sunday of the home schedule at Wrigley Field. The duel was set up by the fact that both pitchers had taken off the day before due to Yom Kippur, the holiest day of the Jewish calendar. And for one day, the twenty-year-old Holtzman outpitched the master. He took a no-hitter into the ninth inning, then barely escaped with a 2–1 victory over the Dodgers.

But Holtzman's greatest teacher was not Koufax. The presence of veteran pitchers Larry Jackson, Bob Buhl, Dick Ellsworth, and Ernie Broglio on the '66 Cubs helped him immeasurably.

"I was probably the youngest guy by ten years, sitting and talking to them about pitching," he said. "A lot of what they said rubbed off on me."

Holtzman's development as the "next Koufax" was slowed in 1967. As with many draft-eligible athletes of the Vietnam era, Holtzman joined the National Guard. He departed for basic training in late spring with a 5–0 record. Amazingly, with little workouts during weekdays filled with military duties, Holtzman won four more games without a loss on weekend passes. The 9–0 record raised expectations even further for 1968.

But Holtzman couldn't live up to the advance publicity. His love–hate relationship with Durocher began. The "Lip" would play cards with Holtzman and other favored players, then sour on them. At one point the amoral, old old-school Durocher called Holtzman a "gutless Jew" when such epithets were uttered without impunity in big-league clubhouses. But he kept Holtzman in the rotation. He began the 1969 season 10–1, the winningest pitcher on a Cubs team that zoomed into first place, seemingly fated to meet its October destiny.

Holtzman's winning pace cooled off after the All-Star break. He was 13–7 when he took the mound against the Atlanta Braves at Wrigley Field before more than forty-one thousand fans on August 19. Staked to a 3–0 lead on Ron Santo's first-inning three-run homer, Holtzman had the Braves beating the ball into groundskeeper Pete Marcantonio's high grass all afternoon. Inning after inning passed without allowing a hit.

And when the Braves hit it into the air, Holtzman had what appeared at the time to be divine help. Henry Aaron hammered a fastball for what should have been the no-hit and shutout-ruining homer in the seventh. But the blast, which according to Holtzman pitching mate Phil Regan actually passed over a couple of rows of left-field bleachers, hit a wall of wind or something invisible. It seemed to take a left turn and settled into the glove of left fielder Billy Williams, backing into the vines at the point where the wall curves outward at the end of the bleachers.

Holtzman faced Aaron again for the final out. He grounded to a slightly wobbly Glenn Beckert at second, who threw Aaron out to complete the no-hitter. Holtzman was engulfed by Santo and his teammates while hundreds of fans poured onto the field. He had pitched a no-hitter without a strikeout—twenty-seven batted balls for outs—while walking three.

"I told everyone that pitching a no-hit game is strictly luck," he said. "It's a well-pitched game with a lot more luck than usual. That day, there were only two, three balls that would have been hits."

Twenty-nine years later, Kerry Wood pitched a superior game to Holtzman's with twenty strikeouts and no walks—and it still was

Ken Holtzman in his coaching mode with one of his athletic students in St. Louis. Photo courtesy of the Marilyn Fox Jewish Community Center.

not a no-hitter, as Houston's Ricky Gutierrez singled off third baseman Kevin Orie's glove. Wood hardly believed a no-hitter could be pitched without any strikeouts. He added that a 20-strikeout performance was more difficult because the pitcher does it all himself, as opposed to the fielders and the elements (as in Holtzman's case) helping to craft a no-strikeout no-hitter.

Holtzman did not finish strong in the Cubs' collapse in 1969, ending up 17–13. But he did pitch better start to finish in 1970, going 17–11 with 202 strikeouts. The rifts with Durocher, though, began to widen, and ruptured in 1971 when he had an off season with a 9–15 record. He had one important highlight, though—his second no-hitter, this time with six strikeouts, at Riverfront Stadium in Cincinnati on June 3. Holtzman was far more dominating, striking out Lee May for the final out in the 1–0 victory. Yet to show the fickleness of baseball, Durocher summoned Holtzman to come into relief two nights later in Atlanta. He served up a game-winning homer to Mike Lum.

Amid an overall fractious relationship between Durocher and the Cubs players, Holtzman decided he wanted out of Chicago. General manager John Holland accommodated his request, dispatching him to the Oakland Athletics for center fielder Rick Monday at the 1971 winter meetings. The deal would be beneficial for Holtzman in two ways. He'd get to become a pitching mainstay, winning fifty-nine games overall for Oakland's three consecutive world championship teams from 1972–74. And homegrown Bill North, the speedy center fielder pushed aside by Monday's arrival, would become Holtzman's teammate in 1973, using his legs to help the lefty win some of those games.

Through the years, Holtzman maintained the Cubs were at a disadvantage playing all day games at Wrigley Field. He compared the conditions to the temperate night air in the Oakland Coliseum, insisting the Athletics had much more vigor toward season's end as a result. Thus he was pleased the Cubs are bumping up their night-game ration to thirty per season by 2006.

"Thirty would be enough to have a positive effect on the team," he said.

The Cubs have never really recovered from Holtzman's departure. Only two left-handed starters have won as many as thirteen games in a season as Cubs—Steve Trout in 1984 and Greg Hibbard in 1993. More often than not, the Cubs would trot out five right-handed pitchers in their rotations with southpaws showing up like the five-year locusts—and just as effective.

Holtzman would return to Wrigley Field in mid-season 1978, but his best days were gone. He had rusted out as a New York Yankee in 1977–1978, somehow never currying favor with manager Billy Martin and appearing only sporadically. He was 0–3 in six games in his Cubs return in '78. The next year, he made twenty starts, going 6–9 before pulling the plug on his career with 174 victories.

But the Yankees-era inactivity, not a bad arm, shortened his career. A stickler for conditioning and mechanics in his present job, he believes the greater number of injuries today can be attributed to not throwing as much while substituting weight training for arm strength.

"We never had weights," he said. "I threw a lot. I threw three hundred innings. Every other day, I threw a regular warm-up. I felt the more I threw, the stronger I got. I don't know why guys twenty-three, twenty-four years old, guys six-foot-five, 240, are breaking down early.

"As a whole, they throw harder now. But I don't see where they have the same stamina and endurance. They go five, six innings, that's their job. Management is different. I have a hunch it's the money."

Holtzman also had a pragmatic side to the first reports Wrigley Field was really showing its age with falling concrete in the summer of 2004.

"The ballpark is ninety years old," he said. "You got to be a little bit naïve if you think the park will last forever. It can't go on forever. I don't think it will hurt the Cubs if they have to change Wrigley Field and make it more modern."

The brass can change Wrigley Field to their hearts' desire. But they can never purge the corner of Clark and Addison of a couple of memories of Holtzman striving for a no-hitter against Koufax, then achieving it by dodging an Aaron bullet. They simply don't make left-handers like him anymore. And if they do, the Cubs usually can't sign them.

Covering a Different Kind of Ground

After bouncing from the playing ranks to big-league managing to business, back to coaching, then athletic administration, Don Kessinger is back in business for good.

Kessinger used to cover ground like few others in Cubs history, using that "boardinghouse reach" to spear grounders in the hole at shortstop, spinning in the air, and firing to first to nip base runners. Now he's still in charge of patrolling real estate, also for a living, albeit at a much slower pace.

Raising his son Kevin to follow in his stead in baseball, Kessinger did not at first realize Kevin had also developed a keen business mind. The younger Kessinger started a real-estate firm in Oxford, Mississippi, home of the University of Mississippi, of which father-and-son Kessinger along with brother Keith are athletic products. Usually a son joins his father's business, but this time Kessinger turned the tables.

"I always loved real estate, so I asked my son for a job," Kessinger said. Don and Kevin now run Kessinger Realty together in a fifty-fifty deal. His wife Carolyn, who possesses a law license, helps with the bills, "but she's a full-time grandmother," Don added.

No way as lean, lanky, and limber in body as in his Cubs days, with white creeping into his hair, Kessinger benefits from location, as any good real-estate person would crave. Much of Mississippi is poor, but college-town Oxford always is stable, if not booming. There's no such thing as a real-estate bust.

"Oxford is an energetic, prosperous town," Kessinger said. "It's great to have the university here. A lot of alumni want to come back. People also buy places for their kids to stay. Oxford's also got a lot of attention as a retirement center."

"Interest rates have been a great catalyst. We haven't had a downturn in real estate in twenty years. We haven't seen the great swing as you do nationally."

And there's no such thing as a Kessinger hard sell . . . or a disingenuous one, when he's showing pieces of property.

"You just have to be yourself," he said. "And absolutely tell the truth."

Kessinger may have had a nice eleven-season run in Chicago, but Oxford is his home. He not only starred in basketball and baseball at Ole Miss in the early 1960s but also settled in long after his playing career as first head baseball coach, then associate athletic director.

He had been successful in business for more than a decade but always left the door ajar for a return to baseball.

"Maybe if the right college or pro job came along, I would do it again," he told Rick Talley in *The Cubs of '69* back in 1988. Sure enough, Ole Miss qualified as the right job.

Kessinger coached the Rebels to a 185–153 record from 1991 to 1996. Kevin Kessinger played for him in his first season, following in the wake of his brother.

"It was a real thrill to coach Kevin," he said. The thrill continued when the Cubs picked the younger Kessinger, a good defensive outfielder, in the twenty-second round in the 1992 draft. But his pro career was short-lived due to injuries. Keith had preceded him into pro baseball, having a cup of coffee with the Cincinnati Reds.

Kevin's aborted Cubs career did not dampen the satisfaction of coaching college kids for his father.

"I always enjoyed the teaching aspect of baseball," Kessinger said. "I loved two things: The challenge of putting it together in a great league, the Southeast Conference. And I enjoyed the day-to-day interaction with kids."

Kessinger, who played the "little man's game" in the majors, did not force that style onto his team.

"You've got to go with what you need to win," he said. "When I played, you used to play for one run. But the game's changed, and you've got to play along with it. You need to adjust. Athletes today are bigger, faster, and stronger."

But Kessinger never tried to mold a player into his own image, baseball or personal.

"You can never take an individual's right to do things his way away from him," he said. "You can't take his freedom away. Certain things you must do, but everyone must be an individual."

Kessinger had to match wits several times each season with a college baseball coaching legend and in-state rival who has produced the likes of Rafael Palmeiro, Will Clark, and Bobby Thigpen.

"Ron Polk has done a marvelous job at Mississippi State," he said. "He's a friend I greatly respect. He set a standard for [Southeast Conference] baseball. We've got a great rivalry in every sport with that school. Both teams respect each other."

For the first time in his life, Kessinger also had to deal with the byzantine NCAA rulebook. He survived the experience, where he said, laughing, "You can break a rule and not mean to."

"The book is about an inch and a half thick," he said. "Things can happen that are quite by accident. One example is, a school can call an athlete once a week. That sounds relatively easy. But if your school is recruiting him for two sports, it's hard to coordinate [the calls] between the staffs. If you find you've done it [broken a rule], you still have to self-report it to NCAA. They'll often tell you not to do it again."

Kessinger did not have to continue to deal with the rulebook frequently when he was promoted to associate athletic director at Ole Miss in 1996. He dodged another bullet in not having to handle pushy alumni in the new role.

"I love dealing with people," he said. "My area was more in marketing and the business and ticket offices. Mine was more an internal situation."

He was proud of the accomplishments of Mississippi's largest school, citing traditionally strong football, basketball, and baseball programs.

"There's a lot of pressure in college athletics today that wasn't there before," he said. "With bad there's the good, too. In running a big-time program, there's a real pressure to succeed. We're fortunate at Ole Miss with an athletic director and head coaches who are wonderful people."

No role in life is forever, and Kessinger left Ole Miss in June 2000, thankful for his decade-long run. It was time for a change, just as it was time to leave the majors when his job as White Sox manager did not pan out two-thirds of the way through the 1979 season, just as it was time to get back into athletics after spending the eighties in the investment business, partnering with former soccer star Kyle Rote Jr. in Memphis, across the Mississippi River from his hometown of Forrest City, Arkansas.

Kessinger, active in Fellowship of Christian Athletes, always has been guided by his deep faith. He excelled in sports, exulted in his success, but did not need to constantly be connected to games. That's why he was able to walk away from the White Sox and why he did not plunge back into baseball after a respite of a few years.

"Nothing takes the place of reaching a goal as a young man," he said. "Everyone who plays sports aspires to be in big leagues. To be there and hang around a few years is great, but eventually you move on with your life.

"I've never been one who missed the thrill of the crowd or the glamour of being there. I appreciate being there and thank the Lord for giving me the chance. But that's not where my life is today. Each phase of your life is different. I do believe there's a reason for things to happen."

Then obviously there was a reason for Kessinger, a poor hitter breaking into the majors, to have learned how to switch-hit. Thus he became a decent hitter, enabling him to stick around for a decade as the Cubs' most spectacular defensive player of his time.

Taking less money to sign with the Cubs out of Ole Miss in 1964 with an obvious near-future need for a shortstop, Kessinger finally broke in to replace butterfingered Roberto Pena two months into the 1965 season. But he was hardly an improvement with a .201 average and twenty-eight errors in just 106 games.

But the light bulb that went on the following year was switch-hitting. Manager Leo Durocher gave him the green light. Kessinger showed amazing improvement by the end of the 1966, batting .274 and cementing his place in the lineup.

Although he slumped below .250 the next two seasons, he rebounded with a spectacular 1969. Kessinger was not the perfect leadoff man, but he still managed to score 109 runs and pull off some deft hit-and-run plays with number 2 hitter and double-play partner Glenn Beckert. Entrenched as the National League's All-Star shortstop, he would go on to win the first of his two consecutive Gold Gloves in 1969. His play in the whole was popularized by Cubs announcer Jack Brickhouse, who described Kessinger as applying his "boardinghouse reach" to spear the grounders and his Ole Miss basketball agility to turn and fire midair to first base.

Since he's a down-home guy, could Kessinger define what "boardinghouse reach" meant?

"When you go to a boardinghouse, they serve a [communal] meal," he said. "If you want food, you have to go get it."

Kessinger made Beckert, a converted shortstop, a better second baseman just by his presence.

"We'd spend twenty to thirty minutes a day in spring training working on double plays, just Beckert and I," he said in *The Cubs of '69*. "We'd go out when there was nobody else on the field so we wouldn't have to worry about dodging line drives from batting practice. We had only one practice field in Scottsdale."

Similarly, the duo became skilled at the hit-and-run, with Beckert hitting behind base runner Kessinger.

"We used the hit-and-run so often that everybody expected it but couldn't do anything about it," Kessinger said in *The Cubs of '69*. "They'd try to pick up our signs, but many times Leo [Durocher] would give the sign when I was at the plate and Beckert was still in the on-deck circle. What it meant was simply that if I got on base, we'd hit-and-run on the first pitch. I'd get on first, and everybody'd try to pick up a sign from coach Pete Reiser, but it had already been given."

The benefit of all those spring drills and crafty sign-giving could not help Kessinger and many of his teammates after Labor Day in 1969. His slump was one of the worst during the Cubs' infamous collapse as the New York Mets rushed past them to glory. Kessinger went just 10-for-65 after September 7 while making errors that were unimaginable a month earlier.

He would long blame the unremitting schedule of home day games for the team's late-season tiredness. Some three decades–plus later, these theories got credence from Cubs brass in their roster and lineup managements along with their push for more Wrigley Field night games.

Kessinger put together another good season in 1970 with one hundred runs scored and fourteen triples. He went 6-for-6 in one 1971 game against the Cardinals. He continued to bat leadoff until

1973, when he yielded that lineup slot to center fielder Rick Monday. But he continued to hit well for a shortstop of his era.

When the Cubs finally cleaned house after the 1973 season, he was a keeper for another two years while longtime partner Beckert was dispatched to the Padres. The nine years the pair spent as the Cubs' double-play combo was—with apologies to Johnny Evers and Joe Tinker—rivaled only by the 1930s duo of shortstop Billy Jurges and second baseman Billy Herman.

Owner Phil Wrigley and GM John Holland could trade away a lot of his teammates, but not their relationships. Those are permanent.

"That group of guys I played with on the Cubs was special," Kessinger said. "It was a real unique relationship, not only between players and fans, but the players themselves. You know where all the players are. You're comfortable picking up the phone, just to have an opportunity to say hello. I probably talk on the phone with Beckert more than with many other people. If things change, you try to let everyone know what's happening."

Kessinger always will treasure the fan–player interaction of the time.

"I think it was a unique relationship that I never experienced on any other team I was associated with," he said. "It was truly a love affair. Cubs players loved the fans. They were great.

"In 1965, we were just not very good, and in 1966 we were worse than that, he said. "You could have shot off a cannon and not hit anyone in the stands in '66. But then we played a lot better, and the fans came out. That game in 1967 when we took over first place for one game, it was an unbelievable moment. You could not get out of the stadium for two hours."

Both the Durocher-era Cubs and fans closed ranks around Ron Santo, their old team captain, during his series of illnesses that cost him his legs and his bladder starting in 1999. Kessinger in particular used his faith to bond with the guy who used to play on his left.

"I prayed for Ronnie," he said.

"Ronnie played every day and played the game hard. You never know how anyone will handle adversity outside the game. But it was a real inspiration to me the way he was able to handle adversities. My locker was beside his all the time on the road—he wore number 10 and I wore number 11. I just watched him in a lot of situations. There was no greater Cubs fan than Ron Santo."

On December 9, 2003, Kessinger, Beckert, and Billy Williams were tapped to honor Santo at the Fans' Choice Awards dinner in Rosemont, Illinois, honoring the top Chicago sports achievers of the previous year. Santo was confined to his home in Scottsdale, Arizona, recovering from the bladder-cancer surgery, but addressed the gathering via videotape. All three of his old teammates took turns paying tribute to Santo.

"His love for the fans and the game and the pride he took in his team, is what made him loved in Chicago," Kessinger said at the podium. "He set the standard for his position that has not been equaled by a Cub to this day."

Santo had retired while his last holdover—Durocher-era teammate, Billy Williams—had departed for Oakland by the start of Kessinger's final Cubs season in 1975. He had a new double-play partner in the slick Manny Trillo, while Bill Madlock was busy establishing himself as a batting champ playing third. Andre Thornton seemed to have a lot of future power promise at first base.

Kessinger was telegraphed the word that he'd be traded after the season, his Cubs career closing with a team record 1,618 games

Glenn Beckert, Billy Williams, and Don Kessinger get together for a tribute to old teammate Ron Santo at the Fans' Choice Awards dinner, held by Sports Profiles, in December 2003 in Rosemont, Illinois. Photo by Chip Zellet.

played at shortstop, 5,346 assists, and 982 double plays. He was dealt to the arch-rival St. Louis Cardinals in exchange for reliever Mike Garman, eventually a flop as a Cub. He kept shortstop warm in Busch Stadium for one and a half seasons until the highly touted Garry Templeton was ready in 1977. With the slugging White Sox (the "South Side Hit Men") flirting with first place in August of '77, Kessinger was dealt back to Chicago but on the South Side instead.

Normally suspicious, if not hostile, to ex-Cubs, Sox fans embraced Kessinger, who still had a little bit of good baseball left in him at thirty-six. He still played a competitive shortstop at old Comiskey Park in 1978 while hitting .255. Then, surprisingly, Sox owner Bill Veeck named Kessinger player–manager for 1979. Veeck took advantage of Kessinger's veteran leadership, to be sure. But with his financial situation increasingly becoming grim, he saved a separate, big salary in doubling up Kessinger's duties.

Kessinger scarcely had a chance to succeed on a Sox roster long on designated hitters and short on depth. He survived the riot of Steve Dahl's infamous "Disco Demolition Night," which cost the Sox a forfeited nightcap of a twi-night doubleheader but pulled the plug on his own career with the team 46–60 and mired in fifth place in the AL West in early August 1979.

His decision had a positive ramification, though. Needing to keep reins on the budget, Veeck promoted his thirty-four-year-old Triple-A manager to succeed Kessinger. Tony La Russa, briefly a Kessinger Cubs teammate at the start of 1973, went on to manage almost continuously for the next twenty-five years.

"I was never asked to resign from the White Sox," Kessinger said. "There was never an indication that I wasn't going to be the manager for the next year. I made the decision in August and went to Veeck. My feeling was the majors was not where Don Kessinger needs to be right now. So I told Bill to go ahead and make a change now.

"It was time to do something else. It wasn't an experience I wanted to continue. The Sox were great to me. I loved Bill Veeck, loved Roland Hemond. But my family is tops to me. I was missing a lot. My two boys were young and were more important to me. After I was traded to the Cardinals, we moved to Memphis [from

Northbrook, Illinois], not knowing I would ever end up in Chicago again."

So he would go on to set himself up in business, toe-dipping in athletics as a radio color announcer for Ole Miss basketball games before getting back into coaching. All the while, Kessinger rooted for both his old Chicago teams.

Like millions of others, he was heartbroken on October 14, 2003, when the Cubs' World Series hopes unraveled in the span of a few minutes during the eighth inning of game 6 of the National League Championship Series against the Florida Marlins. In particular, Kessinger could mentally put himself in the persona of Cubs short-stop Alex Gonzalez, whose boot of a routine, second-out grounder could have put a stop to the collapse.

"Things like that happens, doggone it, it happens," he said. "One thing you've got to learn as a baseball player is that there's not just another game tomorrow but also another pitch coming right up. It was one of those tragic deals."

He knew all too well what was missed by the flop to the Marlins.

"Everyone in the country, except for Marlins and Yankees fans, wanted a Cubs–Red Sox World Series. It would have been great for baseball and an unbelievably watched World Series. I pull so hard for that, not just for the Cubs, but primarily for the fans of Chicago."

Kessinger would have to wait for another twenty-first-century season to take the monkey off the back of the Cubs, particularly his '69 crew. For anyone who ever played in that era in Wrigley Field, the concept of unfinished business never goes away. Yet that never gets Kessinger down.

"I was fortunate to have played in six All-Star games," he said. "But I would have traded them all for one World Series. It didn't happen.

"I think more of the great times in Chicago. They were marvelous. You do that rather than dwelling on what we did or didn't do."

A Guy Nicknamed "Bruno"

G lenn Beckert, who rightfully sported the nickname "Bruno," was one of the Cubs' hardest-working guys of all time. And that style continued well past his playing days when he descended daily into the organized chaos of the trading floor of the Chicago Board of Trade.

All those mental and physical bruises from playing second base and trading long since healed, Beckert started a few years before reaching Social Security age, living the life of a retired squire about ninety miles south of Tampa on Florida's west coast. Everyone figured Beckert would loll about while others had to still slog their way to work. After all, wasn't he the wealthiest of the fabled 1969 Cubs, having bummed everything off everybody, then stashing his money like a squirrel does acorns?

"No, no, no," Beckert protested when rumors of his considerable affluence are brought up. "Maybe I get teased about that. I was somewhat frugal. You just try to save everything up."

Beckert made some money in his postbaseball career, to be sure. He was loaned $130,000 by trading executive Hank Shatkin to buy his seat at the Board of Trade in 1976. Beckert's account was debited for the payback, and he did well enough on the floor to get free and clear of the Shatkin loan in three years. Then, in 1991, having just passed his fiftieth birthday, Beckert began leasing out his seat so he could escape to Florida after Halloween each year. Now he doesn't trade at all, coming back to Chicago to see his two daughters and five grandchildren and attend Cubs conventions and assorted Wrigley Field games while avoiding most of winter's blast.

"When I was younger, I used to love the snow and ice skating and a lot of things, snowmobiling. When I was at the Board of Trade, I'd probably get there at six in the morning, the coldest time of the day, and the wind's blowing. I've paid my dues. I like Arizona, too, but I'm a water person. I like boating and that stuff."

Beckert was not going to keep trading into his sixties. Life is too short in his view.

"There are legendary traders, guys who make zillions of dollars," he said. "I'm not one like that. A lot of people put the almighty dollar in front of everything else. Then, they'll be sixty-five or seventy and realize they've missed out on a lot of things."

With five grandchildren on which to dote, Beckert has to buy a lot of birthday and holiday presents. He knows better than most ex-Cubs how to economize.

"Sam's Club is where I go shopping," he said.

Somehow, hanging with Beckert, you get the feeling you missed out on a lot of fun by not being old enough to cover the '69 Cubs. Beckert and roommate Ron Santo had some adventures on and off the field. Possessed of a sardonic wit, Beckert is the one guy to which you go to put it all into perspective.

He never took his own baseball career for granted. He couldn't, not having been blessed with supreme natural talent. Beckert was all of the blue-collar mentality of his Pittsburgh roots. And he's forever thankful of the warm embrace of Wrigley Field and Cubs fans.

On September 4, 1983, he was persuaded to make his first-ever trip to the right-field bleachers to surprise a longtime fan on her twenty-eighth birthday. After shocking the fan by his appearance, he climbed up into the still-empty center-field bleachers before the game to take in Wrigley Field at its panoramic best. Spreading his arms wide, he proclaimed, "I can't believe the view you get from here."

Twenty years later, on September 28, 2003, Beckert stood in the left-field corner of the ballpark, helping old teammate Randy Hundley raise Santo's number 10 banner up the foul pole in its retirement ceremony. His sometimes stony hands a source of amusement for his teammates during his playing days, Beckert flawlessly raised the banner up the yardarm to fly underneath Ernie Banks's number 14, one of only three numbers retired in Cubs annals.

Wrigley Field's sun-splashed confines were often preferable to the wheat pits at the Board of Trade, where thousands of dollars are gained or lost in the blink of an eye. The nonstop pressure of trading seemed an odd career for Beckert.

But he was in kind of a jam. Injuries had finally washed out his baseball career at thirty-five after two years with the San Diego Padres.

"I still had kids in diapers with a mortgage on the house and no employment," he said.

And he had trepidation when the trading opportunity was proposed to him.

"It was scary," he said. "I knew nothing about commodity trading."

After stalwart trader Shatkin staked Beckert to his seat, he embarked on a learning curve in the soybean pit. He would flash a different set of hand signals from his baseball days while screaming at the top of his lungs amid the one-hundred-decibel din.

"It took me two years to learn the business," he said. "You're an athlete; you have your ups and downs, good days when you get hits and days when you play badly. It is similar to the Board of Trade. But your mistakes at the Board of Trade weren't in the newspapers and on TV."

In another conversation before he cashed in his trading jacket for good, Beckert was glib in describing the wild world of the commodities trader.

"You always have a little bit of fear," he said. "It's necessary. Out of every one hundred people who get into [trading], possibly 65, 66 percent fail. You never set a goal because you never know how you're going to do."

Already in his late thirties, Beckert avoided the T-bond bit, rewarding in financial return but definitely a young man's game in a win-or-lose-it-all mentality. He eventually gravitated to the wheat pit.

"You have older guys in the wheat pit, but it's still pandemonium. There's still the craziness, the yelling and screaming. There's no other system that's ever been devised to buy and sell commodities, so you have to play it that way.

"You've got to adjust to the wave. The biggest thing is how to get out of a loss. And never get too greedy. The first loss is your best loss. Say you buy at $3, then it trades at $2.95. You get out as fast as possible, because it could drop far lower than that."

The risks, in Beckert's view, were worth the reward of doing something he grew to like.

"I just like the freedom," he said then. "In baseball, you were always told what time to be at the ballpark or catch the bus. So many people in life are stuck in a job they don't want to do. There are risks all around—driving a car, for instance. The majority of people always need a security blanket [of a set income]. But how many people say, 'If I only did this or did that?'"

Thus Beckert was doubly lucky, with the lucrative trading gig following up his eleven-year baseball career. He was self-made in both baseball and the Board of Trade.

He grew up watching games at part of the Knothole Gang at old Forbes Field in Pittsburgh, viewing Ernie Banks in his prime when the Cubs came to town. Good enough to get signed by the Boston Red Sox as an infielder, he came to the Cubs in a first-year player draft in 1963. Then tragedy gave Beckert, a shortstop, his big break.

Rising second-base star Kenny Hubbs was killed when his private plane crashed in a snowstorm in Utah just before spring training in 1964. When journeyman Joey Amalfitano, utility player Jimmy Stewart, and minor-league call-up Ron Campbell were found wanting as a Hubbs replacement throughout '64, Beckert was converted to second. He said he couldn't have made the majors any other way.

"I didn't have the tools to play shortstop at the major-league level," he said. "I don't remember playing any second in the minors. I got a crash course in that position in the winter league [1964–1965]. I felt sorry about it [Hubbs's death]. Strange things happen. Why did Lyndon Johnson become president?"

Called up and given the job at second and at leadoff hitter to open the 1965 season, Beckert struggled at first. He couldn't get above the .230 range. But he started to absorb the necessary big-league lessons and began a lifelong friendship with Santo, with whom he roomed on the road.

Beckert learned about overcoming obstacles from Santo, who played despite being afflicted with juvenile diabetes. One day, while Santo was on a hitting streak, he administered his insulin shot in the hotel bathroom. Catching a glimpse of that, Beckert remarked, true to his style, that he wanted whatever Santo was injecting since the latter player was on fire at the plate.

The players had a lot more enjoyment off the field, too. One day, a brawl broke out in a Cincinnati nightspot. Santo and Beckert escaped by crawling underneath the tables. Santo and Beckert could be wrasslin' on the locker-room floor while players stepped over and around them like nothing was happening. Today, such a scene would evoke a huge media controversy.

Players in Beckert's era had their quotient of fun but always were ready when the first pitch was thrown.

"You always hear wild stories about the players," Beckert said. "But you never hear about going to bed early and ordering room service, like we did all the time in New York. Yeah, even in New York.

"We were a looser group. Now there's pressure on players. Every hit means something—thousands of dollars in incentives. There's pressure from the media. The media is not interested in what happened during a game. Now it's all second-guessing of the manager and general manager and where the players' wives went shopping."

Any off-duty hijinks were a welcome respite from the grind of the 162-game schedule in a different era. To survive in an era of one-year contracts and brushback pitches, players had to be mentally and physically tough. Cageyness also was welcome, and Beckert had it in droves with his batting style.

Choking up on the bat when he realized that power would be largely absent from his game, Beckert developed dual talents as an adept hit-and-run practitioner and a tough-to-strike-out batsman. After the tough rookie season, Beckert's average jumped to .287 in 1966 with a career-high fifty-nine RBIs. Kessinger's overall offensive development trailed Beckert's, but the two became well-known throughout the National League for the hit-and-run, with Beckert's short swing punching hits through the vacated shortstop's hole.

"Maybe 99 percent of the guys are down on the end of the bat," he said of today's players, who usually don't mind strikeout totals well above one hundred annually. Beckert averaged just twenty-one strikeouts per season from 1967 to 1973.

"They don't have the makeup to be home-run hitters," he added. "Nothing happens if you strike out. By putting the ball in play, you always have a chance. They could really have a higher average—and make more money—if they just concentrated on hitting the ball. You see smaller guys hitting .200. Do these guys mentally realize they're hitting .200, and why?"

The hit-and-run style had vanished by the late 1980s, which was when Beckert lamented the game's changes in the Rick Talley book *The Cubs of '69*.

"I wish I saw more hit-and-run in baseball today, but I don't," he said then. "I keep watching on TV, but I don't see it. It's too bad because they're taking a great thing out of baseball. . . . When I came up, I was down on the bat, too. Then I moved up about an inch to an inch and a half. My goal was to stay in the major leagues, and I wasn't going to do it down on the bat. I didn't have the power."

Beckert jumped into the .290s in 1968–1969. But his best season was 1971, when he contended for the National League batting title in late summer. At one point in August, he had climbed to .359. He had dipped a bit to .342 when his season ended in early September when he tore ligaments in his right thumb in the artificial turf at Busch Stadium.

The St. Louis ballpark was not a good place for Beckert to maintain his health. Early in the 1969 season, third baseman Santo tried to nab Cardinals counterpart Mike Shannon trying to take an extra base going into second in one game. Realizing the ball was going to beat him, Shannon flattened Beckert, knocking him unconscious and sending him to Jewish Hospital for treatment. Former football player Shannon, now a Cardinals radio announcer, was still proud of the Gashouse Gang–style play thirty-two years later, requesting a videotape of the play that was included on the vintage 1969 Cubs midseason TV special.

"How did I hang onto that ball?" Beckert wondered from the vantage point of a generation later. "It must have stuck in the webbing of my glove. I don't mind. That's how the game was played. I went in hard to the second baseman–shortstop myself."

As a second baseman, Beckert was a target for base runners still rubbing black and blue marks from being hit by mound enforcers like Bill Hands.

"Instead of going to the mound, they took it out on the second baseman or shortstop," Beckert said. "He [Kessinger] can see where they were coming from, but at second base you can't always see. After awhile, you learned to be careful, especially if it was someone with speed coming at you. A big heavy-set guy, you didn't worry about it. You rushed a lot of plays. Back then, the guys were a little more aggressive taking out second basemen, breaking up double plays."

Never the most physically graceful fella, Beckert was a slight hazard to teammates in the field. He earned the "Bruno" nickname in honor of wrestler Bruno Sammartino. Beckert sometimes stumbled about grappler-like, bowling over other infielders going after pop-ups.

Unless injuries were severe, players quickly found their way back into the lineup in Beckert's time.

"Take a guy like Billy Williams, who set the all-time Cubs endurance record [1,117 consecutive games played]," Beckert said. "I remember one game when his ankle was twice its normal size, and he went out and played. We admired him for that."

But there was one malady Beckert could not overcome. Not long after his prime season in 1971, he developed rheumatoid arthritis in his left ankle. Running became more difficult by the month.

"No medicine could get rid of it quickly at the time," Beckert said. He was administered aspirin, analgesic medications, and a series of shots. Eventually he underwent a number of surgeries.

Despite an early twenty-six-game hitting streak, Beckert's 1973 season collapsed after the All-Star break. He was frequently out of the lineup due to the bad ankle, replaced by Paul Popovich. He played just 114 games, hitting .255, by far the worst since his rookie season. Afterward, he was traded to the San Diego Padres for outfielder Jerry Morales, a deal that greatly benefited the Cubs. Morales turned into a run producer while the increasingly crippled Beckert played in just seventy-three games in San Diego in 1974–1975.

He had played a few decades too soon to help his ankle.

"It's finally cured with a new medication from Abbott Labs," Beckert said of the arthritis. "Now I feel wonderful. I feel great."

He wished he felt that great over the Labor Day weekend in 2001. He had a brush with his own mortality while visiting an aunt in Pittsburgh. Beckert fell down a flight of stairs, hitting his head. He had internal bleeding in his skull.

"I caught my foot on a rug going to the bathroom in the basement," he recalled. "I had been sleeping on a couch, not wanting to wake up my aunt."

Beckert was unconscious and in serious condition. "For three weeks, I had no idea whether I was alive," he said. He was totally unaware of the horrors of September 11.

But he recovered in time to attend the 2002 Cubs Convention as if nothing had ever happened.

"I was very fortunate," he said. "The Presbyterian Hospital at the University of Pittsburgh saved me."

He lived to continue playing out his role as an all-time Cubs favorite while cheering up old roomie Santo through his myriad health problems.

Beckert knows he's got a continuing role to perform—honored old-timer from the Leo Durocher–era Cubs. Years ago, he proclaimed that the '69 team was the second-most popular in Chicago history after the Super Bowl XX champion Bears.

"The 1969 legend is good for us and keeps us together, keeps our families together," he said. "We're still amazed at the appeal of that team. Why would they pack a room [at the Cubs Convention] to hear a bunch of old guys like us?"

Sidle up to Beckert, and he'll give you advice on hit-and-runs, turning the double play, commodities trading. Just don't ask him for a loan. Life has its limits.

Always Gentleman Jim

If anyone knows how to persevere, it's Jim Hickman.

After all, he played as an original New York Met in 1962, wondering if senior-citizen manager Casey Stengel even remembered his name or whether he was on the team. All those many hundreds of Mets losses followed. There was the bench in Wrigley Field, followed by a savior's regular role and redemption through so many late-inning clutch challenges answered, sometimes with a Waveland Avenue homer.

And then came the toughest of all obstacles a decade after his last game. There was the bottomless pit of financial ruin during an agricultural depression of the early 1980s, when $700 earned from Randy Hundley's Fantasy Camp tided Hickman and his family over one winter.

So it was a piece of cake, comparatively, when a massive Cincinnati Reds management upheaval ending the year 2003 left Hickman's sixteen-year tenure as roving minor-league hitting instructor in question. That's on top of the chaos that former majority owner Marge Schott had instituted behind the upfront image of her Saint Bernards soiling the turf at old Riverfront Stadium.

Never one to raise his voice or get too upset, Hickman was quietly satisfied when he was re-upped under the new front-office administration for another season teaching the Reds kids. But he never worried too much about regime changes or office politics. He's ever "Gentleman Jim," be it Wrigley Field in 1970 or a minor-league ballpark in Nashville or Chattanooga early in the twenty-first century.

"We've been through a lot of bosses," Hickman said. "We've probably had six, seven minor-league directors. But you try to keep your mind on your business. You do your job the best you can.

"They've been real good to me over the years. They've never told me what to tell the kids."

Always, he is based in Henning. His Tennessee hometown, nearly fifty miles north of Memphis, was made famous by broadcaster Jack Brickhouse whenever Hickman came to bat amid a tumultuous Cubs era. Through all his baseball incarnations and near bankruptcy on his farm, Hickman always knew his emotional base was Henning, a comfortable place for wife Nita to raise their four sons.

Hickman has been able to stay in baseball because he's always able to come home to Henning. Instead of flying all over the country to far-flung farm clubs, the Reds' top two minor-league affiliates play in Nashville and Chattanooga, three and five hours' driving distance, respectively, from Henning. Other minor-league outposts at which Hickman can work, including the Cubs' Jackson, Tennessee, Double-A franchise, are within driving distance. And if he has to extend himself further to drive to Cedar Rapids, Iowa, or Winston-Salem, North Carolina, so be it.

Nita goes with him on his trips, a payback for the itinerant life of a ballplayer's family and weeks of being left home while her husband was on the road as a player.

"Being gone so much was tough on her," Hickman said. "She was a pretty tough gal, to throw those kids in a car and drive all over the country."

Hickman has had the Reds' gig more than twice as long as any other gig in baseball, and it sure was more stable than the farming he reluctantly gave up years back.

"I've been real lucky," Hickman said. "We had a team in Stockton, California, a couple of years and had to fly out there. We now have a [rookie-level] team in Billings, Montana, so I make one trip a season out there.

"If not for [driving with Nita to assignments], I don't know if I could continue to do this. With a lot of these kids, their wives go with them, too."

Hickman stays with it because hitting fundamentals don't change, even if the emphasis of baseball changes. Where the game was more balanced in the 1980s when Hickman started with the Reds, it's now a full-swing-and-damn-the-consequences style, following in the wake of McGwire, Sosa, Bonds, and a slew of middle infielders who muscle up for thirty or more homers. Add to that the questions of coachability of young players.

"You hear all kinds of tales, how kids wouldn't listen," Hickman said. "You always run into a few guys who think they know everything. But I've never had a lot of problems.

"I tell them what I think. The big thing I want is them to not hit the way I want to hit. Keep their own style but improve it. I always believed you can't do more than what you can do."

A lot of talk inevitably goes back to Hickman's own hitting style. He whiffed his fair share of times in his career but not at a pace that's tolerated today.

"The key is, nobody is worried about strikeouts the way they used to be," he said. "Striking out one hundred times a year is nothing. With a guy like Bob Gibson, you wanted to put the first good pitch you saw into play. Some guys who didn't have as good stuff as him, you can carry it a little farther. Some people said I had a pretty good eye at the plate."

"The biggest thing as far as hitters are concerned is you've got to get a pitch you can handle before you can hit it. Billy Williams's hitting zone was bigger than mine. He could handle more pitches around the fringe. Barry Bonds was the ultimate in patience. If he swung at more pitches, his average would come down. These great hitters know they've got talent, and that makes them more patient."

Hickman does not bog down his students with tales of the good ol' days, with the exception of the ultimate example of the qualities of patience: hitters who struggle for years to find the right rhythm.

"I'll tell them I was thirty-two before I learned how to hit," he said. "When a kid's struggling, I'll use that example."

But Hickman limits his comparison of then and now.

"People ask me what I think about players years ago compared to players now," he said. "Kids now as a whole are bigger and stronger. But the superstars of the '50s and '60s would be superstars now. They're just blessed with that ability. Henry Aaron would get to sixty homers. Same with Willie Mays, [Willie] Stargell, [Willie] McCovey."

His contemporaries did not use steroids to add muscle and power. But Hickman refuses to concede that supplements and drugs are the cause of the power explosion of modern times at the expense of the game's finer points.

"Who knows how much good it did?" he said. "Just because you're bigger and stronger doesn't make you a better hitter."

Whatever the style, form and philosophy of modern baseball, Hickman is just happy to be a part of it. He was at a low ebb of his life, farming having almost ruined him financially, when he got back into the game through an age-old connection—the legendary player development man Sheldon "Chief" Bender.

"Chief Bender was the first GM I every played for in [Cardinals affiliate] Albany, Georgia, in 1956," Hickman said. "I went to an old-timers game in Nashville in 1987, and I ran into Jimmy Stewart [a Reds official and former Cub]. He told me then, Ted Kluszewski was retiring, so Cincinnati was looking for a minor-league hitting coach. That was exactly at the time when I went broke. I said, 'I'll have to do something.' Jimmy said, 'I'll tell my boss.' Chief called me, and I took the job."

The scenario was different from what Hickman had hoped in a return to baseball.

"I wanted to work for the Cubs," he said. "When I first got back into baseball, I thought I'd get back with the Cubs. That never happened. I was living in a fantasy world. All the people in the front office changed. The Cubs as I knew [them] changed."

What didn't change was Hickman's financial predicament. He had always lived on the farm. When his career ended after the 1974 season, Hickman simply took up farming full-time. But debt and serving at the mercy of farm prices bedeviled smaller farmers at the time.

Hickman's base property, on which he raised cotton and soybeans, covered 250 acres outside Henning. He also leased additional land, up to fourteen hundred acres.

"I enjoyed it, farming was a good life," he said. "It was a decent living, and good life. I got out of it because I didn't have any money to pay off [debts]. I had to remortgage everything I had. I owed money I couldn't pay. Some [debts] were written off. They [local banks] did that with a lot of people."

Hickman told author Rick Talley in the 1989 book *The Cubs of '69* that, starting in 1980, land prices plummeted from $1,500 an acre down to $5 an acre. He had borrowed to buy $75,000 worth of tractors, but suddenly their value became a fraction of the original cost while he still owed the balance of the notes. Only old family farms that were not in debt around Henning survived the agriculture crash. Hickman had to take his baseball pension early, at age forty-five, drawing just $1,000 a month to start.

By 1983, Henning's People's Bank refused to loan Hickman operating capital for the next season. Eventually the bank claimed his land and house but allowed the family to stay on while they paid rent. At one dark moment, the Hickmans lived for a number of months on the $700 he earned from working as an instructor at a Randy Hundley Fantasy Camp.

Hickman would be the last generation to farm in Henning.

"I didn't want my four boys going into the farming business," he said.

Three Hickmans still live in Henning. Oldest son, Jim Jr., and youngest son, Mike, work in the construction business. Second son, Bill, works in a lumber mill. Third son, Joey, carries on the family athletic tradition as golf pro at the Hickory Club in Nashville. With the depression, financial and psychological, of the farm disaster receding into the past, father and son Hickman can hit the links together and relax.

Joey doesn't have to wait for Dad to tell him old war stories from baseball. All the Hickmans lived it, the old man's station wagon with Nita and four boys a common sight weaving through the postgame crowd of autograph seekers at Wrigley Field in days gone by.

But no golf partner could ever get bored by the rags-to-riches Hickman baseball story.

After putting in six years in the Cardinals farm system, Hickman finally got a break, such as it was, when the expansion Mets needed warm bodies to fill out a roster that was dotted with old New York baseball favorites on the downslide of their careers. He became more or less an outfield regular with the Stengel-led Mets from 1962 to 1965, but never once in any season exceeding 494 at bats, seventeen homers, fifty-seven RBIs, or a .257 average.

"My first couple of years with the Mets," Hickman told Rudy M. Vorkapic of *Vine Line* magazine, "I was one of the young guys there because they basically drafted old guys [in the expansion draft] . . . and I was one of their prospects. But New York's a tough place to play, pressure-wise, especially on a losing ball club. They even stuck me at third one year until I almost got killed. After the first couple, three years, I was already just another guy . . . and that wears out after awhile."

Nita put thousands of miles on the station wagon driving to Los Angeles, where Hickman landed as a pinch hitter in 1967. He reached the pits opening the season in 1968, when the Dodgers dispatched him to the minors.

But then he got his greatest career break. On April 23, 1968, the Dodgers were downsizing while the Cubs sought a relief stopper. Los Angeles traded Phil "The Vulture" Regan to the Cubs—throwing in Hickman as part of the deal—in exchange for outfielder Ted Savage and young lefty Jim Ellis. Hickman almost immediately worked himself into an outfield platoon with Al Spangler and Willie Smith, playing against left-handers.

He flashed the greatest power on the club—occasionally. Chicago broadcaster Les Grobstein claims a Hickman homer in 1968, one of five he slugged for the Cubs, was the longest ever hit at Wrigley Field, landing five houses north on Kenmore Avenue. That's one house beyond the popularly viewed longest homer ever, by Dave Kingman in 1976.

In his typical gentlemanly fashion, Hickman doesn't remember the homer as Grobstein did. It was not the style to stand at home plate in those days.

"I never watched a ball to see how far it went," Hickman said. "I was tickled to death to just hit it. If it went that far, it does astonish me a bit, and gives me a sense of pride."

The '68 blast would be the first of a number of Hickman distance classics, many belted at just the right time. His platoon role, mostly in right field with a few appearances in center, continued into 1969, but Hickman, by now a comparative baseball graybeard at thirty-two, impressed with some late-inning heroics. He hit booming game-ending homers in Wrigley Field against the Montreal Expos in April and the Pittsburgh Pirates in June, prompting some of the loudest Jack Brickhouse "Hey Hey" calls of all time.

Finally, with Spangler slumping, manager Leo Durocher handed the right-field job to Hickman full time on August 3, 1969. It was as if he had been let out of jail for the first time in his career. Hickman almost single-handedly kept the Cubs lineup afloat with ten homers in August alone, including a game-winning grand slam against the Houston Astros in one slugfest. Other Cubs regulars were slowing down, but Hickman continued hitting like a demon into September, finishing with twenty-one homers, as the team collapsed.

He almost made the play of the year during a crucial showdown with the Mets on September 8 at Shea Stadium. Hickman, who always had the Cubs' strongest outfield arm during his tenure on the North Side, rifled a throw to home plate trying to cut down Tommie Agee with the lead run. Hundley appeared to make a swipe tag of Agee, but umpire Satch Davidson ruled him safe. Hundley's fandango dance protesting the call and the appearance of a black cat near the Cubs' dugout are images that are being replayed forever.

"I think about 1969 all the time," Hickman told Talley. "It's hard to forget, and I won't lie—it's still sad to think about. But a lot of happiness came from it, too."

Not the least of which was Hickman's establishing himself as a dangerous hitter. Durocher kept him in the lineup, mostly in center field, to begin 1970. But as Ernie Banks's ravaged knees finally forced him from the lineup in June, Hickman shifted over to first for the rest of the season.

Jim and Nita Hickman with granddaughter Heather.
Photo courtesy of Jim Hickman.

By then, he was a clutch-hitting sensation, his momentum carried over from 1969 without interruption. Another game-ending homer and his reception at home plate was captured as the cover-story photo in a story on Hickman in the old *Chicago Today* Sunday magazine. As the leading Cubs run producer at midseason, he was chosen by National League manager Gil Hodges as a reserve for the 1970 All-Star team; strangely, Billy Williams, in the middle of his own greatest-ever season, was neither voted on by the fans or picked as a backup.

Hodges's choice paid off. Hickman's twelfth-inning single drove in Pete Rose with the winning run as he barreled into AL catcher Ray Fosse. The Rose–Fosse collision is another classic moment replayed for all time. Of course, the low-key Hickman is seen just for a second flicking his bat as the ball sliced into center field.

His dream season continued almost until the very end of 1970, when he slumped in the final couple of weeks. Hickman finished with thirty-two homers, 115 RBIs, and a .315 average, prodigious numbers by the standards of the time.

"As for me, all I could think was, 'Was that me?'" he recalled. "It was . . . really. I guess you'd say over my head. I never thought of myself as a .300 hitter. Probably, I should have. I mean, I might have been a better player."

Few were better around the clubhouse. Hickman was a quiet voice of reason. Such sanity was needed during a famed locker-room confrontation between the increasingly embattled Durocher and Ron Santo, Joe Pepitone, and Milt Pappas late in 1971. At one point, Durocher accused Santo of asking for his own special day, prompting Santo to lunge at the sixty-five-year-old manager. Eventually, cooler heads prevailed. Hickman briefly spoke up, stating that the confrontation was bad for both sides.

"I didn't want to see that happen," he said of the Durocher–Santo rhubarb. "It was one of those things that happen. The whole thing was blown out of proportion."

Hickman probably was not impartial. While the imperious, amoral Durocher eventually grated on the nerves of the majority of his players, Hickman was a Durocher backer. After all, Durocher gave him a chance to play that few other managers had ever matched.

"Leo was great with me," Hickman said. "I can't say anything bad about Leo.

"Leo saved me. He just gave me a chance to play. I can't say enough about the man. I played for some great managers [citing Stengel and Walter Alston with the Dodgers], but Leo did more for me than anybody."

Hickman slugged thirty-six homers combined in 1971–1972 despite illness and a return to a semiplatoon role. But age started to creep up on him in 1973. With Joe Pepitone let go, Hickman could not hit enough to retain at least the right-handed half of a first-base platoon. He slumped to three homers, twenty RBIs, and just a .244 average in only 201 at bats as the Cubs went through a revolving door of Pat Bourque, Carmen Fanzone, Andre Thornton, Gonzalo Marquez, and even Billy Williams at first base.

Hickman was swept out in the post-1973 housecleaning. On March 23, 1974, he was traded to St. Louis for young pitcher Scipio Spinks, who never played for the Cubs. He finished his career as a pinch hitter on the Cardinals in 1974. But despite the quiet wrap-up to his baseball days, the Cubs years stand out loudly front and center in his memories.

"I'm tickled to death that I was there at that time," he said. "I'm proud that it was a well-remembered team. It was fortunate that all of us got along. I roomed with Phil Regan. We were close, and in recent years I got to see Regan when he managed at West Michigan [Class A farm club in Grand Rapids]. Kessinger is close because we're from the same area in Tennessee."

Cubs fans haven't forgotten Gentleman Jim, either. At a youth clinic in Gary, Indiana, led by Pirates manager Lloyd McClendon during the All-Star break of 2001, the subject drifted to the Durocher-era Cubs teams whom Little League star McClendon rooted for in Gary.

"Remember Jim Hickman?" McClendon asked a clinic attendee. That's the impression his clutch hitting had made and held firm over the decades.

"I still get quite a few autograph requests," Hickman said of the inbound mail in Henning. "I usually let them stack up for two weeks, then I sign them and send them back."

A much easier way to get a Hickman autograph is to hang around batting practice of any number of minor-league teams in the mid-South. Look for the tall, lean guy in a Reds uniform, quietly doling out advice to young hitters. That will be the telltale sign of a man who knew how to handle the pressure of winning a game with one swing of the bat in the late innings.

"As long as my health holds up, I still enjoy doing it," Hickman said of his bush-league rounds. "The fire's still there, but it's not as hot as it was. The kids help me out as much I as I do for them."

His Own Wild Kingdom

For a whole bunch of reasons, Rich Nye was born twenty-five years too soon.

Imagine if he could have brought his favorite animals, even a well-behaved dog, to Wrigley Field when he pitched for the Cubs between 1966 and 1969.

Uh-uh. Don't think Leo Durocher would have allowed it. And what would Leo the Lion have thought of a player who even asked? Pansy? Weirdo? Leo never lived to see Cubs reliever Kyle Farnsworth bring his two giant hounds, one of them named Zeus, onto the grass at Wrigley Field a few years back. Or how 'bout Sarah Wood, spouse of Kerry, waiting for her man after the game by the wives' lounge down the left-field line with the couple's little joys, a pug and Jack Russell terrier, straining at their leashes?

"I grew up with animals," Nye said. "I had dogs, cats, and a large desert tortoise. I didn't have any weird things, but I still had a fascination with all animals. When we went on the road, I visited all the zoos.

"I felt I could communicate with animals, that they didn't seem to be tense around me."

Left-hander Nye's mound career didn't last all that much longer after a fine rookie season in 1967. But with baseball over, he had the rest of the animal kingdom to serve as his passion. He attended veterinary school at the University of Illinois in the mid-1970s. Three decades later, he was still practicing his craft as senior veterinarian at Midwest Bird and Exotic Animal Hospital in Westchester, Illinois, about fifteen miles west of Chicago's Loop.

And if you think love of animals has enveloped his life, that's extended to love of humans. His wife, Sue, a fellow veterinarian, had opened the animal hospital with Nye in 1986. More than a decade later, the couple were married.

But the Nyes, in love and on the job, weren't dealing with Fido the dog and Fluffy the cat. Everything but. Always fascinated with birds, Nye decided his clinic would specialize in exotic pets, starting with his avian friends and then expanding to rabbits, ferrets, other small mammals, and reptiles.

While he took a break from surgeries on a platoon of iguanas at the clinic, Nye could analyze why people have kept exotic animals—and why so many misguided folks have tried to treat dangerous wild cats and big snakes as household pets.

"An exotic pet is one where you can carry it into the hospital," Nye said. "If it's a dangerous animal, you can't call it an exotic pet. A monkey can be dangerous. People have done this for a long time. A lot of actors and actresses get involved in wild-animal issues. They see a leopard in a movie in which they're acting, and that gets them excited because it was raised in captivity and seemingly doesn't have quite the same aggressive nature. But it still has its wild instincts.

"Domesticating dogs took thousands of years. Dogs became part of man's habitat when man became their source of food. The ones that would hang around man would breed generations just like them, and they'd develop a human–animal bond. It's different with wild animals."

But just as dogs and cats are different from wolves and leopards, people who keep wild animals are different from the average pet owner. A good example was flashy, eccentric former Cub Mel Hall, who during his Yankees years paraded around Manhattan with a couple of wild cats that the city of New York eventually had to clamp down upon.

"When someone has a big cat, a gorilla, any other large primate, or a twenty-foot dangerous snake, something else is driving it," Nye said. "When people have pets like that, have interests in these animals, they want to be different. Look at many owners of big reptiles; they've got tattoos and [body] piercings. That's got to be the perception of pet owners when they have a big boa constrictor around their neck. They can get in trouble quickly. If the animal gets angry or spooked, there's no way to handle it."

"Most of the time, the people are impulse buyers for pets. I had a woman bring me a baby alligator, a foot and a half long. She had a four-and-a-half-year-old daughter. In three and a half years, her daughter will be eight, while the alligator will be five feet long. It's not going to be a calm, relaxed pet. That will be a dangerous mix, a wild animal and a still-small child in the house."

There had been more of a fascination with keeping monkeys as pets. But Nye has soured on treating them. "They carry diseases that are a threat to the staff at this clinic," he said.

With all his warnings about keeping wild or untamed animals, a somewhat adventurous and conscientious pet owner can own an unusual pet. It takes the same research as buying a dog or cat. Nye said the pet owner's lifestyle must conform to being able to care for and handle the animal. Workaholics who are gone sixteen or eighteen hours a day do no good service to any pet.

"We'll see large constrictors at the clinic," he said of the huge snakes. "But if they're handled a lot, fed, and well-cared for, they can make for very interesting pets. Snakes and turtles are fascinating to watch. But you have to learn the ins and outs."

Same with iguanas, another more common household companion in the last few decades.

"They're 100 percent vegetarians," Nye said. "But this is a wild animal. It's not as tame as you want. The tamest iguana can get pissed off and bite. All these animals have a biting instinct."

The pet that has grown most in popularity, though, is not as exotic as one might believe.

"There aren't many who realize that rabbits make neat pets," Nye said. "Rabbits have grown in our practice from perhaps 2 percent to 35 percent. Birds are 45 percent. Another 15 percent are ferrets and 5 percent are reptiles."

But even though he sees literally a wild kingdom of patients, Nye still is most stimulated by treating birds and observing their behavior. It was the reason he formed his own specialized clinic after getting his veterinary feet wet at the prominent Niles Animal Hospital, where he treated dogs and cats. Now, he has the challenge of handling the often-beautiful birds, who can be outwardly intimidating with their size and giant, sharp beaks.

"Macaws and cockatoos generally sit still, but Amazons tend to squirm and move around," Nye said. "But with proper handling, you won't injure the bird—or yourself."

The supposed intelligence of several breeds of parrots, especially the African gray, has been under increasing study while Nye has specialized in birds. The more hopeful of pet lovers have been waiting for researchers to proclaim birds possess deductive reasoning due to their superior verbal skills. But the gray or Amazon that does a perfect mimic of his owner's voice and other sounds may not be figuring the world out the way humans believe.

"Anything that happens in an animal, the written-down observation is a human interpretation of what the animal is doing or saying," Neye said. "It's not a computer that spits out an answer that is scientifically oriented. The thing that's interesting about it is not everybody looks at the animal the same way.

"A bird, like a child, repeats phrases heard all the time. It's not any different than you learning something. If it's repeated enough times, you learn when to say it. It's not deductive reasoning. It's how the learning process goes."

Nye had to be committed to the science of handling animals to attend veterinary school in the first place. The academic course of study is difficult, be it in the 1970s or 2000s. What has radically changed is the gender composition of veterinary graduates.

"Then it was a male-oriented population," Nye said of his rookie days. "From 80–20 percentage males, it's now 80–20 females."

One aspect has not changed, though. The huge salaries drawn by some MDs won't be repeated by their DVMs.

"It's a good living," Nye said. "You're fulfilling the opportunity to make people and animals happy. Money is not the motivating aspect. You've got to love people, too, because they're owners of the animals. Love of animals is not enough. The job requires excellent communication skills. There's obviously some instincts needed about problem solving. When you're trying to solve a problem and you're treating a human, a doctor asks questions and you get answers. But you won't get that from an animal."

Longtime vets like Nye now enjoy better understanding of animal-borne diseases and employ better diagnostic techniques than in their younger years. But the basic goal of the profession remains the same.

"Our job is educators [of pet owners]," he said. "We're not healers. We choose the right medicines to help animals heal themselves."

But as he enters his sixties, Nye may soon be ready to put away the tools of his trade. He and Susan have interests, such as gardening, enjoying nature, hiking, and others that cannot be pursued fully when emergencies at the clinic beckon on a regular basis.

"One thing I need to be looking at is what I'd be doing the rest of my life," Nye said. "Are there other things I'd like to do? I've had a good thirty-year run as a vet. And I've built up a clientele that are trustworthy of my fellow staffers at the hospital."

Symbolically, Nye's own home-based menagerie has been trimmed down. In the mid-1990s, his Downers Grove, Illinois, house hosted three cats, a schnauzer-mix dog, a parakeet, a cockatiel, ferrets, frogs, snakes, rats, chinchillas, hedgehogs, tortoises, and a tarantula. Ten years later, he was down to five canines—two Chihuahuas, two American Indian dogs, and a Shiloh shepherd—along with a pair of birds, a Pacific parrotlet, and a red-bellied parrot.

"We really trimmed it down at home," Nye said. "Our animals lived their lives fully and passed away."

Nye never was able to live his baseball life fully. He was part of a promising corps of home-grown Cubs pitchers coming up starting in the mid-1960s that included Ken Holtzman, Joe Niekro, Bill Stoneman, Jim Colborn, Joe Decker, Archie Reynolds, and Larry Gura. All but Holtzman enjoyed only fleeting success as Cubs because of the archaic way Leo Durocher, a man out of his time as manager, handled them.

A fourteenth-round pick in the June 1966 draft out of the University of California–Berkeley, Nye pitched in just sixteen minor-league games before he was rushed up, as was general manager John Holland's style, to make his debut at the end of the '66 season.

As a left-hander, Nye had an advantage in staking out a rotation spot on a team searching for starters. As the Cubs revived in 1967, going from a 103-defeat tailender to an 87-victory near contender, Nye rose with the tide.

"If I had to pick a time to be associated with baseball, it would have been the mid- and late 1960s," he said. "It was one of those times when Chicago fans were looking for a team to bring them excitement. We made an awful lot of new Cubs fans."

Nye was 11–9 going into September. In the first game of a Labor Day doubleheader against the Dodgers at Wrigley Field, he hurled six perfect innings, losing a 1–0 victory on a two-out, ninth-inning homer by once-and-future Cub Lou Johnson. He'd get a no-deci-

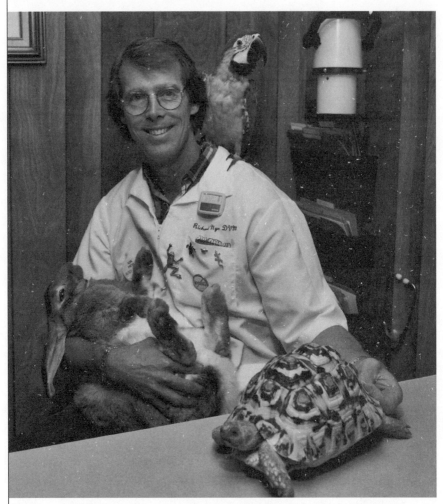

Rich Nye, former Cub and current exotic animal veterinarian. Photo by Chip Zellet.

sion as Ernie Banks homered to win the game 2–1 in the tenth. In his next start, Nye fanned ten Giants in his hometown of San Francisco. He finished with a 13–10 record—ranking second in wins to Fergie Jenkins's twenty—along with a 3.20 ERA and just fifty-two walks and 179 hits allowed in 205 innings.

"It's absolutely a feat to do that as a rookie," Nye said. "You can learn all you want, learn the hitters, but to be successful you need some luck. There were times I warmed up great, had great velocity, and felt I hit my spots during the game, but the batters still hit you."

Nye couldn't keep up the momentum into 1968, enduring tough-luck losses early on and finishing with a 7–12 record and 3.80 ERA during the "Year of the Pitcher." But Durocher's acerbic style did not help a twenty-three-year-old trying to mature.

"I don't think there's any doubt about that," he said of missing out on a better career due to Durocher. "You don't manage everybody the same. And he managed everyone the same.

"I'll give you the example of my brother, Bob, and I. Bob was a catcher. When he would do his best is when the coach would get on his back. I'd do my best with praise. I'd bust my butt and try harder. He was always a smart ass with Holtzman, but Ken gave it back to him. Not everyone could be like that. Leo did not know how to make a team, and we had twenty-five individuals as a result."

That's contrary to a lot of remembrances of the late 1960s Cubs—until those with long memories recall media criticism of the time that the team was indeed made up of too many individual stars. Even so, Durocher's clubhouse style has been largely discredited over the decades. And the Cubs of his day did not achieve their maximum potential due to the manager.

Nye's mound time decreased in the famed 1969 season before he moved on to the Cardinals and Expos. Shoulder problems made matters worse. He was ready for a change when his career finally ended in the Oakland Athletics organization in 1972.

And he made the change, all right, to the advantage of those critters that squawk and slither through their lives and of those owners who love them.

A GM with Some Special Jewelry

You wouldn't expect a guy with business horse sense like Bill Stoneman to lack the tools of his trade.

As his red-clad Anaheim Angels filtered out on the field below, general manager Stoneman was all set up in the office with a laptop, cell phone at the ready, and stacks of reports and statistics that left no stone unturned in the quest for the World Series. Remember, here's a man who was prepared to put graduate school ahead of baseball way back in 1966; who worked in financial services in a city that spoke a different language; who always had his head on straight whenever he was on the mound with the Cubs, Angels, or Montreal Expos or in a three-piece suit in corporate headquarters.

But Stoneman's experiences in both baseball and financial services also taught him a basic lesson: you don't go far unless you've got enough operating capital and a boss passionate enough to give the OK to spend that money.

He had one such boss in the Disney Corporation, who once agreed to increase the player payroll to get a player Stoneman wanted, even though Disney was attempting to sell the team. He has another one in former billboard magnate Arte Moreno, who must be a dream of an owner for so many fans who experience the nightmare of the same. Here's Moreno, half a year after buying the Angels from Disney, ensuring the franchise wouldn't be run Mickey Mouse–style by approving the spending of $146 million in free-agent money to Vladimir Guerrero, Bartolo Colon, and Kelvim Escobar. And, to boot, baseball-fan Moreno even lowered beer prices at Edison Field in Anaheim.

With a 2002 World Series ring in his possession and Moreno telling him to press the forward button, Stoneman's life is a far cry from Wrigley Field in the summer of 1967, when as a rookie pitcher he answered to, in succession, manager Leo Durocher, general manager John Holland, and owner P. K. Wrigley.

Stoneman was one of a cadre of homegrown Cubs pitchers who gave the bedraggled franchise one of its biggest jump starts in history in 1967. He was joined by Ken Holtzman, Rich Nye, Joe Niekro, and Chuck Hartenstein. Only Holtzman would still be pitching in Chicago beyond 1969, but it gave Stoneman a lesson he took with him through the decades into the baseball executive suite: there's no substitute for a good farm system. The 2002 world champion Angels had largely been assembled by the time Stoneman took over as GM the year before, and he knew that the winners were largely developed from within.

"The core of that team was homegrown," Stoneman said. "That's fun. Everyone likes that. The fans like it. The ownership likes it. The team likes it. You take a lot of pride in that. We did bring in some people from the outside—we traded a homegrown guy in Jimmy Edmonds [to St. Louis] for Adam Kennedy and Kent Bottenfield. We got a guy who was the American League Championship Series MVP in Kennedy. We got [David] Eckstein off waivers. He was a second baseman we turned into a shortstop. It clicked with Eckstein at shortstop and Kennedy at second.

"We signed Brendan Donnelly as a six-year free agent. We got Ben Weber off waivers. There were some little pieces we put together, but the core were guys who started their career as Angels and were there when I got there."

How Stoneman "got there" as GM of the surprise World Series winners, who rallied from a three-games-to-two deficit to beat Dusty Baker's San Francisco Giants, couldn't have been mapped or choreographed back to the days when Stoneman had to answer to Durocher for throwing a curveball at a time the "Lip" wanted a fastball.

In fact, the erudite Stoneman never gave a thought to staying in the game when the Angels handed him his release in July 1974. He had been working in public relations in Montreal in the off-season for O'Keefe Brewery. But a few years before, Royal Trust of Montreal had offered him a full-time job. Unable to take the offer while he was still playing baseball, Stoneman went back to Royal Trust to ask if he could still work for them. He then began a decade-long career in finance, moving to Toronto when company headquarters were relocated due to the French separatist movement in Quebec.

One day in 1982, Stoneman visited Olympic Stadium to say hello to some old contacts on the Expos, such as Steve Rogers, Gary Carter, and Rudy May. By chance he crossed paths with Expos president John McHale.

"He asked me if I ever thought of getting back into baseball," Stoneman said. "I said I was doing well and happy with Royal Trust Company. McHale said, 'You have a business background; baseball's becoming more of a business. We need people like you.'"

Stoneman and McHale talked for a year and a half until he finally took the job with the Expos at the end of the 1983 season. The timing was good when Royal Trust wanted to move him to the marketing department, not his preference. Stoneman would be charged with handling the more complicated contracts that began to dot the baseball landscape in the 1980s.

"At first, I didn't know what a contract looked like," he said. "I had to learn basic agreement, learn who agents were. I was totally green at it. It was a learning-on-the-job sort of thing."

Stoneman also had to learn to handle the fire-breathing agents of the day.

"It was a much more combative environment with the club–agent relationship," he said. "If you've been a player, you're used to competing, so you're not used to getting knocked down without knocking the other guy down. I figured I'm up for this; this is not a big deal. There were people who, you could get deals done without being so combative; others were trying to bully you. Now there are very few combative negotiations. It's more businesslike. You develop knowledge of the other guy, respect for the other guy."

Stoneman had to be tougher to keep as many bucks as possible in the Expos' pockets. Despite the large population of Montreal, the corporate support base began to thin out as the 1980s progressed and the separatist movement prompted a business exodus. Meanwhile, player salaries mushroomed.

"We had a market which produced the lowest revenues of all clubs," Stoneman said. "Sure, Montreal was a huge hockey market back then. But when players' salaries were lower and pressure to garner revenues wasn't as much, it worked well there. When salaries grew, pressure grew even on the Montreal Canadiens. They started to get squeezed.

"My company moved to Toronto. The Bank of Montreal moved its head office to Toronto; so did other companies. Jobs moved. It changed the tax base. There weren't enough of the big companies to provide corporate support. There was a time when the Expos had one of the better broadcast deals in baseball, and it dried up to nothing."

Owner Charles Bronfman, the Canadian liquor tycoon, always covered team deficits at the end of each season. But after the debilitating 1994 strike when the Expos incurred debt, Bronfman tired of propping up the team, which had been the National League's strongest when play was interrupted in mid-August.

"Bronfman sold the team to a consortium of individuals," Stoneman said. "Going into debt in sports is not a wise thing to do. It's an endless type of thing."

But the financial squeeze under which Stoneman, now in charge of baseball administration, and a succession of GMs had to operate did not cause him to gnash his teeth in frustration.

"You do the best you can under the circumstances," he said. "We took a lot of pride in our ability to locate and draft very good talent, especially from Latin America. One thing we couldn't control is outbidding other clubs. We had to sign and develop players better than anyone else. We took it as a challenge. People didn't complain."

But Stoneman finally had to think about making a change after the owners grew more restive and sold out to Jeffery Loria. "Like Royal Trust, it looked like a good time [to make a job change]," he said. Looking for a new GM, the Angels called the Expos to ask permission to talk to Stoneman. He interviewed with Angels president Tony Taveras, then climbed the ladder in talks with number 2 Disney honcho Sandy Litvak and finally corporate chairman Michael Eisner.

"I knew corporate discipline, and that probably helped," he said of the Disney interviews. Installed in the job in his mid-fifties, Stoneman turned the team's scouting emphasis more toward Latin America. Then he passed his first test of corporate salesmanship.

"In the winter prior to 2002, we went over budget to get Aaron Sele and get Brad Fullmer by trade," Stoneman said. "I picked up the phone and called [Disney team supervising executive] Paul Pressler. I said we're already over budget.

"The public perception and media is that these decisions are done by committee. That's not how it works. In this case, the parent company had a lot of money. The baseball entity was relatively small. To spend another couple of million bucks wasn't that huge a deal, but explaining it was. Remember, the club was for sale. They were looking at that, if the club does well on the field, it would help their effort to sell it.

"I told Paul, this Fullmer will be an important piece for us and will cost us a few bucks. It was pretty easy to get a go-ahead. He said if that's how you feel, let's go. There's a trust that has to develop between you and your boss."

A similar fascination exists with trades. The process is considered mysterious, yet Stoneman said deal-making is simply a matter of two teams reaching agreement. No smoke signals go up from the top of the tower.

"We all know each other; there aren't that many of us," Stoneman said of the GM fraternity. "It's more, two clubs have come to an understanding that they'd like to adjust their roster."

He cited a deal in which the Angels dealt catcher Jorge Fabregas to the Milwaukee Brewers in mid-season 2002 for outfielder Alex Ochoa.

"In the Ochoa deal, it was more a thing of moving a guy that saved them some money," he said. "They were looking to get some backup catching help. They benefited by getting a catcher right away, and they liked our minor leaguers. We said we're coming on strong, got a shot at it, let's bolster our outfield. Each club could help the other obtain their objective."

Stoneman witnessed the Angels achieving the ultimate objective as October 2002 ebbed. And as he marveled at the comeback over the Giants, he would soon see a familiar face in his private box at Edison Field.

"It was an exciting series," Stoneman said. "The fan excitement was there. They fed off one another. It's an experience that you can't describe. You have to live it. It's tremendous excitement but also tremendous focus on what's going on. By the time you get to the postseason, the GM doesn't have a whole lot to do with what's happening. You've done what you can do. It's in the hands of the players, manager, and coaches.

"You do think of people you played with or been associated with who haven't had the opportunity to experience what we did. Ernie Banks was at the World Series. He lives out in the LA area. He had a sip of wine with us. He came into my booth, and a bunch of friends were excited because it was Ernie Banks. He chatted and was gracious to talk to some of my buddies. So at the World Series, there was a Cubs connection."

Stoneman couldn't celebrate too far into 2003. The Angels' pitching slumped, forcing him to think of retooling the staff. And Disney finally completed the sale to Arte Moreno, who formerly had a piece of the Arizona Diamondbacks. Normally a change of ownership makes a holdover GM walk on eggs, but Stoneman and Moreno hit it off immediately.

"I had an opportunity to meet Arte prior to his making an offer," Stoneman said. "He wanted to find out what he was getting into. He met with me and met with others. What I'm looking at is what kind of an owner will he be? My biggest concern is will the new owner understand the importance and support of signing and developing your own talent. It's patience and an understanding. The owner has to understand that's critical to long-term success of business.

"Arte is a big baseball fan. He had been very passionate. Disney called in spring training, said he wants to meet with you. I asked him how long he wants to meet. They said probably an hour, hour and a half. That hour, hour and a half meeting turned out to be five and a half. It really went quickly. He's an easy guy to talk to. I was able to find out what I was able to find out. He talked about players, talked about philosophies. It didn't seem like it was a five-and-a-half-hour meeting."

In his first full off-season as owner in 2003–2004, Moreno would learn how expensive a big upgrade of a big-league baseball team would be. He did not blink in committing to the $146 million in contracts that made him George Steinbrenner Lite.

"Number 1, we knew we had to bolster starting pitching," Stoneman said. "Number 2 was outfield. The free-agent period hit; we went after Colon right away. He was number 1 on our list. But we weren't going to dwell on one guy. If he won't sign with us right away, we'll move on. We then moved to Escobar and quickly got the deal done. Then we said, 'Do we go to an outfielder?' Instead, we're going back to Colon's guy [agent]. He was surprised we called after signing Escobar. We ended up getting a deal done."

The Angels finally turned their attention to the outfield.

"We got [Jose] Guillen first and thought we were pretty well done," Stoneman said. "We got the opportunity to get Colon at a lower number than we expected. Vladimir Guerrero was still available. I knew what he meant to a team with his personality. I knew if he were part of the Angels, he would really make a huge difference to what would be a pretty good team. One more hitter on the club, wow. What I also knew was that we were a good team for him. That he would feel at home, that he landed in the right spot."

Former Expo Guerrero signed, joining his old exec three thousand miles away from his baseball roots. Guerrero went on to win the 2004 American League Most Valuable Player Award. "Arte was elated," Stoneman said. And Angels fans could toast their acquisitions with cheaper beer.

After three generations of being rooted in Chicago with a three-decade detour to Montreal, the Stoneman family reputation has been transplanted to Orange County. William Hambly Stoneman is the third male member of his family to bear his name.

"I was born in Chicago, and my parents and grandparents were Chicagoans," Stoneman said. His father, William H. Stoneman Jr., moved to Indianapolis when his son was young, but the Windy City connections held firm. "My grandfather worked for years for Montgomery Ward and Sears in executive positions," he said. "We had some real roots in Chicago. My mother's mother and a good friend of hers all attended the Babe Ruth 'called shot' game [in the 1932 World Series]. She was a Cubs fanatic."

Despite moving away from Chicago, Stoneman was elated that pitching-savvy West Coast scout Gene Handley recommended him to the Cubs' front office. He was drafted in the thirty-first round in 1966. Graduate school took precedence over attending spring training, but the Cubs didn't mind, as the student deferment kept Stoneman out of the Vietnam-era draft for awhile. When he finally came up around the All-Star break in 1967, he had joined a club on the move upward.

"We had a groundswell of young talent and guys who could play," he said, citing the young pitchers. "There was also our double-play combo, Don Kessinger and Glenn Beckert. Randy Hundley was young. All of a sudden, we're there together.

"What happened, the minds opened up. People got opportunities. I was on the receiving side of an opportunity. The value of granting opportunity, opening up minds, make good things happen. Having not finished in the first division since 1946, the Cubs finished in the first division [third place]. All of a sudden, we all knew we were pretty good. We view that as a huge plus. It happened because they trusted a bunch of twenty-three-year-olds."

In twenty-eight games—all but two in relief—in 1967, Stoneman was 2–4 but sported a fine 3.29 ERA with fifty-one strikeouts in sixty-three innings with four saves. Only five feet ten, Stoneman succeeded just like a later Cub, Steve Stone, with a crackling curveball. But current events of the day sidetracked a repeat in 1968. A slot had opened in the Arizona National Guard. Stoneman grabbed it and underwent six months of basic training and duty. He missed spring training in 1968 and got a late start. In eighteen games, Stoneman had a 5.52 ERA.

With shadows creeping one late afternoon in '68, Stoneman hung a curveball to the Pittsburgh Pirates' Manny Sanguillen, who banged the pitch off the wall for a game-winning double. Durocher screamed at Stoneman from the dugout. The next day, the two met.

"They didn't give you that $100,000 signing bonus for your curveball," Durocher proclaimed. "They gave it to you because of your fastball." But the Lip confused lower-pick Stoneman with Dean Burk, the Cubs' number 1 draft choice in 1966. "I want you to throw your fastballs late in the game until they hit if off the [scoreboard] clock in center field," Durocher added.

Even with such a tirade, Stoneman felt no enmity toward Durocher as did a slew of other homegrown Cubs pitchers who would go on to success elsewhere.

"I never hated Leo or anybody like that," he said. "I would have managed differently. Leo was much better with veteran players than young players, and we were a team of young players. But to me, opportunity is so valuable, and I had an opportunity."

The Cubs let Stoneman go to the Expos in the 1968 expansion draft. He was initially disappointed. "I loved the Cubs," he said. Now he would lose nineteen games as a rotation starter for the ragamuffin 110-game losers in cozy Jarry Park.

"Every time you take the field, you think you were going to win. It didn't matter who you were playing," he said.

For two years, Stoneman put it together as a starter. He was 17–16 for another mediocre Expos squad in 1971. He struck out 251 in 294 2/3 innings with a 3.15 ERA. The next year, Stoneman was 12–14 with a 2.98 ERA. However, the wrap-up of one part of his baseball life was near in coming, and the path toward his first world championship ring had begun.

Once on the receiving side of opportunity, Stoneman is on the granting end now. With a lot bigger payday for those who get the nod.

Close-Cropped but Still Fun-Loving

When you meet Jose Cardenal as he greets fans and flashes that familiar smile, he's wearing a baseball cap pulled smartly down on his head.

But something very important is missing.

Where's Cardenal's Afro?

Cardenal's hair is now so closely cropped that Roger Maris would have been proud. Can this be the same exuberant guy who dashed through the Wrigley Field outfield with seemingly a hairpin attaching his cap to that billowing thatch atop his head?

It is. Players became expressive, verbally and stylewise, in the 1970s. The brush cut or less has been in vogue since the dawn of the 1990s. Cardenal likes to go with the flow.

"Not really," he said when asked if he misses his luxuriant growth. "You couldn't pay me enough money to bring my Afro back now."

Cardenal is making other changes. Forty-two years in a baseball uniform after signing out of his native Cuba at age seventeen in 1960 mandated a break. So he closed up his longtime home in Prospect Heights, Illinois, a Chicago northwest suburb, to move to the Sarasota, Florida, area.

Maybe he'll come back to the coaching lines, after the better part of two decades in the Cincinnati Reds, New York Yankees, and Tampa Bay Devil Rays organizations. Maybe Cardenal will just be happy coaching kids in Florida. But don't worry, he'll always be identified with the Cubs first and foremost.

"I got three rings with the Yankees, but to me I feel like [Tom] Lasorda. My blood is blue like the Chicago Cubs.

"The Chicago Cubs are my number 1 team."

When Cardenal played in old-timers games, Cardenal always wore a Cubs uniform. "Like I played here all my life," he said.

That wasn't true, of course. Cardenal was close to a baseball vagabond. He started with the San Francisco Giants in 1963, moved on to the Anaheim Angels in 1965, and then alighted in blighted Municipal Stadium with the Cleveland Indians in 1968.

Tours of duty in St. Louis and Milwaukee in 1970–1971 preceded his six-season stay in Chicago, where he was one of the most popular Cubs—and even with that Afro, a favorite of owner Phil Wrigley. Then there was a move to Philadelphia, a little time with the New York Mets, and a wrap-up on the Kansas City Royals World Series team in 1980.

It's hard to get Jose Cardenal down. Happiness is his byword. Sometimes he's a showboat. Some called him a "hot dog," a common put-down against Latin players of the 1960s and 1970s. But then the south-of-the-border expressive style was pretty foreign to Wrigley Field. Folks had to get used to Jose Cardenal, the Cubs' first true Latin star, a decade after many other teams welcomed representatives of a baseball-crazy part of the planet.

He did it with his particular style, but he did it all, with the exception of hitting homers in bunches. But don't relax. Lay one into Cardenal's five-feet-ten, 150-pound wheelhouse, and he was liable to deposit the baseball onto Waveland Avenue. Pitch him carefully, because he was twice a .300 hitter as a Cub. He once got six hits in one game as a Chicago mainstay. And he was named Chicago Player of the Year by the local chapter of the Baseball Writers Association of America in 1973.

Sure, "Junior" Cardenal was a baseball clown at times, colorful and entertaining in a manner not seen anymore. But the amassing of 1,913 career hits and 329 stolen bases meant there was a good accumulation of baseball knowledge and savvy that could be passed down to the next generation. That's exactly what Cardenal starting doing as soon as he retired in 1980.

He ran a youth baseball camp before taking a detour into community relations with the Cubs. Then he spent a summer as a minor-league instructor in the short-lived Hawk Harrelson general-manager regime with the White Sox in 1986 before hooking on for the first of three gigs with the Reds.

He settled into a routine of teaching base running and reading pitchers on steal attempts. But Cardenal soon found that the late twentieth century was a different era compared to when base stealers were prized. He learned from the masters and tried to pass along the techniques.

"I was blessed—all my life I was a good base runner," he said. "When I was at San Francisco, I saw Willie Mays run the bases. I learned a lot of things from Willie.

"Then, with the Cardinals [in 1970], I had the opportunity to play with Lou Brock, so right there, it really helped me a lot."

But Cardenal didn't have as many willing pupils as in previous decades. By the dawn of the 1990s, the thirst for power had supplanted the Astroturf-fueled speed game.

"Today, most of the players are big and strong with the weight-lifting and nutrition," he said. "They forget about running the bases. All they have in mind is to hit the ball as far as they can.

"It was a different time when I played. To be a complete player then, you had to do everything: run, throw, and steal bases, like Roberto Clemente."

Cardenal's coaching tenure was interrupted by near tragedy in spring training in 1990 in Tampa. He was struck in the head by a batted ball in a hitting drill. Emergency surgery was performed, during which three parts of Cardenal's skull were wired together. He missed most of the 1990 season recuperating.

"I was scared because I didn't know if I was going to be normal or not," he said. "I have a little brain damage. Everybody was joking with me by saying you don't have to worry because you have had brain damage since you were born. But [the brain damage] concerned me the most. I didn't know if I could do the same things I love to do in life. Thank God everything came into place. Nothing came easy."

Cardenal went on to work with former Cubs teammate Jim Hickman, the roving hitting instructor, in the Reds farm system. He found the secret to longevity in an often-chaotic Reds organization of the time. "I get along with Marge Schott," he said in 1992, referring to the eccentric, Saint Bernard–loving owner of the time.

Later, Cardenal served as a big-league coach with the Reds, Yankees, and Devil Rays. Cardenal was lucky to catch the Yankees in their prime in the late 1990s as a member of manager Joe Torre's big-name coaching staff.

But the Cubs will always take precedence in his own ratings.

And Cardenal is now secure as the answer to several of the more off-beat trivia questions in team annals.

Cardenal had been a journeyman top-of-the-lineup outfielder, a guy who would hit leadoff or number 2 for you, but you wouldn't necessarily keep for the long run.

"I lasted eighteen years in the big leagues, so I had to show some talents," he said. "The problem was that in the late '60s and early '70s—it was hard to get some money. I was putting good years back to back, and nobody wanted to pay me. I used to go to the people in the front office and tell them to trade me. That's how I made my money. Each time they traded me, I would get a raise."

The trade to the Cubs during the winter meetings of 1971 provided a long-sought answer to a nagging lineup hole. The Cubs had dealt outfielder Brock Davis and young pitchers Jim Colborn and Earl Stephenson to the Brewers for his services. Right field had literally been wide open since Lou Brock held down the position, shakily, for one and a half seasons in 1963–1964. Desperate, the Cubs often shifted Billy Williams over to right in order to get a supposedly good-hit, no-field guy in left field. When the left fielder

Jose Cardenal and fan. Author photo.

didn't hit, Williams went back to that position while the Cubs tried yet another right-field candidate. The Len Gabrielsons, Ted Savages, Clarence Joneses, Lee Thomases, Al Spanglers, and Johnny Callisons just kept coming and going.

Cardenal put an end to the revolving door, holding down right field until he switched positions with left fielder Jerry Morales by the 1975 season. In his first Cubs season in 1972, Cardenal injected a long-awaited dash of speed into the lineup with twenty-five steals. He had seventeen homers, seventy RBIs, and a .291 average.

"My first year here, we had a chance to win," Cardenal said. But the Pittsburgh Pirates beat the Cubs twelve out of fifteen times and finished eleven games ahead of the second-place Cubs.

Cardenal kept hitting when the rest of the lineup slumped, prompting a wholesale Cubs collapse from first place in the second half of 1973. His .303 average, thirty-three doubles, and sixty-eight RBIs earned him the Chicago Player of the Year award.

By now Cardenal was a favorite of both the fans and owner Wrigley.

"I was one of those lucky guys," he said. "I was lucky to have a great year. I was the fan pleaser. I played hard. That's the reason the Wrigley family liked me.

"I think it was my style of play. I was nice to the fans. Every organization, they like to see the players being nice to the fans."

Cardenal stories brightened up the otherwise-drab Cubs seasons of the mid-1970s.

He was reputed to have stashed a baseball in the ivy to point to as a ground-rule double. "I did it once," Cardenal admitted. "In right center. Somebody hit the ball to the wall, and two balls came down. The double was supposed to score the winning run, but it was ruled a ground-rule double."

Cardenal supposedly could not play one day in spring training because of a "stuck eyelid."

"Jim Marshall was the manager," he said. "I got a little eye infection. I told Marshall I can't see the ball, so Marshall made a big deal out of it."

Still another time, Cardenal supposedly complained he couldn't play because of lack of sleep. A cricket had kept him up. Or at least someone named Cardenal.

"That was my wife [Pat], but I got blamed for it," he said.

So why aren't such funny stories told about today's players?

"I believe players make a lot of money and they see this game more like a business," he said. "When we played, we didn't make big money, and it was more like a sport. It was a fun game to play. But the more money you make, the more you should enjoy the game."

Humor aside, Cardenal kept producing. He had a stellar all-around season in 1975 with career highs of .317 and 182 hits, along with a Cubs-high thirty-four steals. By now, he was the veteran among the Cubs' first sizable group of Latin players. Morales was a clutch-hitting bookend in the outfield, while the slick-fielding Manny Trillo took over at second. By 1977, speedy shortstop Ivan DeJesus formed a good double-play combo with Trillo. Willie Hernandez established himself in the bullpen as a setup man for closer Bruce Sutter.

But Cardenal's Wrigley Field days would be numbered. He and manager Herman Franks did not hit it off as 1977 wore on. Greg Gross and Gene Clines ended up as the lefty–righty platoon in left field, while Morales had moved over to center with newly arrived Bobby Murcer in right. By season's end, Cardenal had just 226 at bats spread over one hundred games, finishing with a .239 average. Both he and Morales moved out of town after '77, Cardenal to the Phillies and Morales to St. Louis. Cardenal helped the Phillies win the NL East in 1978, while enjoying a final burst of .340 in fifty-three at bats down the stretch for the 1980 AL champion Royals.

But, always, he returned to Prospect Heights after the season when he easily could have established roots in some warmer-weather clime.

Not Cardenal the Cub.

"I love the city," he said of Chicago. "It was great to me. How are you going to forget Cubs fans?"

Don't Coach As He Was Coached

How not to coach was taught to Burt Hooton at the most impressionable age for a big leaguer.

He was twenty-two, ballyhooed out of the University of Texas and possessed of a dipping, never-seen-before pitch called a knuckle curve. That was not good enough for those who were labeled as coaches in the Chicago Cubs organization of the early 1970s.

"I wasn't going to get all my pitchers to pitch the way I did, which kind of happened to me," the now middle-aged pitching coach said. "I was a straight-over-the-top four-seam pitcher, curveball pitcher. When I got here, I was told I needed a sinker and a slider, and I never had a sinker and a slider in my life. I'd been pretty successful without it. I listened to them, started throwing sinkers and sliders, and became a worse and worse pitcher.

"It wasn't 'til I got to the Dodgers where I ran into a pitching coach named Red Adams, who I thought was one of the best: low-key, humorous. There's a few things he said to me: 'The worst thing a kid can come up against is a coach who thinks he has to coach.' That always stuck with me."

Hooton had several memorable games, including a no-hitter in his fourth big-league start, before the malaise of the Cubs organization at the end of the Leo Durocher era negatively enveloped him and most of his teammates. He'd enjoy far better success with the Dodgers. And through 2004, Hooton coached longer than he had thrown that knuckle curve for pay in the majors.

Nicknamed "Happy" Hooton early in his career for his outwardly dour makeup, Hooton laughs a lot more easily today. Maturity obviously has taken over. So has satisfaction in a coaching career that has returned him to his native Texas for much of the time since 1990.

But his most recent assignment with the Houston Astros, which ended in a housecleaning the day after the 2004 All-Star Game, taxed his own philosophy. How do you coach a Roger Clemens and an Andy Pettitte after all their world-championship experiences in New York? All the while, Hooton had a firehouse of great young arms to tutor—Billy Wagner, Octavio Dotel, Roy Oswalt, Wade Miller, Brad Lidge, Carlos Hernandez. Just like the Cubs of his youth, the organization produced a mess of good arms. The difference was the Astros kept the majority of those young pitchers and enjoyed the benefits of their talents, at least for awhile, until mounting pressure and an underperforming team led ownership to sweep out Hooton along with manager Jimy Williams.

He got some unplanned time off in the game. The last time he had taken such a breather was voluntarily, after his pitching career wound down.

"I just needed a little time away from the game," he recalled of his career wrap-up with the Texas Rangers in 1985. "I spent a couple of years going to school. The Dodgers called and asked if I'd be interested in coaching in the minor leagues. I didn't have any aspirations then."

Hooton's entry-level pitching coach's job was the short-season Class A team in Salem, Ore.

"My wife, Ginger, and my two kids went up to Salem in the summer of 1988," he said. "We enjoyed it. They asked if I wanted to do it again in '89. After the '89 season, they asked me if I wanted to continue coaching. I told them I'd like to go to a higher level than short-season 'A.' There was a big gap between what I knew and how to relate it, to what those kids knew and what they could accept."

But in the long run, Hooton benefited from such an apprenticeship.

"I probably learned more, though, in those first two years coaching," he said. "Bottom line, those guys aren't very good. I had a lot of knowledge, but I had to learn patience and tact, and learn how to say the same thing several different ways. When I first went into coaching, I thought I was going to set the world on fire, but that brought me down to reality. Maybe you should go a little slower."

Five more years at Double-A and two in Triple-A in the Dodgers system brought Hooton back to the University of Texas as pitching coach from 1996 to 1999. Then he joined the Astros organization for the 2000 season as pitching coach of Double-A Round Rock, near Austin. On June 23 of that season, the firing of Vern Ruhle opened up the Astros job, and he was summoned to the brand-new ballpark in downtown Houston.

Remembering his own pitching days, Hooton is no tinkerer with his charges' motions or repertoires in his job. As an example, he's never pushed his old knuckle curve on a young pitcher. That offering was a freak pitch, requiring the utmost dedication and a world of patience in an attempt to learn it.

"They got signed for a reason—they had talent," Hooton said. "They make it to the big leagues for a reason. I want to see what that reason is. I'm not a good enough pitching coach to see a guy for one day and totally change him and make him start doing other stuff. I call that pitching out in the wilderness. That's the way I was for three, three and a half years. And as a young kid, I wasn't smart enough to realize that.

"It took a pitching coach like Red Adams to tell me to ditch the sinker, ditch the slider, and go back to pitching the way I used to, to how I got here. Immediately, everything fell into place again because I was back in familiar territory. That's where I want to keep all my guys. I want to find out where their familiar territory is. It becomes a lot easier to relate to them.

"I would never teach anybody to have the delivery I had. I happened to think I had a good delivery, but most guys didn't have that. I'm looking to find out what they do right, build upon that, and keep them within that."

The mental and instinctive part of pitching is Hooton's emphasis.

"There's a lot of information around, but all that information that's around may not necessarily help that guy. If you start taking in all that information and trying to digest it, it becomes difficult. You want to keep it simple, keep things that work for you.

"Most every pitcher I've ever coached—they've thrown a pitch, they've gotten hit. I've sat them down, and I've said, 'What do your instincts tell you?' They might reply, 'My instincts tell me to throw this, but I went with this.' I've done that, too. Best thing is to listen to your instincts. Your instincts are 99, 100 percent right. I'd rather you throw what is deemed the wrong pitch but you're 100 percent confident in it, than throw whatever seems the right pitch and be 50 percent confident in it. If you use your instincts, that's naturally going to happen. Bottom line, be yourself.

"I don't teach new pitches. I teach where they get something out of their effort. Most of it is mental. You get a lot of pitchers up on the mound where they don't mentally practice. You need a strong mental fortitude. I've had guys who've had bullpens who don't go anywhere—they just throw a ball. When they get on a mound to practice, they're a lot more disciplined. You've got to practice over and over the pitches you want to use in a game."

Starting out 2004, Hooton became caretaker for Clemens and Pettitte, who zeroed in on employment with their hometown Astros. In the case of the Rocket, Hooton could have been learning as much as he's teaching.

"He's been around (more than two decades), and has a pretty good idea what he's doing," Hooton said. "I've become an observer. If I find out he's varying from anything, I tell him. But what I found out about Roger is that everything he does is calculated. He knows what he's doing. Things that happen with him don't happen by accident. He creates things pitch by pitch. Most generally he can put it into practice.

"He's got tremendous talent, a tremendous baseball mind. He's a tremendous competitor, not willing to let down on any pitch."

Clemens continued a Longhorns tradition of pitching excellence that Hooton pretty much started in the majors. After pitching Richard King High School in Corpus Christi to the Texas state title in 1968, Hooton amassed a 35–3 record, thirteen career shutouts, and a 1.14 ERA for the Longhorns in three years. His excellence got him selected number 1 by the Cubs in the secondary phase of the 1971 draft.

Nine days later, on June 17, 1971, impatient Cubs GM John Holland allowed Durocher to start Hooton fresh out of college against the St. Louis Cardinals at Wrigley Field. Although Hooton struck out Lou Brock, the first hitter he faced, he was soon routed. Optioned to Triple-A Tacoma for seasoning, Hooton was a sensation with the new-fangled knuckle curve. He struck out 135 batters (including nineteen in one game) in 102 innings while leading the Pacific Coast League with a 1.68 ERA.

Hooton was no less sensational in his late-season call-up in '71.

On September 15, he fanned fifteen Mets, tying the Cubs' all-time strikeout record, in a 3–2 win at Shea Stadium. On September 21 at Wrigley Field, he pitched a two-hit shutout against the New Yorkers. But the most compelling start had to wait until the following April 16, after the season had been delayed one week by the first players' strike.

At a chilly, windswept, forty-degree Wrigley Field, Hooton was off-kilter in his control against the Philadelphia Phillies. And the northerly gales blew a homer-panting drive by Greg Luzinski back into the glove of center fielder Rick Monday. Yet as the innings passed, Hooton hadn't allowed a hit. He completed the no-hitter by fanning Luzinski for whiff number 7. Minutes later, Hooton told Jim West and Lou Boudreau on the postgame WGN broadcast interview that he had dreamed he'd pitch a no-hitter. Such precognition was no freak event. Twenty-eight years later, Glenallen Hill said he dreamed he cleared the big advertising sign across Waveland Avenue with a homer. Sure enough, two weeks after that, Hill slugged a titanic blast atop the building across Kenmore Avenue from the sign.

The rest of Hooton's 1972 season was less successful in the won–lost category. He was only 11–14 but was the team's tough-luck starter with a 2.80 ERA. All five Cubs starters in '72 had ERAs of 3.21 or lower. One other highlight of the season was a grand-slam homer off Tom Seaver in an 18–5 victory over the Mets, quickly becoming Hooton's favorite opponent.

He got off to a bad start in 1973, pitched better in the second half, and yet still finished 14–17, a collapsing Cubs lineup doing none of the starters any favors after July. Hooton backslid further in 1974, going 7–11 and losing his rotation spot. He made twenty-seven relief appearances as his ERA soared to 4.81.

By now Hooton was thoroughly confused. Mel Wright had been his pitching coach when he arrived at the end of '71. Wright was replaced the next season by Larry Jansen. In 1974, Hank Aguirre took over as pitching coach. And for the 1975 season, Marv Grissom was pitching coach.

"Each of the pitching coaches had their own ideas," Hooton said. "Some of the coaches thought they had to coach, and as I said before, that's the worst thing a kid can come up against."

Durocher was replaced by Whitey Lockman as manager at the

Andy Pettitte with Burt Hooton at Wrigley Field in 2004. Author photo.

1972 All-Star break. Almost exactly two years later, Lockman stepped down in favor of Jim Marshall.

"In the early 1970s there wasn't a lot of stability in the organization," Hooton said. "I'm a twenty-one-year-old kid coming out of college. Pretty much I had four pitching coaches in three and a half years, three managers in three and a half years. So there's no stability, no continuity. To me we had a very, very good team on the field. When I went to the Dodgers, you had to be bad for two months before they'd put you in the bullpen. Here, you only had to be bad for a couple of starts in a row before they shuffled you off to the bullpen. There was no chance to get on a roll.

"In Los Angeles, [Walter] Alston managed twenty-three years, then [Tom] Lasorda 20 years. You had a bad year, everyone didn't get fired. It wasn't retooled and started all over again. To me continuity speaks volumes."

But Hooton did not help himself by not reporting to work in the best of shape. He was overweight. When Hooton went to pitch in the Dominican winter league after the 1974 season, his manager was Lasorda, then the Dodgers' third-base coach. Lasorda, no lightweight himself, had an idea to slim down Hooton, then persuade Dodgers management to trade for him.

The tact worked. One month into the 1975 season, the pitching-rich Dodgers—who already had finagled the likes of Ron Perranoski and Jim Brewer out of Holland—landed Hooton in exchange for lame-armed lefty Geoff Zahn and overemotional right-hander Eddie "King" Solomon. The rest of the season, Hooton was 18–7 with a 2.82 ERA for the Dodgers, who got him in shape physically and mentally. Zahn and Solomon flopped around with the Cubs and were out of the organization two years later.

In 1978, Hooton was 19–10 with a 2.71 ERA in Los Angeles. He came through in the only world championship run with that group of Dodgers in 1981, earning the Most Valuable Player honors in the National League Championship Series against the Montreal Expos, then winning the clinching game 6 of the World Series against the New York Yankees. He'd finish in career in 1985 with 151 victories.

Through all those decades, Hooton offered up a consistent reason why the Cubs couldn't win: too many day games at Wrigley Field.

"It gets hot and humid in the summer, and it takes a toll on a team," he said. "It's a lot different playing here in the high 80s and high humidity compared to playing at night in LA, low or mid 70s, with no humidity. The hardest thing about playing baseball is the schedule. You add all day games for one team and every other team is playing night games, then it's the logical outcome."

The thirty night games the Cubs will play by 2006 is an improvement.

"If they played all night games, it would be a great place to play," he said. "By all rights, half the season it's the best park to pitch in with the wind blowing in. It can be the worst park to pitch in and the best park to pitch in. I haven't seen a ground ball go out of the ballpark.

"Chicago can be a wonderful place to win."

Fleet Afoot, Careful in the Markets

The fleeting pace at which Bill North's Cubs career flashed by—seemingly at the same speed at which he won two American League stolen-base titles in subsequent seasons in Oakland—is not quite matched by North's present work style.

"I'm relatively conservative," North said, having traded one type of pinstriped "uni" for another as a financial planner—a "glorified stockbroker," he mused—for Raymond James Financial Services in Kirkland, Washington, a suburb of his hometown of Seattle.

"What I can do is inform clients, do right with their money," he said. "I'm pretty basic. I like my clients. I try to do the best I can with them. I don't like to use big [financial] words. What I have them do is break it down and understand the market. Do it for the long term. If you're a short-term speculator, you're smarter than me, so go do your own stuff."

Like many players, North did not quite know what to do with his career once his legs and bat slowed down. Then he noticed that Equitable sponsored an old-timers game in which he was playing in the early 1980s. A few calls later, he began working in financial services with Lincoln. Then he shifted to Equitable. A job with Great Western brought him back to Seattle. Now he's spent the last decade with Raymond James.

Part of North's work life is guiding investments, and the other part is calming the jittery nerves of clients buffeted by roller-coaster markets.

"I like to educate my clients," North said. "People thought that in the 1990s, you could have only one flat year. You'd be making 25, 30 percent every year. Well, things increase in the long run, but not at that pace.

"I don't want to ever see it like that again, balloon up. I'd just like to see it go up twenty points one day, go back five points next day, up ten points next day."

An advocate of putting an investor's biggest allocation into large domestic growth funds, North projects a future growth area in financial companies, services, and durable goods.

While keeping one eye on Wall Street, North gazes somewhat amazed at the baseball salary market. He definitely missed out on his big payday.

"My top salary was $260,000, and I was broke," he recalled. "I didn't spend my money well. Agents in the late 1970s and early 1980s put you in tax shelters that was later disallowed by [President] Reagan. I had $70,000 a year in phantom income. Billy Williams told me it's hard to be smart and good at the same time."

That said, North insisted that owners did not pay out money they didn't have during the era of $250 million contracts.

"It's still a market," he said. "It dictates itself. They're not getting money that isn't there. With the Alex Rodriguez contract, there was a reason he [Texas owner Tom Hicks] had that kind of money. He owned a lot of land around the ballpark. He was a real-estate guy."

But North also aims a few barbs at modern-day players who don't know who trailblazed their way to riches.

"Players ask who Curt Flood is, and nobody knows," he said. "There was not one active player at Curt Flood's funeral.

"These players are doing well. If they're making $20 million, they're living a $20 million lifestyle."

North thought he'd be living a nice big-league lifestyle as a Cub. The switch-hitter was a twelfth-round draft pick out of Central Washington University. Succeeding the traded Oscar Gamble as the organization's best outfield prospect, North led the Class AA Texas League with forty-seven steals while scoring ninety-one runs at San Antonio in 1971. He figured he'd plug up a longtime hole in center field and lead off for a perpetually slow team after he had a debut of sixteen at bats at the end of the 1971 season.

But he came into the majors with a little bit of a tempestuous reputation, not an asset for an African American Cub at the time.

He tussled with right fielder Pete LaCock in San Antonio.

"He'd come flying by and catch some balls from center that should have been mine," LaCock recalled. "I told him if I'm standing under the ball, he couldn't do that. I told Bill if he did that again, I'd punch his lights out. He did, and I jumped him in the dugout."

North would later become friends with LaCock. But in the short term, his problems began and ended with general manager John Holland, both conservative and impatient at the same time.

Although Holland had North coming on fast, he instead traded lefty Ken Holtzman to Oakland for young-veteran center fielder Rick Monday after the '71 season. That left no room in the outfield for North with Billy Williams in left and Jose Cardenal in right.

Although manager Leo Durocher told North to get an apartment while he broke him into the majors slowly, he was optioned to Triple-A during a St. Louis trip in which he was supposed to meet his family.

Angered, North threatened to quit to go into teaching. Warning him that he was ruining his career, Holland eventually recalled North. After ten days, he was sent down again.

"They told me if I didn't go to the minor leagues, I'd be suspended for the rest of my life," North said. "They had lied to me and told me to get an apartment, that I'd be staying. I had been raised principled."

Put off by North's outspoken nature, Holland sent him to a psychiatrist in Arizona, insisting North be made ready to handle "the big city." That puzzled a native of Seattle, not exactly a cow town.

"I was from the Northwest and relatively smart, and that threatened the Cubs," North said. "Ability wasn't the only criteria for playing with the Cubs."

North did heed the warnings by African American teammates about relationships with white girls, a capital offense in Cubs management's mind-set of the time.

"Cleo James and Brock Davis pointed to some girls sitting there," North said of some groupie types. "They said, 'Don't mess with them.'"

North's up-and-down Cubs season in 1972 produced a paltry .181 average in sixty-six games. He did provide an interesting preview of his own future with six steals in as many tries. He almost gained a measure of infamy on September 2 of that season at Wrigley Field. He was playing center in the ninth inning while Milt Pappas had a perfect game going against the San Diego Padres.

John Jeter sent a fly ball to center leading off the ninth, but North slipped and fell on the damp grass. Left fielder Williams, backing up North, raced over to snare the fly ball to preserve the perfect game, which ended moments later on a controversial walk. But Pappas still ended up with a no-hitter.

As with many other young players who did not pan out quickly, the way he desired, Holland cut his losses with North. Already an easy mark for Oakland owner Charlie Finley, who was based in Chicago, Holland dealt North to the Athletics for aging reliever Bob Locker on November 21, 1972. Locker soon became a regular on a Chicago–Oakland shuttle. He was traded back to the Athletics after the 1973 season for reliever Horacio Pina, then returned to the Cubs as part of the Billy Williams deal a year later.

While Locker's pitches dove in more slowly in each Cubs tenure, North turned on his afterburners. Given a chance to play every day, with 544 at bats in 1973, he stole fifty-three bases while picking up his first world championship ring. North gathered a repeat piece of jewelry in 1974 while pacing the American League with fifty-four steals. He stole a career-high seventy-five in 1975 as the Athletics made the playoffs again.

Like all the A's stars of the era, North eventually was sent packing by the penny-pinching Finley. He played part-time in the outfield for another World Series team with the Dodgers in 1978. Then he moved on to the Giants, where as a center-field regular in 1979–1980 he totaled 103 steals. For his career, which ended at age thirty-three in 1981, he totaled 395 thefts.

Along the way, he had an interesting time. He did not quiet down in Oakland, getting involved in the clubhouse rows for which the Swingin' A's were noted. And he met future Cubs manager Dusty Baker way back in 1969 on the Arizona State campus, then got reunited with him in Los Angeles in 1978. They've been friends ever since.

"I'm the least surprised person in the world. Dusty is special," he said of Baker's revival job on the Cubs.

Baker's in the money. So is North, every day, to his satisfaction, market up or down.

He's in Idaho, but He's No Spud

B ill Buckner craved the outdoors, and he got plenty of it
the day he traipsed around the woods in Montana only to
endure a close encounter with a mother grizzly bear and
her cubs.

"She got up on her hind legs," Buckner said. He added that it
was "fifty-fifty" that the grizzly would attack him.

Ol' Cubs teammates Bruce Sutter and Mike Krukow were on the
hunting trip with Buckner but not out in the woods at that moment. But with the grizzly eventually going her way and Buckner
his, he has come back for more in his bow-hunting jaunts.

If Buckner was the toast of Wrigley Field as a master batsman
known popularly as "Billy Buck" in the late 1970s and early 1980s,
an even .300 hitter as a Cub who was comfortable as a big fish in a
big pond, he's even more happy out in the Mountain time zone.

Having always hoped to settle in Idaho dating back to his Cubs
days, he now lives with wife Jody and their family on five acres ten
minutes outside Boise. The Buckners are near enough to civilization to enjoy entertainment, college sports and minor-league basketball and baseball, and an airport large enough to whisk them to
bigger cities when necessary. But they are far enough out to lead
the quiet life while getting Buckner closer to his outdoor haunts.

"We have a couple of dogs and three horses," he said. "But either a coyote or mountain lion ate a calf we had. That happens."

Buckner may dabble in car dealerships and commercial real estate to keep some fresh cash flow coming in. But his full-time role
is outdoorsman and dad/coach.

"I had planned to move here for some time," he said. "I bought
a ranch here in the mid-1970s. I knew I'd eventually move to Idaho
if had the opportunity. I told my wife when I met her, 'Before this

goes any further, I'm moving to Idaho in the future.' She accepted that.

"I really like the outdoors. I do fly-fishing, a little bit of hunting, and play golf. We've got a small-town atmosphere. It's great for kids. But they've got some entertainment with concerts here. Rod Stewart played here. There's stuff to do other than the outdoors."

Buckner won't be bound by the wilds of Idaho and Montana. After having learned to bow hunt, and bagging elk and even a couple of black bears in the sticks, he planned to go to Alaska "to get a moose."

Hosting the likes of Sutter, Krukow, Bob Boone, and the late Tug McGraw made the trips into the woods like a reunion. And mind you, Buckner doesn't have one thousand miles of separation from baseball. Son Bobby, now in high school, is trying to make his way as a shortstop. He's not exactly a chip off the old block as a right-handed hitter, though.

"I try to give him a little constructive criticism," Buckner said. But he has to restrain himself from being too involved as a parent.

In his midfifties, Buckner will be close at hand for Bobby's development as a ballplayer. He won't go traveling throughout the majors as a coach anymore. He last worked in the game as White Sox hitting coach under manager Terry Bevington in 1996–1997.

"Baseball's a good life, but the tradeoffs are just too much," he said. "The time away from family a big one. If I was single, I'd probably stay in the game." But staying married twenty-four years and getting out of the rat race allowed Buckner to raise his two daughters, now in their twenties, and be a baseball parent.

Buckner's obviously a man who started saving and investing his money early, never losing momentum as he amassed 2,715 career hits.

"When making a lot of money in your twenties, you're not the smartest guy in the world," he said. "Guys a lot smarter than me lost all their money. I tried to stay on top of that. My rookie salary (in 1971) was $11,000. My top salary was $825,000 with the Red Sox. With the Cubs it was $600,000. If I played now, I'd probably be making $8 or $9 million."

"It's starting to level off. It's just crazy with the amount of money available. If you make $10 million in a year, after you pay taxes, you've got $6 million left. You should be able to live on that the rest of your life."

Buckner probably could have retired to Idaho just on his Cubs earnings. But a love of baseball and an incredible pain tolerance kept him going twenty full seasons, through a chronic ankle injury and the trauma of a game-busting error that was a part of the Boston Red Sox's game 6 collapse in the 1986 World Series.

"When you look back at my career, I wasn't the best player out there," Buckner said. "But I don't think a lot of players could have done it with the situation I had and been productive."

Buckner started out his baseball life as part of a golden crop of homegrown Los Angeles Dodger prospects who all came up around 1970. Most played for Tom Lasorda at Triple-A Spokane—Steve Garvey, Ron Cey, Davey Lopes, Bill Russell, Joe Ferguson, and Steve Yeager. In 1972 Buckner hit .319 as a hustling left fielder with speed. Two years later, he batted .314 with 182 hits with the Spokane alums as they won their first National League pennant together.

Buckner hurt his left ankle sliding in 1975. He developed a staph infection, making matters worse. He came back, had a decent year at .301 in 1976, had more surgery, then was traded to the Cubs in the off-season along with shortstop Ivan DeJesus for center fielder Rick Monday. The deal would turn out in the Cubs' favor in two ways. Both Buckner and DeJesus would go on to produce on the North Side. And in late 1981, GM Dallas Green would trade DeJesus to Philadelphia for Ryne Sandberg.

Starting in 1977, Buckner occasionally would have to leave the Cubs' lineup because of the sore ankle.

"I would have loved to have been close to normal," he said. "I could have probably gone up another scale. I could have hit a lot better with more power. You couldn't put enough drive into that back leg. But I'm proud of what I did. You put the effort in, do the best you can do."

Buckner's daily preparation with Cubs trainer Tony Garafalo was extensive.

"We had a lot of ice and a lot of anti-inflammatories. The whole [ankle] joint was disintegrating. It was amazing I went on to play that long. Position-wise was lucky, playing first base."

Bill Buckner with wife, Jody, and children at Flathead Lake, Montana. Photo courtesy of Jody Buckner.

But the pain was nearly unbearable. Sometimes fans and media could see the hurt etched on Buckner's face.

"I was so competitive, I was able to do that. Usually the first half of the game it felt best. As games rolled on, it would get more sore. In a fifteen-inning game, it was really sore."

Despite the pain, Buckner began to contend for the NL batting title. He hit .323 in 1978, driving in seventy-four runs and just five homers. Two years later, he finally won the batting crown with a .324 mark on a ninety-eight-loss Cubs team.

Buckner had an old-school approach to hitting—put the bat on the ball at all costs.

"Back then, guys didn't know that much about hitting," he said. "Growing up [in Vallejo, California], we played whiffle ball all the time. I had a knack for putting the bat on the ball. I had good hand–eye coordination.

"It's a different game now. As a manager you want a guy who can put the bat on the ball. But everybody wants to be a Sosa or Bonds. When I played, three, four, five guys a year struck out one hundred times. But I saw a number recently. It blew me away that there were 250 guys who struck out more than one hundred times."

Buckner kept getting better even as the Cubs were reduced to little better than an expansion franchise in talent level by 1981. He had seventy-five RBIs with a .311 average in 106 games in the strike-shortened '81 season. The Cubs hardly improved under Tribune Company ownership in 1982, but Buckner was at his Chicago peak. He had a career-high 201 hits, driving in 105 runs with just 15 homers while batting .306 in 161 games.

But Buckner wasn't a Dallas Green "guy." After mulling over trading Buckner on several occasions, Cubs GM Green tried to sign Steve Garvey as a free agent after the 1982 season. Garvey played Buckner's position—first base. Garvey instead opted to go to the San Diego Padres, granting Buckner a reprieve as a Cub.

After some declining production in 1983, Green decided Leon "Bull" Durham needed to play his natural position at first base the following year. Forced to the bench, Buckner played in just twenty-one games early in the season before Green dealt him to the Boston Red Sox for pitcher Dennis Eckersley.

The trade helped both teams. Eckersley was a key cog in the rotation in the NL East title season in 1984. Playing in all 162 games in 1985, Buckner drove in a career-high 110 runs in 1985.

Another 102-RBI season should have made Buckner a longtime Fenway Park hero in 1986. But one of the most famous World Series errors marred his Boston tenure for all time. Joining other Fall Classic goats, Buckner allowed that snaking grounder from the New York Mets' Mookie Wilson to go through his legs as the winning run scored in game 6 after the Red Sox seemed oh-so-close to finally shaking their World Series curse.

The fanatic Red Sox Nation blamed Buckner and not his teammates, such as the shaky performance of reliever Bob Stanley. He was literally hounded out of Boston. For years Buckner got no peace about the error and had to try to keep a low profile even out in Idaho.

He's more mellow about the misplay almost two decades later, though.

"It's just part of sports," he said. "There's a lot of tension with [would-be] winners. That's all the East Coast people [the reaction].

Most people know what the real story was. Now, to my face, people are nice."

Of all people, Buckner could sympathize with Steve Bartman, the Cubs fan in the wrong place at the wrong time in game 6 of the 2003 NL Championship Series at Wrigley Field.

"He shouldn't worry about it," Buckner said. "He didn't do anything anyone else wouldn't have done in that situation." Still, Bartman's profile will forever be far lower than Buckner's.

With the Red Sox error fresh on everyone's minds, Buckner moved on to the Anaheim Angels in midseason 1987. By the following season he was a part-time player with the Kansas City Royals. He finished out his career at age forty with a twenty-two-game stint back with the Red Sox in 1990.

But through all of Buckner's travels, Chicago remains the highlight of his career.

"Wrigley Field and the fans helped," he said. "I was very lucky it happened. LA was a great place to play, Boston too. When I think back at places I played, Chicago was the best."

Gimpy ankle and all, Buckner gave the fans their money's worth.

Kong in Repose

Dave, we hardly knew ye.

And that's the way it will stay, apparently. The day won't come soon when we get to examine the usually inscrutable Dave Kingman under a microscope, to figure out what makes the ultimate strong, silent type tick.

"I'm still on the quiet side, I guess," he said back in 1992. "Once people get to know me, they realize that the Dave Kingman the press portrayed never was and certainly isn't today. My close friends know the person they tried to portray never existed."

But just try to separate legend from fact. Kingman sightings are like the will-o'-the-wisp. You'll see him, then he'll go off the radar for years before unexpectedly reappearing. You can find him if you look hard enough in the country around South Lake Tahoe, Nevada. But if you're waiting around Chicago, his hometown and the place of his shining baseball moment, you'd better be prepared to wait out a decade to catch him.

As much as retired all-or-nothing slugger Kingman insists he's a "private person," he can't sever his Cubs ties. He appeared at the Cubs Convention in 1992 and 1993. Then, after a long absence, he showed up at Wrigley Field for a special giveaway day of his old baseball card in 2002. A year and a half later, Kingman was back at the Cubs Convention, still tall and angular, but with longish hair turning from gray to white as his fifties progressed.

Relocating to South Lake Tahoe in the late 1980s, soon after his baseball career ended, the former "Kong" likes the quieter life, away from the media mainstream that almost always pained him.

"It's hunting, fishing, and skiing—all-around activities," Kingman said of the attractions of the area. "It's outdoor living; it's not big city by any means. It's easy to get around and very few traffic jams."

Fishing obviously was a big attraction. Kingman always loved the water, and was famed for the boat he docked in Belmont Harbor, near Wrigley Field. "He either wanted to ride a motorcycle or go fishing," recalled Lloyd Meyer, his old American Legion coach, circa 1967, just after Kingman graduated from Prospect High School near Mount Prospect, Illinois.

Kingman also tries to keep up with the activities of his three children, Adam, Abby and Anna. "All are very active in all different sports," he said.

End of details. "I'm private and I enjoy my private life," he said.

The Kingman who excelled at bashing a baseball into the outer limits does not want a major commitment to the game. But when he is so moved, he'll be available for autographs and fans' greetings.

"I enjoy being around fans and the people who have supported major league baseball, the Cubs in particular," he said. "I really don't do very many events. So it's always fun coming to Chicago because the fans are so good, so supportive, even though you're not playing anymore. Even the different generations, they keep up with what happened in the past.

"I'm so active in my kids' activities that I really don't want to miss that portion of their growing up. I miss the competition in baseball. For the next few years, I got my hands full with kids' coaching and all those activities."

That seems Kingman's speed. He never desired the celebrity, the seeming role-model status that comes with the big bat or golden arm. And he could have been bigger than anybody in Chicago this side of Michael Jordan, had he so desired.

The list of logical attributes was long. Former all-everything prep baseball and basketball star. Local boy makes good. The first free agent ever signed by the Cubs, in late 1977. Tall, powerful, and perhaps stronger than anyone else in the major leagues. Handsome face, a good speaking voice. A natural for an endorsement superstar who could have held Chicago in the palm of his hand after belting forty-eight homers, the upper limit of the power standards of the time, as a Cub in 1979. Kingman's power output was the second-highest home-run total by a Chicago player up to that time.

"We're all different," he said. "We all put our pants on different, I guess. Everybody goes about their business in their own way. I probably wouldn't have made too many changes if I had to go out and do it all over again. We all do our job the way we feel it's best for us.

"We all do things we enjoy doing and those [the trappings of celebrityhood] are things I probably wouldn't have felt comfortable in. There's other things I had more confidence in and was comfortable with."

The touchy subject that separated Kingman from revered personality then is broached.

"Avoiding the press was the way that gave me peace away from baseball," he said. "I'm still a very private person, and that hasn't changed."

The more the media wanted to know about Kingman, the more he retreated. He shed very little light on his dream season in 1979, declining most interview requests. Further putting him into his own shell was a joking feature by *Chicago Sun-Times* beat writer Joe Goddard in spring training '79. An informal poll of Cubs players had named Kingman their worst-dressed teammate. The poll was all in jest, but Kingman apparently took offense at its publication and retreated into a cone of silence.

Sometimes he gave it back to the media in strange and inappropriate ways.

In spring training 1980, he dumped a bucket of ice water on beat writer Don Friske of the *Daily Herald*, the Chicago northwest suburban–based paper that had chronicled Kingman's high school feats more than a decade earlier. Good-guy Friske, now the newspaper's night sports editor, hadn't written anything to provoke Kingman. He just happened to be sitting there, talking to infielder Lenny Randle, when Kingman approached him and doused him, a la Denny McLain to a Detroit sportswriter ten years earlier. Kingman would be made by Cubs management to offer an apology to Friske, while assorted teammates told the writer they were embarrassed by the incident.

Six years later, while he was a designated hitter on the Oakland Athletics, sportswriter Susan Fornoff opened a gift package. It contained a rat in a cage, courtesy of Kingman. Female journalists in clubhouses still were relatively new on the scene in the mid-1980s, a fact that Kingman apparently did not accept easily.

These were serious transgressions that would have netted more severe punishments in the politically correct days of a new millennium. Perhaps that was Kingman's juvenile side. Perhaps he simply didn't take media–player relations seriously. When he opened an ice cream parlor called Kingman's Landing two miles west of Wrigley Field in April 1981, the men's room was labeled "pressroom." That day, as owner of the short-lived business, Kingman could laugh about the analogy.

By 1992, he tried to explain himself.

"Sportscasters on radio and TV can tell it like it is," he said then. "They have no way of misinterpreting or inserting their feelings into their report. When they ask you a question, the public can make up its own mind.

"In print, a writer will interpret his feelings toward an individual. Sometimes it's unjust and unfair. The reader at times comes away with a tainted feeling toward an athlete. I wasn't out there trying to be in a popularity contest.

"I feel if you have a bad game between the white lines, you have a right to be criticized. If you lose a game, drop a last-inning fly ball, that's their option. I don't think sportswriters should get carried away with what happens outside the white lines."

Kingman claimed he actually respected some scribes back in '92.

"There are quite a few writers who I respect and enjoy reading and who have become close friends. But there are many, many bad writers out there who will write their columns, never venture into the clubhouse, and never make the effort to really get to know somebody before they write their articles. These are the people I don't have any time for."

Trying to figure out something, anything about Kingman requires tracing his athletic roots back to the mid-1960s and Chicago's northwest suburbs. Lloyd Meyer, still coaching American Legion baseball in his early seventies, recalled a talented slugger–pitcher who could blow hot and cold, performance-wise and emotionally, as a just-graduated high school senior in 1967.

"He had been a first-round pick as pitcher coming out of high school, but he was going to USC [University of Southern California]," Meyer said. "He had a big-league curveball. He played on the best team we ever had. We won twenty-five games in a row. Overall, he was a good kid who never caused you problems except for one thing. He wanted to play for two weeks, and hit homers.

Then we had the big [tournament] game, and he said he didn't want to pitch. He did end up pitching, but he got hammered and we got beat. At the plate, he'd strike out six, seven times in a row. He was very moody."

Both Meyer and Bob Frisk, then sports editor of the *Daily Herald*, described the youthful Kingman as "different," performing in front of an involved father whose schedule as a United Airlines executive permitted him to attend a lot of Kingman's baseball and basketball games.

"Dave never gave us any problems," said Frisk, now assistant managing editor at his paper. "Most of these high school athletes are so anxious to talk to media. At that age, they jump at the chance to see the media. I never had the idea that Dave really cared one way or another. He was kind of aloof. You usually don't see that in a high school kid."

Years later, at his Cubs peak, Meyer witnessed two moods of Kingman at different games at Wrigley Field.

"The first game, he comes into the dugout, and I reach around the corner, holler at him," Meyer said. "You knew he recognized my voice. He would not look up. I must have stood around for five minutes before he turned around and said 'Hi.' At another game, he asked me, 'Where have you been all season?' It was like Jekyll and Hyde. I've never tried to figure him out. I like him. I've had bad kids, and Dave was not a bad person."

Kingman's talent carried him beyond Mount Prospect into Southern Cal and right into a San Francisco Giants uniform with minimal minor-league prepping in 1971.

"He was big, he was good, he had a future," Frisk said. "The last high school game I saw him play, he hit three of the most towering home runs I ever saw. They kept rolling down streets. He was a tremendous strikeout pitcher, and he could dunk a basketball."

In his first full Giants season in 1972, Kingman belted twenty-nine homers but struck out a then-astounding 140 times in 472 at bats. Those numbers foreshadowed the typical production for his career—monstrous homers that often were canceled out by his air-conditioning of ballparks with strikeouts.

"He was one of those kids where I wish I could have taught him to hit to right field," Meyer said.

Dave Kingman. Author photo.

Moving on to the Mets, he slugged seventy-three homers in 1975–1976. Included was what has commonly been rated the longest homer ever at Wrigley Field, landing four houses down on the east side of Kenmore Avenue early in '76. For the next three seasons, an X marked the touchdown point of the blast on the sidewalk in front of that fourth house.

Teams often didn't quite know what to do with Kingman, with holes in his swing made worse by erratic outfielding skills. He played with four clubs in 1977, moving from the Mets to the Padres to the Angels and finally the Yankees. In the ensuing off-season, the Cubs signed him, an apparent panacea to a power shortage.

In 1978, Kingman slugged twenty-eight of the Cubs' seventy-two homers, a puny total in the post–World War II era for a team playing in Wrigley Field. He might have had forty or more that season but missed forty-two games with a shoulder injury.

Then he really turned on the power to lead the National League in homers in 1979, his most complete season, which included a .288 average and acceptable left fielding. Kingman twice belted three homers in one game (including in the famed 23–22 loss to the Phillies on May 17) and had one streak of five homers in two games. All of Wrigley Field would quiet to a hush of anticipation when Kingman came to bat. Single-handedly slugging the Cubs into contention through late August, Kingman won over legions of fans.

One rooter was a nine-year-old Peoria youth baseball player named Jim Thome. He would mimic Kingman in playground games.

"We played with the tennis ball against the brick building," Thome said. "I liked the way Kingman hit the ball out of the ballpark. Dave Kingman was one of those guys who was all or nothing. My dad [Chuck] loved him. I had this obsession with Kingman."

Jim searched for Kingman's boat while the family drove down Lake Shore Drive to Wrigley Field. Once at the ballpark, the kid took matters into his own hands in an attempt to meet Kingman. He slipped away from his parents and sneaked into the Cubs' dugout.

"[Cubs catcher] Barry Foote ended up carrying me out," Thome recalled. "It was a great story. It's like any kid—when they have a player they admire, they'll do anything to get their favorite player's autograph. That's how I was."

With two autographs in tow, Thome was proud and never forgot the incident. Two decades later, he'd match and even exceed Kingman's distance classics as a slugger for the Indians and Phillies.

Kingman flashes back to 1979 from time to time.

"It's just one year where you put it all together," Kingman said. "It was a fun year. Unfortunately as a team we didn't do better [a 13–28 finish for a final 80–82 record]. That was probably the one thing that would have been more highlighted. But hitting forty-eight certainly was fun.

"Everything went right. Sometimes those line drives that are caught went out of the ballpark. But I don't think any one person can describe the contributing factors going into a great year."

As positive as 1979 turned out, the following year was in stark contrast, as Kingman quickly wore out his welcome in Chicago. The ice-water incident with Don Friske immediately made media relations go from bad to worse.

"I was stunned when that incident with Friske occurred," said Bob Frisk. "A lot of people thought it was me [due to the name similarities]. He just changed. It's too bad, because he had enormous talent."

Kingman then was paid by the *Chicago Tribune* to pen a regular column, a rare occurrence of the slugger taking advantage of his high profile. But the column was ghostwritten by a Chicago Park

District official chum. Reporters from competing newspapers frozen out by Kingman in the clubhouse were made even unhappier by the column. The piece soon was pulled to the ridicule of then *Chicago Sun-Times* columnist Mike Royko, who branded Kingman "Dave Ding Dong."

As the Cubs slid toward last place at midseason, Kingman left the lineup again with several injuries. The team scheduled a Kingman T-shirt giveaway promotion during his disablement. He did not even show up at the ballpark that day, and some claim to have spotted him riding a jet-ski off Navy Pier during a lakefront festival. He ended 1980 with just eighteen homers and fifty-seven RBIs. The following spring, Cubs general manager Bob Kennedy finally tired of Kingman and peddled him to the Mets for his second tour of duty at Shea Stadium.

Kingman returned to his feast-and-famine ways in New York with thirty-seven homers and a .204 average in 1982. But he seemed to find a niche in 1984 in Oakland, serving as the designated hitter. He had his second-best overall season with thirty-five homers, 118 RBIs, and a .268 average. The next two years he belted thirty and thirty-five homers, respectively.

And then there was no contract offer for 1987. Not from Oakland, not from anywhere. His career was over, with 442 homers and a .236 average. Kingman blames it on the owners' collusion to hold down salaries at the time.

"I wanted to play two, three more years," he said. "I wasn't slowing down a bit in my last year. I really enjoyed [being a] designated hitter. I would have had five hundred [homers] with no problem. Not many players end their career with those kind of numbers [thirty-five homers]."

Getting over the disappointment of 1986, Kingman said he had "no regrets" with the course of his baseball life. "I'm very happy and content with the career I had and the numbers I put up," he added. "If anything, I would have enjoyed playing on one team, without moving around so much. But I was single at the time, so it didn't affect my family."

Now he watches players reach and surpass his best power numbers with ease, no doubt aided in some cases by steroids, which only began creeping into the game at the end of Kingman's career.

He prefers not to comment about the illicit juice, instead lauding present players for their feats.

"I will say it's hard to compare things happening now with days gone by," he said. "Guys are getting bigger and stronger, not just in baseball, but in all sports. You still have to hit the ball with good hand–eye coordination."

Both Andre Dawson and Sammy Sosa passed up Kingman's best year, Dawson with forty-nine homers during a Most Valuable Player season in 1987, then Sosa with the first of his three sixty-homer seasons, also winning the MVP, in 1998. He has met both players.

"I wish Sammy well," he said. "He's an incredible ballplayer."

With a smile and a series of corny one-liners, Sosa won over the fans and the majority of media until his 2003 corked-bat misadventure, season-long slump in 2004, and AWOL status on the season's final day soured his image. But until then, Sosa possessed the persona and appeal that Kingman could have easily had.

But as the man said, there are no regrets, no turning back. Only South Lake Tahoe and the outdoors life. Dave Kingman never had a lot of wants. He has what he needs just fine now.

Well-Rounded Instruction in Fort Worth

Arlington Stadium lives. The former open-air home of the Texas Rangers was not totally ground to dust. One area entrepreneur ensured as much when he snared the old ballpark's batting cages for his Ray Burris Academy of Sports Instruction in Fort Worth.

But you don't know Burris as well as you could have if you think he's just a baseball guy, trying to relate his experiences of pitching in Wrigley Field in the 1970s to new generations.

The Burris academy not only teaches baseball but also softball, football, basketball, volleyball, soccer, and personal training. Burris himself handles instruction for baseball, softball, basketball, and personal training. Yeah, he played some hoops back in high school in Oklahoma, while also rigorously practicing the art of training body and mind for athletic challenges as a player. The results weren't always to his satisfaction, but he tried to put himself in the best position possible in a less-enlightened era of personal training and sports medicine.

With a nine-thousand-square-foot facility on the east side of Fort Worth, better geographically to serve the entire metroplex including Dallas, Burris has carved out his own identity. He no longer is compared to others. Nobody calls him "Little Fergie" or suggests he looks like Bob Gibson anymore.

"This probably will be my last [career] stop," said Burris, eloquently spoken and candid without raising the decibel level ever so slightly.

"But I still wouldn't mind being a Cubs pitching coach."

Burris will never dodge his Chicago connections. But there are a lot of folks ahead of him in line to get the call for any openings on

Dusty Baker's staff. So he'll be content to follow the path on which he began to trod while working for the Texas Rangers in the early 1990s.

Burris always was business minded. He had started a sports promotions company on the side in 1982 while he pitched for the Montreal Expos. His instructional bent had begun when he was dumped from the Rangers coaching staff upon the appointment of Kevin Kennedy as manager in 1992. Burris switched to the front office, where he got to know Rangers managing partner George W. Bush.

"One on one he was very congenial, very warm, with a passion for baseball," Burris said of the future president. "He loved talking baseball. He didn't try to push you away. He was down to earth."

Burris didn't have any inclination to handle sports instruction. But he started anyway in August 1992 as a favor to Tom House, a Rangers colleague who would develop a gig as a private pitching coach, developing the likes of Mark Prior.

"The next thing I know I'm doing forty hours a week for the Rangers, then forty hours a week for instruction," Burris said. Soon he rehabbed an old warehouse and imported the Arlington Stadium batting cages when the Ballpark at Arlington opened. Now Burris employs nineteen instructors out of his total staff of twenty-nine, while using six indoor batting cages and six outdoor fields. For basketball and volleyball, the academy has portable courts that are set up inside the facility.

Burris said seventeen thousand fledgling athletes pass through his academy each year from far and wide. "Our demographics go as far west as California, north to Chicago, east to Georgia, and south to Corpus Christi. We gave traveling clinics and specialized things, such as a right-handed pitchers' camp and a catchers' camp."

Recognizing the number of injuries to pitchers, Burris's instructional methods focus on prevention.

"I try to teach them how to stay healthy," he said. "They produce movement that will eliminate additional stress on the arm. I was able to keep healthy in my career. I wasn't a pitcher who broke down. I didn't throw a lot across my body on a regular basis. The fortunate thing is I was blessed with good genes and good body chemistry.

"Everyone is now concerned about velocity. Parents get hung up about that. What's lost in that element is how the kid is throwing the ball. When a kid breaks down, they overpitched him in high school or college. Nobody is showing them the proper way of pitching the ball. The thoughts are wrong. Evidently not too many teach proper mechanics."

At the same time, the baseball talent pool has dwindled, with many potential pitchers and everyday players now opting for basketball.

"In our society, it's the get-rich-quick scheme," Burris said. But when he attended high school thirty-five years ago, the only way for a young athlete to make money out of high school was signing a baseball contract. The NBA did not take high school players, and most college players had to play through their senior year.

Burris is a baseball guy all the way through. When he couldn't pitch anymore in the majors, he switched to the short-lived Senior League, taking the mound in 1990 for the West Palm Beach Tropic. He returned to the Milwaukee Brewers, his last big-league pitching stop, as bullpen coach and assistant pitching coach before moving on to the Rangers.

By then, Burris had used the sum total of his major-league experiences in a career that was pegged for stardom at the beginning, with the Cubs in 1973, but eventually settled in to a journeyman's existence through fifteen seasons.

Burris had the classic small-town athletic upbringing in Oklahoma, playing all sports and learning how to pitch through constant repetition and in makeshift style.

"One thing I did have is, I had ability to play the game," he said. "My approach was much different than kids today. . . . We didn't have all that much growing up. We had to be creative and threw rocks building up your arm. We hunted with rocks—that's how I learned accuracy. Baseball was a passion to me."

A high school and semipro star, Burris was an NAIA All-American at Southwestern State College in Weatherford, Oklahoma. That earned him the attention of Dallas-based Cubs scout Bill Capps. Burris was drafted in the seventeenth round in 1972. He was so impressive pitching batting practice for the Cubs' Bradenton (Florida) rookie team that he was promoted to Double-A Midland without ever getting into a rookie-league game.

Burris used his time in the Texas League well, listening to a legendary pitching coach who would soon teach Bruce Sutter, another Cubs farmhand, how to throw the baffling split-finger fastball.

"Freddie Martin taught me how to make the ball sink, how to apply proper finger pressure, and throw it off the meat part of my fingers," he said.

Burris did not stop in spring training 1973. He led all Cubs pitchers with a 1.80 ERA, winning a spot as a middle reliever on the parent team with just that half-season of pro experience. Again, Burris did not disappoint. Sandwiched around a demotion to Triple-A Wichita, he was 1–1 with a 2.91 ERA in sixty-five innings.

Since he was six feet five and African American, he naturally was compared to Fergie Jenkins, who had just come off six consecutive twenty-victory seasons with the Cubs. And the likening to Gibson also was natural, as the Cardinals' ace was still an effective starter in 1973 despite advancing age. Burris always swore off the comparisons, insisting that he "couldn't be like Fergie."

But Jenkins's presence was helpful in getting Burris in the right frame of mind.

"I was fortunate because I was surrounded by great players, who helped me understand what the game was all about," Burris said, citing Jenkins, Billy Williams, Ron Santo, Randy Hundley, Milt Pappas, Jose Cardenal, Rick Monday, and Bob Locker.

"We were policed by our teammates. If we didn't get that 0-and-2 pitch where we needed it, our players told us how to correct it. We got on-the-field training. When you came up, you listened to older players. Now you see [young] guys talking trash."

But then a wrinkle was thrown into the baseball educational process. Many of the veterans were dealt away in a massive housecleaning after yet another pennant-race collapse in 1973. Burris endured a sophomore jinx in 1974 with a 6.60 ERA in forty games, all but five in relief. Again, he was demoted for a spell to Triple-A to get straightened out.

"There was a new group of young players coming in from other organizations," Burris said. "I was still young. I didn't have the know-how and experience of pitching in that ballpark. I had to still continue to grow and learn to pitch in that ballpark."

Burris's future was still uncertain in spring training 1975. But he quickly gained an advocate in new pitching coach Marv Grissom.

He went to bat for Burris with manager Jim Marshall, not a big fan of the pitcher off his 1974 performance.

"He saw an aggressive, take-charge, get-after-the-hitter type," Burris said. "He told Marshall I'd win more games than any other pitcher on the staff."

Grissom was proved right after Marshall put Burris in the rotation. He was 15–10 on a pitching-poor team that finished 75–87. Only future announcer Steve Stone had a winning record at 12–8 among the other starters.

Seemingly solid, Burris got off to a poor 4–11 start in 1976. But the type of conditioning that he would teach in later life paid off for him. He had enough energy to turn his season totally around. He won eleven of his last thirteen decisions, including nine complete games and four shutouts. Burris was named National League Pitcher of the Month for August, 1976 with a 6–1 record and 1.89 ERA. He ended up with a 3.11 ERA to go along with his second straight fifteen-victory season.

Unlike other Cubs of the time, Burris was not bothered by the all-daytime schedule at Wrigley Field.

"Playing all day games was great for me," he said. "I had to learn how to eat right, get my rest. It's up to the player to adjust to the schedule."

Further progress for Burris wasn't linear. With seemingly a twenty-victory season in his future, he regressed in 1977. Burris was 14–16 with a 4.72 ERA. Worse yet, he became the easiest-to-hit Cubs starter since Dick Ellsworth in 1966, allowing 270 hits in 221 innings. To this day, he'll give a justification for being hit so freely.

"In 1977, those balls that fell in could have been hit at somebody," he said. "There's no defense for a walk. I knew what I was. Nobody said you should be striking out hitters. Letting them put the ball in play [to the fielders] was my job. That's how I was taught to play the game. If I give up anything, I was taught to never beat yourself. If you were going to lose, make the other team beat you with a hit, not a walk."

Burris's strikeout totals were very much unlike Jenkins's, so the last of the comparisons had ceased by 1977. From 1975 to 1977, Burris struck out 108, 112, and 105 batters while hurling 238, 249, and 221 innings, respectively.

The constant change in pitching coaches did not help him, either.

From 1973 to 1978, Burris was tutored by Larry Jansen, Hank Aguirre, Grissom, Barney Schultz, and finally Mike Roarke. The continual turnover in pitching coaches was one of the biggest detriments to Cubs pitching throughout the entire seventies.

Burris also had to concentrate on trying to improve himself through mossified racial attitudes by the front office. Even in the seventies, while Phil Wrigley was still owner, African American Cubs had to be careful whom they were seen with and what they said. The top capital crime, resulting in banishment from the Cubs, was any hint of interracial romance. Backup player Wayne Tyrone found his playing time cut to nearly nothing in 1976 when his white girlfriend started showing up at Wrigley Field, a situation corroborated by Burris.

The pitcher's fan club was headed by a white female. She was seen by a front-office type talking with Burris in the Wrigley Field parking lot after one game. Burris was then told by the honchos upstairs not to be seen with the woman again in public. He also recalled a front-office representative traveling on the road to monitor players' off-the-field activities—especially the African Americans.

The front-office policies would have provided grist for hard-hitting stories about the Cubs' losing aura if the newspapers of the day could have exposed them. "But no one asked," Burris said of the beat writers and columnists of the day. Blackballing awaited any player who sought out the media to complain.

However, it was not subtle racism by the front office that held Burris back even as he became one of three African American pitchers—along with Donnie Moore and Lynn McGlothen—on the roster for the first time in Cubs history in 1978. He faulted himself for not continuing his earlier progress. By later in the '78 season, Burris had backslid in the rotation and started to be used out of the bullpen in a 7–13 season.

"Those seasons, 1978–1979, were transition years for maturity," he said. "I wasn't preparing myself right. I thought a lot of things would happen based on what I did. I got comfortable in those first three years thinking it would just happen for me. It was not knowing how to put things in their proper place. My performance was affected. I had to regroup, change my thought process."

A change of scenery also was involved. More than a month into the 1979 season, Burris was traded to the New York Yankees for setup man Dick Tidrow. The trade became lopsided in favor of the Cubs with Tidrow enjoying two excellent years working the seventh and eighth innings, paving the way for Bruce Sutter's saves. Meanwhile, Burris struggled as a Yankees reliever, moved on to the Mets near the end of the '79 season, and then was 7–13 as a Mets starter in 1980.

But then Burris caught a break with a trade to the Montreal Expos, a team on the rise that made the NLCS in the strike-fractured 1981 season. He was 9–7 with a 3.05 ERA as a starter, then pitched well in the postseason.

"That brought my value back up, my ability to perform well in playoffs," he said.

Again, the success did not last. Burris was back in the bullpen, at his request, later in the 1982 season. Then he had one more last gasp as a quality starter at Oakland in 1984, amassing a 13–10 record and a 3.15 ERA. He finished up with the Brewers, the Cardinals, and then the Brewers again in 1987, his final record 108–134 with a 4.17 ERA.

Burris will accentuate the positive when he talks to his younger baseball students. Nobody can take those 108 victories away from him. How many pitchers from small towns in Oklahoma make the majors, let alone win more than one hundred games?

"I'm not sad about my career," he said.

Rather than the second Fergie, Burris was himself, start to finish. That alone is satisfaction enough.

The Backstage Operator

At ninety, Herman Franks doesn't impress too easily.

But when the former Cubs coach, manager, and general manager set foot on Wrigley Field for the first time in twenty-two and a half years on May 18, 2004, with the San Francisco Giants in town, he sported the look of the nearly awestruck.

It was lights, cameras, action in a manner Franks and his fellow Cubs employees of the late 1970s could only fantasize about back in the day. The ballpark lights were blazing; the daily capacity crowd was assembling; assorted folks were scrambling around for pregame ceremonies; and the folks were filtering in on those rooftop bleachers. When Franks stepped out on the field, cane in hand, he remembered looking out at the rooftops a quarter-century previously, when there were just cozy gatherings of residents sitting on lawn chairs and a stray Weber firing up.

If Franks had come a little bit earlier, he probably could have cut some deals before chatting with Andy MacPhail, a 1981 vintage front-office assistant now Cubs president. Front and center as Cubs and Giants manager, he was always brokering business or people deals behind the scenes in those days. The game was his passion, but managing money and helping move people around was a close-behind pastime.

"I retired in 1981," Franks said of his final year with the Cubs, serving as general manager for the final two-thirds of the last season of Wrigley family ownership.

"I retired too young. I should have kept going. My mind was very clear, very healthy."

Franks had done very well for himself through a series of investments and businesses that always dovetailed with baseball roles. Operating from his longtime home in Salt Lake City, retirement offered a little bit of golf along with a cabin in Montana and a condo in Coronado, California. Three children and seven grand-children make sure family matters are close at hand. There's a cir-cuit of phone calls to old chums like Willie Mays, Buzzy Bavasi, Joe L. Brown. He also counts the likes of Joe Torre, Don Zimmer, and former Cubs pitching coach Billy Connors as friends.

"I never made a lot of money in baseball," Franks said. "I thought I'd have to invest in a different business. In 1955, I retired from the Giants, went home, and got into grocery stores. We came up with nine, ten stores, then sold those to Mayfair in California.

"In the meantime, I got into the mobile-home business and was in that for years. During that time, Willie Mays was having prob-lems with taxes. A banker out in San Francisco was handling his affairs. I was managing the team, so I said let's see what we can do for you. I signed a note for Willie and put him into real estate. We got into a lot of real estate for him. Willie then referred me to Juan Marichal and other players."

Soon Franks was running a business entitled Man-Invest, han-dling the business affairs of a number of baseball players. And while Franks ran a small business empire, he just couldn't stay away from baseball. He retired and unretired so many times he would have put Michael Jordan to shame.

He's now in the role of elder storyteller, so you just let him rip. His life connected with so many interesting characters in Cubs his-tory that his reach kind of extends to the present day, even though he had finally retired for good in Ronald Reagan's first year in the White House. Franks had been a faithful servant and confidant of Leo Durocher, dating back to his role as backup catcher and third-base coach for the "Lip's" Giants teams in the early 1950s. That association would ensure that he'd have almost as significant of a role as Durocher's.

First he traces how his many comebacks started.

"The Giants called me in 1958 and asked me to come back as a coach after their move to San Francisco," Franks said. "I told them I'd go out for one year, and I retired again."

A couple of years later Franks was asked to serve as general manager of the Triple-A franchise in Salt Lake City. "But I didn't want to work for anybody," he said. "I ended up owning the club. I made quite a bit of money." His manager in 1962 was Bob Kennedy, which was only a prelude to a crucial later association in Wrigley Field.

In the meantime, the Giants just couldn't live without Franks. Manager Alvin Dark summoned him again to coach in 1964. "That started the cycle again," he said. Franks succeeded Dark the following year, managing the Giants of Mays, Marichal, and Willie McCovey to four consecutive second-place finishes. He broke the late Bobby Bonds into the lineup in 1968.

Franks retired again after the '68 season. But he was sitting back, minding his own business and others' investments, when he got a call from Cubs owner Phil Wrigley late in July 1969. Durocher had been caught sneaking off to his stepson's summer camp in northern Wisconsin while the first-place Cubs were playing a weekend series against the Los Angeles Dodgers at Wrigley Field. A livid Wrigley wanted to fire Durocher on the spot and offered to replace him with Franks.

"I told him, 'You can't fire him, that would disrupt the team too much," Franks recalled. " 'I'm not going to replace him.' At the time, I was handling Leo's business affairs and making investments for him."

The Cubs finally persuaded Franks to join them in 1970. Durocher began bickering with Ron Santo, so general manager John Holland wanted Franks to play peacemaker. Franks initially told Holland to rig it up so that he appeared to be consulting with Mays while in San Francisco and then would also help the Cubs. However, Holland then got a logical entrée for Franks when pitching coach Joe Becker went off duty with a heart problem. With an opening for a coach, Franks hired on for the remainder of the season.

Franks immediately was put in charge of the colorful Joe Pepitone, just acquired from the Houston Astros. His main duty was trying to moderate Pepi's overactive social life.

Another retirement followed the '70 season. Half a decade passed before the Cubs called again with another unusual request. On behalf of Wrigley, team president Bill Hagenah wanted Durocher's number. The Lip had departed the Cubs midway through 1972, managed the Astros in the 1973 season, and then retired. But Wrigley, at his wit's end as to who would succeed the aging Holland as GM, wanted to summon Durocher back to take that job.

Franks called Durocher at his home in Palm Springs to inform him of the Cubs' intentions. But the deal soon got gummed up when Durocher also learned that Wrigley wanted to make broadcaster Jack Brickhouse, with whom he had long feuded, team president. Instead, park operations director Salty Saltwell was elevated to general manager while continuing in his old role in another of the eccentric moves that marked Wrigley's stewardship.

But soon Franks himself would return to Wrigley Field. By now Kennedy had been working with the neophyte Seattle Mariners as that franchise started up. Bill Wrigley, Phil's son and successor as owner, recruited Kennedy to take over from Saltwell.

"Bob calls me at my club and asks me to be manager," Franks said. "I asked him, 'What the hell you talking about? Seattle?' He said, 'No, Chicago. I'm the new general manager.' I had to talk to [wife] Amy. I then called Kennedy to say I'll take it."

But Franks's return to the Cubs caused some bad blood with Durocher.

"Leo thought I screwed him out of the Cubs job," he said. "For a couple of years, we didn't talk." Eventually the two patched things up.

Despite the sour aftertaste of dispatching two-time batting champion Bill Madlock to the Giants in a money dispute in exchange for outfielder Bobby Murcer—in fact the Cubs paid Murcer more money than Madlock had demanded—Franks's 1977 Cubs got off to a fantastic start. They were 47–22, eight games ahead in the National League East by the end of June. Then the wheels came off, one by one. The Cubs grimly hung on to first place through early August, then steadily nose-dived. They still had to lose the season's final five games to finish at 81–81. The odds were in doppelganger territory that the Cubs would be twenty-five games over .500 after three months, then finish at .500.

Franks actually tried to employ too much of a good thing—Bruce Sutter. The second-year stopper's split-fingered fastball baffled almost every hitter in the first half. Franks used Sutter two or three innings at a time. By July, he developed a knot in his pitching shoulder and only worked sporadically in the second half.

"The last couple of months we had injuries you can't believe," Franks recalled. "I lost my catcher, Rick Reuschel, Jerry Morales. But I had more fun with that ball club than all the great players I had in San Francisco. This was a very mediocre club. The way they were winning, and the fans gave them standing ovations every game."

Chastened over his handling of Sutter, Franks was much more judicious after 1977. By 1979, he started using Dick Tidrow and Willie Hernandez as setup men in the seventh and eighth to get to Sutter in the ninth. "All I strived to do is get one run out in front going into the seventh inning," he said.

By 1979, the Cubs clubhouse was one crabby place. Franks often growled at assembled media, his ever-present tobacco juice just missing the pen-and-mike crowd's shoes. Media-unfriendly Dave Kingman and Bill Buckner were twin anchors of the team, while clubhouse lawyers like Barry Foote and Ted Sizemore abounded.

Away from the media gaze, Franks tried to figure out how to handle Kingman.

"I admired him," Franks said. "He never drank or smoked, but Dave would get up at four or five in the morning to go fishing. When he came to the park, he was tired as hell. He'd go in the training room to take a nap. In Philadelphia, I had a run-in with him. He's a great guy but did certain things I didn't agree with. When I retired, I told him, 'I'm retiring because of you and Buckner.'

"He's really basically a good guy. He called me here about a year ago to tell me he bought some trailer in Provo. I've gone to his house. We just didn't agree on how to handle baseball. Baseball was kind of secondary to him."

Franks's assessment of Buckner was more harsh.

"Buckner was selfish. The ball club knew it," he said. "If he got a base hit, everything was great. All he cared about was himself. He was jealous of Kingman."

With less than a week to go in a 1979 season in which the Cubs were 67–54 in late August but had fallen to near the .500 mark, Franks announced he was quitting. He cited disgust with a number of the players. After the season, Buckner wrote a letter of apology to Franks, who would like to visit Buckner at his getaway residence in Idaho, where he has tried to put distance between him and the nightmare of his error that helped cost the Boston Red Sox the 1986 World Series.

Franks was fated for one more tour of duty with the Cubs—as

general manager. Bill Wrigley's inheritance-tax problems after the mid-1977 deaths of his parents prompted him to order Kennedy to shave payroll, including Sutter's. Shorn of talent even after a 64–98 finish the previous season, the 1981 Cubs got off to a horrific 6–28 start. Kennedy walked the plank, and Wrigley summoned Franks back from Salt Lake City to take over.

"I said, 'I'll take this job, but I want to spend some money to get ballplayers,'" Franks told Wrigley. "The first guy I signed was Joe Carter. We gave him $125,000 [signing bonus]. Bill said, 'Do what you want to do.'"

Franks even got money back. Believing Reuschel was going downhill, he traded the ace to the Yankees for several lesser pitchers, but also got $400,000 in return. Wrigley later told Franks that the George Steinbrenner cash cost him even more in taxes owed.

MacPhail, then assistant director of scouting, recalls that the sometimes bombastic Franks impacted positively on the downtrodden front-office employees in the spring of 1981.

"He brought a lot of energy to the front office when he came," MacPhail said. "He showed a lot of faith in the scouting department. We had the second pick in the draft. [Scouting director] Vedie Himsl was adamant about taking Joe Carter. He walked into Herman's office and said if this guy wasn't in the big leagues in two years, he'd resign. That was all Herman needed to hear, so he said to go ahead and draft him."

Franks's reputation as a good baseball man was long-standing.

"I was in the Dominican recently and spent some time with Marichal," MacPhail said. "Juan went out of his way to talk about what a good manager he was, one of the best he ever had.

While Franks was settling into the front office in '81, he sensed Wrigley was trying to sell the team. He told the owner he was interested in buying the Cubs, too, but likely would have needed more time to round up an investment group. "Hell, yeah, we could have rounded it up someplace," Franks said of the desired $20 million purchase price. But Wrigley did not want to make the sale a public bidding, so he quietly dealt with white-knight purchaser Tribune Company, across Michigan Avenue from the Wrigley Building.

Just after baseball shut down due to a strike in June 1981, the sale to the media conglomerate was announced. On the day the sale was formally approved, Tribune Company honcho Stan Cook called Franks, asking for a meeting to explain how the new owner operated. With Cook subordinates at his side and Cubs manager Joey Amalfitano joining Franks, Cook asked for advice.

"I said, 'Mr. Cook, I would fire everyone here, including me, and start over,'" he said. "Cook said, 'We want to keep you.' I just felt the whole thing should be started clean."

Initially under the impression Cook wanted him to return, Franks worked with new team chairman Andy McKenna, a veteran of Bill Veeck's ownership group with the White Sox, who had helped broker the Cubs' sale to Tribune Company. The pair worked together the remainder of the 1981 season. At one point, Franks wanted to dump third baseman Ken Reitz, owed $900,000 for another season, but McKenna opposed to the move on the theory that Tribune Company would be perceived as cheap. Sox chairman Jerry Reinsdorf, also new to baseball ownership in 1981, said he would take Reitz off Franks's hands—possibly moving the third baseman to another team—if the Cubs would agree not to try to steal broadcaster Harry Caray away from the South Side. Reitz ended up staying until he was released in spring training 1982 by new GM Dallas Green. But the Cubs did end up employing Caray, who did not want to stay on in the Reinsdorf regime and work games on pay-cable TV.

Green's arrival was effected without Franks's knowledge. Immediately after the end of the 1981 season, McKenna started actively wooing the voluble Phillies manager, who had a long background in player development.

"After the end of the season, I get up one morning, open the paper, and Dallas Green is the new GM," Franks said. "McKenna never called me. I thought that was pretty bad."

Almost immediately, Green strode into the ballpark like the new sheriff in town.

"All the people were worried about their jobs," Franks said. "I told Dallas to tell the people what's going on. He calls a meeting in the Pink Poodle [the old front-office/media lunchroom]. Dallas rolls up his sleeves and says, 'I'm a working GM. I get out here at 7:30 AM.' He told people they didn't know how to win. After he was done, I go into his office and told him, 'You talk too much.'"

Franks agreed to stick around to help out for the 1981 winter meetings. "Dallas was up in the room, while I was in the lobby talking to people," he said.

That would turn out to be Franks's last official baseball gig. He returned to Salt Lake City. There would be no more calls to return to the big leagues, no more backstage posturing and deal making. Just memories of a long life.

"I've got a wonderful family," Franks said. "They take care of things for me. For ninety, I'm doing good. I still drive."

And still tell a good story, sans tobacco juice.

Green Acres

Dallas Green may have been salt of the earth, or just plain salty. Never would one think that either could be taken literally.

To those who heard him boom and bluster through six years in the big office at Wrigley Field in the 1980s, the sight of the now white-thatched Green, always an imposing six feet five, happily tending a garden, mowing a huge lawn with a tractor, or soothing a horse doesn't compute too well.

But that's the other side of Green that has existed for twenty-five years, put on the sidelines most of the time while he blew through the Friendly Confines, verbally and physically. Dallas and wife Sylvia have had their getaway, a sixty-acre farm in West Grove, Pennsylvania, more than thirty miles west of downtown Philadelphia, since before he was summoned by Tribune Company to rouse the Cubs from too many years of ownership-induced competitive drowsiness in 1981. Now the couple have acquired an even bigger farm, a two-hundred-acre spread twenty-three miles across the state line in Maryland, to which they'll soon move.

Green now leaves the farm in the spring and summer to watch Philadelphia Phillies games as an extra set of eyes and ears for general manager Ed Wade. He'll make day trips to Phillies farm clubs in Reading and Scranton. But make no mistake about it, baseball has to coexist now with the land.

"Sylvia and I both enjoyed the outdoors," Green said. "She loves her flowers and trees and started a small nursery. It kind of grew and grew out of a hobby.

"It's a great getaway. I jump on the tractor, mow grass, get away from the telephone. I love to piddle around with the vegetable garden. I take a lot of tomatoes, corn, beans out to the ballpark and give it away to all the people I know."

The Greens rent out much of the acreage to a farmer who works it for cash crops. But they've also had a few head of livestock on the property. One was a recalcitrant bull. Green chuckled at the memory of a recruiting visit by Andy McKenna, first Cubs chairman under Tribune Company ownership. "Andy was a city boy, and while he was here, we had a bull that got out from the fences," he said.

Mind you, the tall, strapping Green is no farm boy by upbringing. He grew up in the modest municipality of Newport, Delaware, but was a townsperson, through and through. Yet the idea of living in the country tugged at Dallas and Sylvia for years while he was director of minor leagues and scouting for the Phillies in the 1970s.

The couple discovered the West Grove property in 1979. The farmhouse was built in 1749. They were at first outbid on the property, but a family squabble involving the buyers enabled the Greens to acquire the farm.

Through the years they always would return to West Grove when they had the chance. Sylvia stayed on the farm much of the time when her husband managed the Yankees and Mets, giving her the option of making the two-and-a-half-hour drive to New York whenever she desired.

But not having gotten enough of the bucolic surroundings, the Greens bought the second farm in Maryland. This farmhouse was newer—of 1833 vintage. Several portents convinced them this was the right place to buy. The seller was named Taylor, which also was Sylvia's maiden name. A creek running through the property was named Green. Eventually, two of their children, John and Dana, lived on the property. Now Dallas and Sylvia will prepare to take their turn after selling the West Grove farm.

Now, mind you, it wasn't living on the farm while engaging in a stress-free baseball job that softened up Green. That came naturally.

"We all mellow with age to a degree," he said. "Things aren't as important to me as when I was younger. Everyone says Dallas Green can't change. Well, people don't change, they adapt. I was able to adapt a lot better than people give me credit for.

"There's a side I had that was always there. Check with all the people who worked with me. I'm a really pretty easy guy to get along with."

Wonder what the fly on the wall said about the meetings between two strong-willed, blustering men—Green and Yankees owner George Steinbrenner—when the "Boss" had hired Green to manage his team in 1989? At that point, having just been told to pack up and leave Wrigley Field by Tribune Company suit John Madigan, Green wasn't yet ready to retire. Green had been itching to manage anyway and had suggested he take over the Cubs in the dugout after the 1987 season, a plan that was vetoed by Madigan and Company.

"I have a desire, something I really enjoy doing, to change something that's not going well and make something of it," Green said of managing.

He had won a World Series in Philly in 1980 being his voluble self. It didn't quite work with Steinbrenner and not because he couldn't outshout the owner. The Yankees simply did not have the baseball organization and commitment to homegrown players that benefited Joe Torre more than half a decade later. Steinbrenner's millions weren't spent wisely, and Green's Yankees were 56–65 under his direction before he was fired.

"I think we did get along," Green said of Steinbrenner. "He respected me for what I did. When we fell apart, I said pretty much how I feel. I said a little too much to the press. George was in the firing mode in those days, so Dallas Green got the ax. Say anything you want about Steinbrenner, he puts his money where his mouth is."

Green returned to West Grove, then was summoned back into baseball by good friend Frank Cashen, then boss man of the Mets, to scout games out of Veterans Stadium. But when Jeff Torborg's tenure as a highly paid manager at Shea Stadium disintegrated in bad performances and discipline problems, the sheriff-like Green was summoned to clean up the ballpark early in the 1993 season.

"The Mets experience, I went from the frying pan [at Yankee Stadium] to the fire," Green recalled. "I was called into a situation where the media hated the players, and the players hated the media."

The specter of labor problems haunted the franchise, too. Green was on duty when the strike shut down the game in August 1994. He had to preside over the temporary use of replacement players the following spring training. And when the game resumed and some sense of normalcy returned, Green had to relive some of his Cubs experiences when top pitching prospects Bill Pulsipher, Paul Wilson, and Jason Isringhausen all got hurt.

The Mets never cracked the .500 mark in any of Green's four seasons. Fired late in the 1996 campaign, he put his managerial career to rest with a 454–478 mark.

"I was by then in my sixties, and I knew I was not getting back into the revolving door business of baseball," he said. "I didn't *need* a job. Obviously, the Chicago job had set me up financially. I had spent all my life in professional baseball. I was not going to work in some office building or be a guy who goes nine to five.

"Baseball was a natural thing for me. The Phillies made their changes. [Bill] Giles went upstairs, Dave Montgomery came in to run the team, and Ed Wade came in as GM. Paul Owens was still alive. 'Pope' knew I would like to stay in baseball. He let Eddie know that I would be interested. Some guys pushed for me. Eddie and I had a conversation."

Green became a special assistant to Wade. He'd start out his days in West Grove and then either go to the ballparks in Philadelphia or the minor-league clubs.

"It's really a good marriage, and I did contribute my thought processes," Green said. "Scouting and development is what I love. I evaluate the minor-league staff and evaluate the minor-league players for Eddie. I try to be creative and thoughtful as I can."

Cubs fans thought Green was anything but creative and thoughtful when he burst on the scene in the fall of 1981, proclaimed a "new tradition," imported players and front-office staff from Philadelphia, demanded the installation of lights and gave many the impression that Chicagoans were unsophisticated when it came to baseball.

The years, though, proved Green right. Charging in like the bull on his farm proved to be not the right tact, but the message was on target. The Cubs had to be dragged kicking and screaming into the latter twentieth century in installing a quality baseball organization and applying marketing techniques that were by then common in pro sports.

Appointed general manager while McKenna served as liaison between the team and Tribune Tower, Green had to start rebuilding from the bottom up. Buffeted by inheritance-tax liabilities that would total $40 million, owner Bill Wrigley had starved his team for operating capital even worse than his late father Phil Wrigley. The Cubs had virtually been stripped down to expansion-team quality by 1981. Some baseball operations folks hung onto their jobs like patronage workers in a political machine.

Green applied the unkind cut to some but didn't toss everyone overboard. Scouting chief Vedie Himsl and park operations boss Salty Saltwell stayed on, along with such venerable scouts as Buck O'Neil, Gene Handley, and Bill Capps. So did young front-office types like John Cox and Bill Harford. Green wanted assistant scouting director Andy MacPhail to stay on, but MacPhail was offered a better job with the Astros, starting a career journey that would lead him back to Wrigley Field twelve years later.

Tribune Company gave Green an infusion of capital to spruce up Wrigley Field while improving the player development system. He also hired the first full-fledged marketing directors in team history—the husband-and-wife team of Bing and Patty Cox Hampton.

"What we left behind is a change in philosophy, retraining Cubs fans that you have to buy tickets," Green said. "The Wrigley family had the philosophy that they will open the doors and they will come. I had worked under a marketing genius in Bill Giles. I knew that it was something that had to be instructed. We worked very, very hard to understand that a ticket to Wrigley Field was a special ticket and would be more special if we played good baseball."

But Green's best hire was the courtly Gordon Goldsberry, a top associate from the Philadelphia player development department. Goldsberry "no question" was Green's better half, he said. Where Green beefed up to eighty decibels, Goldsberry turned down the volume. Where Green was bullheaded, Goldsberry was conciliatory. Green was the Cubs' tough cop, Goldsberry was the good cop. Almost twenty years later, another front-office dynamo, Jim Hendry, said he aspired to be the quality person and baseball exec Goldsberry, who died in 1996, was.

Goldsberry rebuilt the scouting and farm systems, although the Cubs still trailed the likes of the Dodgers, Pirates, and Blue Jays in Latin American scouting, a hole that would not be closed until later in the 1990s. But when Green made some critical trades, importing Rick Sutcliffe, Dennis Eckersley, Gary Matthews and Bob Dernier, that boosted the 1984 team to a surprise National League East title, the farm system was still several years away from providing help.

"Everyone asked if I had a timetable," Green said, mindful of past failed "five-year plans." "I didn't. But in 1984, we won too quickly. Scouting and development hadn't kicked in to help us when we needed help and had breakdowns."

One by one, in 1985, the rotation that Green had spent millions to re-sign as free agents fell to injuries. At one point in August of that season, the entire starting five of Sutcliffe, Eckersley, Steve Trout, Scott Sanderson, and Dick Ruthven were on the disabled list at the same time. None would regain their pre-1985 effectiveness on Green's watch. One train of thought is that Tribune Company executives looked askance at a hefty portion of one of baseball's best payrolls being allocated to a quintet of pitchers who spent more time in the whirlpool and trainer's table than on the mound. Continuing the logic, that put Green on the slippery slope to departure.

He disagrees. Green believes his hiring of Gene "Stick" Michael as manager to replace Jim Frey nearly one-third through the 1986 season prompted discussions in the Tribune Tower about him.

"Gene didn't want to manage," he said. "I didn't have another guy in mind. John Vuckovich [then a Cubs coach] wasn't quite ready. The Michael thing started people distrusting the decision-making process."

By 1987, the likes of Rafael Palmeiro, Greg Maddux, Jamie Moyer, Shawon Dunston, and Dave Martinez, all drafted by Goldsberry, had established themselves as regulars at Wrigley Field. Mark Grace was moving up fast and would make his Chicago debut the following year as part of a flow of even more talent. Atlanta scouting impresario Paul Snyder, who built up a great development system of his own, said at the time the Cubs system was among the game's best.

All of the '87 crop would play as at least quality big leaguers through the year 2000. Maddux, Moyer, and Palmeiro were still regular contributors in 2004. But despite the influx of young talent, other factors were pulling the rug out from under Green.

With his vocal style and title as team president, Green had to deal directly with the button-down, bottom-line crowd at Tribune Tower. When Jim Finks had been team president in 1984, he served as a buffer between Green and the corporate crowd. Green was suspicious of the decision to rehire Frey as radio color analyst only a half-season after he was canned as manager. By the end of 1987, with Michael having quit and the Cubs collapsing in September to finish at the bottom of the NL East, Green was ready to be the center of a shakeup.

"The obvious key was when I offered to go back down on field [to manage]," he said. "They wanted to put someone from Tribune Company in charge of baseball operations. We had worked too hard to build things up. I said Gordy and John Cox could handle the GM situation. Then I suggested I should train the replacement for me while Vukovich became the manager. I can't work six or seven years and have someone we don't know or trust on the job."

The behind-the-scenes showdown came down to Green and Madigan. The latter won. Green was upset at Madigan, whom he considered a friend, for the quick hook more than a decade afterward. But his positive Chicago memories far outweighed the negatives of his departure.

"We're proud," Green said. "Every time we talk about Chicago, I think about the guys I hired. We left with people feeling that they were part of an organization, which they were never part of before. We left baseball operations in great shape, from a development standpoint. The organization was made to last. Gordy did a great job. Everything was set for the next guy to keep the momentum going."

The fact that the momentum would grind to a halt, and even go backward, in ensuing seasons under three different general managers did not dim Green's enthusiasm for his work. He will not comment on the strategies of his successors. But he's pleased that the elevation of MacPhail to team president finally is paying off, particularly with the combo of Hendry as GM and Dusty Baker as manager.

"I think it's a great model," Green said of the present-day chain of command. "Andy's done a great job in handling the workings of Tribune Company. He was trained very well in Houston, but Minnesota was where he earned his spurs. He worked in tough [economic] circumstances in Minnesota."

Although Green came through Wrigley Field for four seasons as Mets manager, he didn't really get a feel for the long-term changes he started until he visited the ballpark early in the season to sing in the seventh inning. In Chicago for the christening of his grandson, Green made his first appearance connected with the team in sixteen and a half years on May 9, 2004. He had never been in the upper-deck press box and luxury suites, on the drawing board during his tenure but not constructed until after his departure.

"It was quite a different look, to see the bleachers up on the rooftops and the super boxes the way they were constructed," he said. Green could have never dreamed the rooftops were so popular and lucrative that they'd have to cut a deal with the Cubs for 17 percent of their gross revenues in order to avoid legal action.

Green sang during a Sunday afternoon game. But he also could not have figured that the night games which he was so pilloried for demanding would now be a part of the Wrigley Field schedule, with more to come. Four more games each season were being phased in to reach the proscribed limit of thirty per season starting in 2006.

Green knew the demands of network TV for postseason night baseball could not be resisted. One other longtime theory about the players getting tired from the all-daytime home schedule has been proven to have some credence. And yet halfway through his Chicago tenure, Green came to understand the appeal of daytime baseball that made Wrigley Field so unique.

"I had come from night baseball," he said. "I didn't have a good feel for day baseball until a couple of years into my Chicago time. I found if you can do it, that's the way to play ball."

While the Wrigley family had poured the lion's share of its resources into maintenance of Wrigley Field's physical plant, instead of building up the baseball organization, Green's arrival began a stepped-up program of ballpark renovation. In the twenty years of Tribune Company ownership, more than $40 million was poured into the old ballpark, which celebrated its ninetieth birthday in 2004.

"It's a great ballpark," Green said. "It's great for the industry, great for the city of Chicago. It contributes to Cubs fans loving the game of baseball. . . . I don't know how many people came up to me and said, 'My grandma brought me to my first game.' It was a pleasure to see young people come into the ballpark."

He can relate to the young 'uns because he'll never feel old while connected to the game. And whenever he can get out and stomp around his own Green acres, be it Pennsylvania or Maryland, he gets the zest for life that keeps him going.

Putting the Hammer Down

During his pitching days, Chuck Rainey wanted to be known as a craftsman.

Little did Rainey know that would literally be his fate, well beyond baseball.

He'd move his fingers on the baseball for different grips and never did it better than one late August 1983 afternoon at Wrigley Field when he came within one out of pitching a no-hitter. Now he uses his hands all the time in a contracting business in his native San Diego.

"I do it all, a little bit of everything," ol' right-handed pitcher Rainey said. "I specialize in carpentry. I was always able to [work with my hands]. It was an aptitude scale that was high on my list."

So high that he did not dawdle or explore other lines of work when the pitching trail ran dry in 1985. He went right to work with hammer and saw, now specializing in renovations and additions in residences.

"The thing that's weird is that every year it seems that I'm not going through some transition in the biz standpoint but also a transition as I get older," he said. "First was making the transition from baseball player to average, everyday working stiff."

Even though he endures backbreaking physical labor, contracting is like baseball in another respect. It is mentally challenging. Those who attend to details get ahead, but it isn't easy by any means.

"The hardest thing is there's so many things you've got to think about," Rainey said. "Even on simple jobs, the hardest thing is to make sure everything gets done. In the course of doing everything, you're constantly, every day and every night, knowing that something needs to be done.

"You can get involved in a job where there is no plan. You just need to spend some time with it. I went out on one Monday morning where I did not know what to do on a job. But you get there, and it falls together. It's probably a lot like baseball."

And like his former calling, pain is never far away. If a pitcher like Rainey had to suck it up when he took the mound through all the aches and pains, think of the contractor who has lifted heavy materials one too many times or has not moved his hand out of the way fast enough to avoid a hammer or sharp tool.

"Nowadays the hardest tools are anything I use over my head, because my shoulders don't allow it," Rainey said. "I knew how to use tools from the time I was a little boy, so I had a relatively high comfort level. You always have to be a little bit afraid of them. A saw, it can take your finger off, take your legs off."

The contractor cannot afford to let his concentration slip at mid-afternoon, when many office workers need a sugar fix to avoid nodding off.

"They say most accidents happened at end of day," Rainey said. "The toughest time is 2, 3 PM. There are not too many days where I don't have a tool at least scuffing myself."

Many construction workers will not retire with body parts that look normal.

"The worst thing to happen to me was the index finger on my right hand looks similar to Yogi Berra's," he said. "I cut the back of my finger to the bone. I cut ligaments, severed all the stuff, and had microsurgery on it. It looks deformed, but I can use it."

Making matters worse is Rainey's inability to get affordable treatment for injuries.

"It's a big problem for this business," he said. "The way my business is set up, I can't get worker's comp. I'm an employer, not an employee, even though I'm a hands-on guy. I don't have health insurance now. I was turned down from having a preexisting condition. There are some unrealistic parameters for having health insurance."

In his early fifties, Rainey knows all too well that his business is a younger man's game. Even though he knows of men in their sixties who are still contracting, he says that "every year I delegate more and do less with tools. There were things I could do ten years ago that I absolutely won't do today. Now if I swing a hammer all day, I won't sleep at night without Vicodin.

"My goal is to look at my [baseball] pension each year, to see what it's good for. Maybe in five years . . ."

But Rainey would not have continued in the business if there wasn't some satisfaction in working for yourself and not having to answer to bosses.

"My business is fine," he said. "I'm not real aggressive about growth. I tell people I'm busy. My bills are paid, and I've got money in the bank. I've been pretty lucky. It's all referrals."

Rainey started off in the apartment-building development business after his baseball career petered out. "I took the money I made in baseball to parlay into a living," he said. But then he shifted into contracting when the development business nose-dived in the deep California recession of the early 1990s.

Rainey's jobs range from $10,000 to $200,000. Those who aren't buying new homes are fixing up their old ones with the likes of room additions and general remodeling.

He works with more than a dozen subcontractors.

"I just respect them," he said. "They know when I come to a job, it's clean. They're not going to waste their time, and they're going to get paid."

Rainey was an everyman when he pitched and hasn't changed.

"I go to a Padres game and don't get recognized," he said. "I tell people I was a journeyman pitcher. I told Dallas Green one day in the trainer's room that I don't want to be a million-dollar pitcher. I didn't want that kind of responsibility.

"I had a different attitude. I was more humble. Every day I was in baseball was a miracle."

After starring in amateur baseball in and around San Diego, Rainey was the Red Sox's first pick in the January 1974 draft. After five seasons in the minors, he made the parent club but was able to work only on the fringes of the Boston rotation from 1979 to 1982. He had a 7–5 record with three shutouts but also a 5.02 overall ERA in '82. In parts of his four Boston seasons, Rainey was 23–14 with a 4.38 ERA. A pitching-desperate Green picked him up in a deal for right-hander Doug Bird during the 1982 winter meetings.

Suddenly he thrived in manager Lee Elia's rotation in 1983. Rainey put a lot of men on base (219 hits and seventy-four walks in 191 innings) while batters made frequent contact (only eighty-four strikeouts). But he won on a mediocre team. Rainey lost his first three decisions, then got hot in boosting his record to 14–10 before losing his last three decisions of the season. He had a 4.48 ERA.

"Being the type of pitcher I was, I had to rely on people behind me for support," Rainey said. "We had high grass, and sand in front of home plate. You look at my stats. Now, an ERA of 4.50 or 5.00 is acceptable. It's almost the norm. I look at stats, it's pretty incredible what they're getting away with. When I was in Boston, I was out of the game before the sun set."

But there was one Chuck Rainey start where he was unhittable until the last possible moment.

The Cubs were listing to port with a 55–70 record on August 24, 1983, at Wrigley Field. Two days earlier, Elia had been fired, replaced by interim manager Charlie Fox. That didn't bother Rainey as he took the mound in front of a Wednesday afternoon crowd of 17,955. He no-hit the Cincinnati Reds into the sixth, seventh, eighth, and ninth. He was in such a rhythm, it looked like the no-no was a sure thing.

"I've never been in that situation before," he said. "It was uncharted waters. It was mind-boggling."

The last Red between Rainey and the hitless gem with two outs in the ninth was outfielder Eddie Milner. Rainey and catcher Steve Lake agreed on the pitch to start Milner off: "a little back-door slider," in Rainey's words.

Milner guessed right, though. He laced the pitch into center for a single.

"I could have created a different scenario," Rainey said. "It gave me something to second-guess. I should have thrown a fastball. My first thought was to get on the mound, get the next guy. After the game, it was pretty emotional. I was pretty well worn out."

His exhaustion made sense. The one-hitter was Rainey's only complete game of the 1983 season. Perhaps he was tired from running the bases, too.

"That was the only game where I outhit the whole [opposing] team," Rainey said. "I got two hits myself."

No Cubs pitcher has thrown a no-hitter since Milt Pappas on September 2, 1972. Rainey and Jose Guzman in the second game of the season in 1993 have come closest at two outs in the ninth. Otis

Nixon of the Braves broke up Guzman's budding gem with a single to left.

Rainey's record was 13–10 after the almost no-hitter. Afterward, Rainey's Cubs career did not last much longer. Although he opened the 1984 season in the rotation, his 5–7 record was deemed expendable after Green traded for Rick Sutcliffe and Dennis Eckersley. Rainey was traded on July 15 to the Oakland Athletics for a player to be named later, which turned out to be outfielder–infielder Davey Lopes.

"The word I got was that I was the most marketable guy on the team," Rainey said. "I consider myself fortunate that I played for two teams [Red Sox and Cubs] that had a lot of tradition and played in two great old ballparks."

"I really enjoyed Chicago. The whole day-game concept was good for me. It felt like an ordinary job. You got the rest of the evening off to have time for yourself."

With the trade to the noncontending Athletics, Rainey missed out on the stretch run of the 1984 NL East titlists. But he's not hanging crepe over missing the postseason in Chicago.

"It was more of an emotional thing being traded from Boston to Chicago," he said. "The Red Sox were the team I was born and raised with."

He doesn't want to hear about how teams are built and then torn down, though. Rainey endures the real-life version of building and demolition every day. It's honest work, a true successor to the way he worked on his former job on the mound.

Running like a Deer . . . in His Teachings

Bob Dernier still appears to be in shape. The hair's thinner, but the face is still handsome and familiar. The deep voice hasn't changed and probably is being cultivated for the better.

Don't expect Dernier to run like a deer anymore. The "Deer" nickname stuck because of the former center fielder's trademark speed. But now the Kansas City–area resident just talks a good game, teaching the concept that speed never takes a day off, that playing the "little man's game" often adds up to big results.

When he was not trolling for a new broadcast opportunity, the leadoff man of the 1984 National League East champion Cubs teaches the fine arts of the game at the Old Ball Game Sports Academy in Kansas City. He's also a part of the second wave of former Cubs to work as so-called instructors at Randy Hundley's Fantasy Camps, where overage Walter Mittys live out a baseball dream, putting on the uniform, swinging the bat, and swapping lies with their ol' heroes.

Dernier is joined by such former teammates as Jody Davis, Keith Moreland, Lee Smith, Leon Durham, and Ed Lynch at the Hundley camps. Joe Pepitone, never without his hairpiece, has dropped by in recent years.

"It's more about having fun. I get a lot of gratification from those camps," Dernier said.

Dernier has done a little bit of everything since his career faded at the cusp of the 1990s. He has toe-dipped in and out of the majors, via a roving minor-league instructor's job with the Texas Rangers and a fill-in color analyst's role on Cubs telecasts when Steve Stone was ill at the end of the 2000 season.

Basically, Dernier is a baseball guy and would love a baseball field or broadcasting gig.

"I was working with an insurance-related annuity company," he said of his employer when he worked for WGN-TV. "That's long since passed. It wasn't my cup of tea."

Somewhere along the line, Dernier will get his true postplaying career calling.

"I reflect back to 1990–1991," he said. "I had an opportunity to meet Neil Armstrong. He's often asked that question about what you're doing now. I told him we get that question now. Neil said, 'What do you do after you walked on the moon?'

"I look at the opportunity to play in the major leagues as like walking on the moon. There's not a false belief as to being able to find something equal to that. I kind of trust in my path. If I'm pretty good at it, I'll enjoy it, dig my heels into it. I enjoy teaching, working with young kids. I'm a notary and do some closings for title companies."

Although he worked with the Rangers, Dernier would regain some of his old speed to snare a job with the Cubs or Phillies, his old teams. And a long line of people suggested Dernier take advantage of his natural dulcet tones to work in radio or TV.

"John McDonough [Cubs marketing and broadcasting chief] always was a good friend," he said. "He's urged me to pursue the broadcasting end of things."

McDonough was instrumental in summoning Dernier to take over for Stone, stricken by kidney stones and a respiratory disease, to finish out the lost first season of manager Don Baylor. Dernier had been at Wrigley Field to sing in the seventh inning, so he was in the right place at the right time to hear McDonough's pitch.

"I did the last forty games, and the Cubs must have won eight of them," Dernier mused. "I had a lot of fun, hanging out with Chip [Caray], Pat [Hughes], and Ronnie [Santo]."

Stone still did not feel up to working in the winter of 2000–2001, so he announced his retirement from the booth. With the job open, Dernier threw his hat into the ring. So did Randy Hundley, who had done fill-in work for Santo on radio in recent years. But instead of these obvious Cubs connections, WGN-TV hired Joe Carter as analyst. Carter had played a handful of games as a Cub at the start of his career before being traded to Cleveland and performing a series of heroics elsewhere. But even discounting his lack of Chicago connections, nice-guy Carter was a near disaster on the air, his contract not being renewed two years later when a recovered Stone came back to claim his rightful position.

"I wasn't disappointed it didn't develop into something better, but I didn't have any expectations," Dernier said. "My real desires lie in radio."

He can go anywhere, do anything that interests him. Dernier's children are grown. He's now a grandfather. But he stays mentally young when he reunites with old baseball friends.

"Life's about relationships," he said. "I don't miss playing. It would be selfish to say that. What I miss is the relationships. I feel pretty fortunate to have a large circle of friends."

In a homer-happy age, a cagey front-office chief might like a fellow like Dernier handling instruction of the finer points of the game.

"What I had kind of an edge in was working with outfielders, base runners, leadoff hitters, table setters," he said. "It's the 'little man's' game. Things that don't necessarily make headlines."

Dernier could teach attitude, if that could possibly stick with a new generation of players.

"I bring some integrity to what I say," he said. "What I always share with players, kids, or young pros is, I never worked one day of baseball. I played every day. It was fun—I didn't treat it any other way. There's also a certain level of mental toughness that you have to have. I was raised that way. It's a 'won't quit' attitude. I was just one of those who outhustled you.

"I teach the intangibles of the game. What I share with you is not Bob Dernier's book on baseball. It's many, many players I learned from, like the Mike Schmidts, Pete Roses, Ryne Sandbergs, and others."

A teammate of Sandberg for three full seasons in the Phillies' minor-league system in the late 1970s and early 1980s, Dernier finally made the parent club as a fourth outfielder in 1982. He played on the Phillies' 1983 World Series club, then found his way to Chicago along with Gary Matthews Sr. in a famed spring-training trade the following March 27 that virtually rounded out the budding contender. Cubs GM Dallas Green had remembered Dernier's speed and hustle.

"I always keep a fond memory of Dallas Green in my mind," he said. "He was my mentor. I felt his pat on my back and his boot on my butt. Five of us former Phillies on the Cubs either had Dallas as manager or farm director, or both. I give him credit for believing in me as player.

"It was a good fortune that I was traded with Gary. He was the guy I looked up to for support and advice."

His path to regular duty in center blocked by the likes of Garry Maddox and Von Hayes in Philadelphia, Dernier thrived the instant he took over in center in '84. He and Sandberg formed the "Daily Double," promoted on the airwaves by Harry Caray, as the Cubs' most productive one–two lineup punch in memory. Dernier would slash hits to get on and then trot out his running game as Sandberg, with his newly minted power style, drove pitches in the gaps and beyond.

Dernier hit over .300 in the first half, including a .344 average in May. He had a pair of five-hit games against the Braves in one six-day span. The Cubs never had in the post–World War II era such an efficient leadoff man.

Bob Dernier and grandson Kobe. Photo courtesy of Bob Dernier.

"I liked to believe I was always a threat at the plate," he said. "Just to irritate the crap out of the guy [pitcher], I found different ways to reach base. Bunting, singles, and doubles. But it was no surprise. I hit at or near .300 my whole career in the minor leagues."

Dernier was carried by his legs even more than his bat. He had three seasons of at least seventy-two stolen bases in the minors. He stole seventy-seven bases as a part-time Phillie in 1982–1983. So he was not surprised when he stole forty-five, getting caught seventeen times, as a Cub in 1984. Only Sandberg's fifty-four thefts in 1985 exceeded that total, of any Cub since the Frank Chance deadball era of the early twentieth century.

"There were three-run homers looming," Dernier said of the hitters that followed him. "You had to be sure [of the stealing situation]. The main thing is you pick your spots well. You've got to know the game situation. You've got to know if the guy behind you is swinging the bat well and has a nice streak going. But I can't ever remember a guy I played with telling me not to run while he was hitting."

Dernier's careful eye helped set up one of the most memorable Cubs games in history on June 23, 1984, at Wrigley Field.

Trailing by two runs with two outs in the bottom of the ninth against ex-Cub Bruce Sutter, by then the Cardinals' closer, Dernier squeezed out a walk on a close 3-and-2 pitch. That brought Sandberg up, and the rest was history. Sandberg's first of two gametying homers off Sutter that afternoon provided much of the impetus for the '84 Cubs' success.

"It was a pitch down and in, with Sutter throwing his split finger," Dernier said.

"The whole idea was to reach base safely and get the tying run up. Ryno had a way of rising to the occasion like no one else. It didn't surprise me and didn't surprise anyone on the bench.

"I feel that was the turning point of the season."

The Cubs sprinted into first place even as Dernier started losing steam in August. Although he stayed in the lineup, his average dropped below .300, finishing at .278.

"By the time mid-August rolled around, I was getting beat up," Dernier said. "You had to know when to rest me. I would reach fatigue levels the way I played."

Dernier got a second wind, figuratively and literally, when he led off the Cubs' first in game 1 of the National League Championship Series against the San Diego Padres at Wrigley Field. He slugged a booming homer to left, touching off a 13–0 Cubs rout.

"If that big fence wasn't there, it probably would have hit a building," Dernier said. "The wind was blowing out fifteen miles per hour, and I got it up into a gust."

Despite the Cubs' inopportune exit from the NLCS, Dernier expected to repeat his success in 1985. But his legs were cut out from under him. He underwent surgery for removal of a bursa sac and ganglion from the top of his left foot in June. Robbed of both their leadoff hitter and healthy starters, the Cubs fell apart. Even when he returned, Dernier was not the same. He stole just four bases out of his season total of thirty-one from May 31 to September 6 in '85.

Dernier was injured again in 1986. He strained his right rotator cuff trying to throw across his body while cutting off a ball in the gap hit by the Cardinals' Willie McGee. By now, the Cubs brought up rookie outfielder Davey Martinez, who took playing time in center. That arrangement was formalized in 1987, with Dernier playing just against right-handers.

"That was the nature of the game," Dernier said. At least he boosted his power totals with a career high of eight in the juiced-ball summer of '87. One wind-blown homer to the green in center at Wrigley beat the Reds' John Franco in the bottom of the ninth. Franco threw a tremendous fit on the mound, realizing he had just lost to a pitch-and-putt hitter. Dernier still smiles at that memory.

Even though he batted a career-high .317 in '87, Dernier moved back to the Phillies. Strangely, new GM Jim Frey did not stick long with Martinez in center, trading him to Montreal in midseason 1988 for Mitch Webster, not a center fielder by trade or experience. By 1989, rookie Jerome Walton was holding forth in center.

But Dernier did not feel he missed out on anything as his career wound down in Philadelphia in 1989.

"I have no regrets," he said. "I got to play 'til I was thirty-one, thirty-two. For an old running back, that's a long time. I knew when to go home."

Now Dernier likes his freedom to go in any direction.

"I enjoy my alumni status very much," he said.

"Zonk" Aims for a Golden Voice

Sitting around and shooting the breeze with conversationalist and ex-Cub Keith Moreland, you automatically detect a different kind of vocal cadence compared with your memory of his playing days two decades ago.

Moreland always was a decent talker with that Texas twang, but he did not have that cultured, trained voice. Now he's close. Ten years' experience as radio color analyst and play-by-play man, first for Texas Longhorns baseball and later football, will school the vocal chords to eliminate a lot of the "ums" and stutters and pregnant pauses that are part of conversation in the rest of the world.

And, if the truth be known, there's a certain enthusiasm that pushes him to be the best announcer possible. Building upon the self-made player's work ethic that made Bobby Keith Moreland, nicknamed "Zonk," one of the Cubs' best clutch hitters in the late twentieth century, he'd like to return to the major leagues as a radio color analyst.

"One of the things I've done is have satellite radio in my car," Moreland said of his routes in and around his native Austin, Texas. "I don't spend as much time listening to announcers on TV as radio, because they're two different styles.

"On TV, you've got to be quieter, give your points, and let the picture do the talking. I don't go anywhere in the car where I don't look for a live [radio sports] broadcast. It doesn't matter if it's two women's softball teams. If you don't continue to listen and watch and see what's going on, you're not going to get any better."

But while Moreland has his eyes on a big-league job after son Cole gets into college, he's trying not to get ahead of himself. If he can't broadcast Cubs games right now, he's just thrilled handling his alma mater's games on radio in parts of all four seasons of the year.

"You cut me, I bleed orange. I'm an avid backer of the University of Texas," the former Longhorns linebacker/catcher said of his sales spiel to station management when his school's football color analyst's job came open in 2002.

Moreland's a busy man. When he's not on the air or working one of the Longhorns' practices to gather information, he's running an Austin-based candy distributorship called Moreland's Munchies. And when he's not giving others the sweet tooth, he heads up the Baseball Academy of Texas, running clinics, providing individual instruction, and sponsoring traveling amateur teams. That leaves precious little time for four-day hunting expeditions with old friend Jody Davis, which date back to their first Cubs seasons in the early 1980s.

But broadcasting is the firm direction of Moreland's life as he plunges further into middle age. The road to wherever he's going started back in his Chicago days in tandem with a late, popular WGN-Radio personality.

"Bob Collins, God bless his soul, used to have me on a couple of times," Moreland said. "He said, 'You need to do some stuff,' so I did a few talk shows, sat in with him, wrote for *Vine Line* [the Cubs' monthly magazine]," he said. But broadcasting was set aside after Moreland's career finished in 1989. He went back to Austin and the Texas classrooms, where he finished his degree in business.

Moreland's first impulse was to rejoin Longhorn athletics on the coaching lines. He naturally became an assistant to baseball coach Cliff Gustafson, helping the team make a couple more College World Series appearances. But when the NCAA, through one of its many reform programs, limited the number of assistant coaching positions, Gustafson had to wield his own ax. An old teammate from Moreland's college days in the mid-1970s was set to get chopped while Moreland would stay. But Moreland persuaded Gustafson to keep his chum while he bowed out; he had saved up enough from his baseball days while he cast about for another job.

He did not look for long nor move more than a few feet away from the coaching lines.

"My other mentor in business was Bill Schoening, now the voice of the San Antonio Spurs," Moreland said. "Bill then was the voice of the Longhorns. He asked if I'd like to do some color for baseball.

Bill was a Philly boy, a big Phillies fan from the days I played there. I started periodically doing some games, ten to twelve per season.

"I knew what I was doing with my communication skills. Bill said I was getting better. I started working at the craft, started improving. I started doing almost forty games in 1996."

In a football-mad state, Longhorns baseball has its own popular niche. All fifty-six games are broadcast on radio. Crowds of seven thousand, like a popular minor-league team, are common for the home schedule of Tuesday and Friday night games and Saturday and Sunday day games.

Once on the radio, Moreland started to soak up other broadcast gigs. He lived in the Austin Westlake area, also home to Drew Brees's high school alma mater.

"The station that did Longhorn games also did Brees's high school football Friday night games," Moreland said. "They asked if I wanted to be the sideline reporter after having played football for the Longhorns. That's where I drew attention, for my versatility. It is a big production. We had wireless technology with engineers." Soon he added color analyst's work for the central Texas high school football game of the week.

While he expanded his broadcast work to football, he got a promotion for Longhorns baseball. Schoening left for the Spurs, enabling Craig Way to take over. However, Way also was the play-by-play voice for Longhorns basketball. The baseball and basketball seasons overlap in late winter, so Moreland took over to do six innings' worth of baseball play by play in 1999 while Way was absent working basketball games. And when Texas's season ended, Moreland helped out on the minor-league Round Rock Express radio and TV broadcasts.

With his existing work and Longhorns playing history, Moreland was the logical choice over even more experienced candidates when the football color analyst's job opened up in 2002. Moreland spends a goodly number of hours each week during the football season gaining insight on Texas's game plan from the Longhorns offensive and defensive coordinators while taping pregame programming.

Moreland is no Jimmy Piersall–style critic in his analyst's roles in either baseball or football. While Texas is as big time as college athletics are rated, it is still not the pros in his mind.

"It's an eighteen- or nineteen- or twenty-year-old kid out there," he said. "They can make mistakes. I never go in the direction very often of being critical of an eighteen-year-old on scholarship. He's not being paid.

"I try to explain 'why.' One of the kids gets beat on a pass play. There's not so much pressure from the line. The quarterback did a good job hitting the receiver. The receiver ran a good route. I'm not a second-guesser at all on collegiate kids."

Game officials and umpires, though, don't get the kid-glove treatment from Moreland.

"I'm probably very critical if necessary," he said. "Stuff that's very obvious in my opinion should not be missed. With umps behind the plate, what you want as a player and broadcaster is to know that right arm is coming up. If he calls a pitch that my eyes in the booth see as a strike in the first inning, you want that same strike in the ninth inning. Umpires' strike zones floating around drives me crazy. It drove me crazy as a player. Just stay with it."

With on-field strategy, Moreland tries to anticipate situations as they develop and then sketch them out on the air.

"I'll say this is a good opportunity for the manager to hit and run," he said. "Will he bunt in this situation? I'm a little more critical of the manager and his sense of execution. People are listening for an opinion, but they also want analysis. My job is to explain why a team got beat."

Moreland could not adopt the style of Harry Caray, who both praised him and zinged him as a Cub. In fact, when he thinks more about it, the Caray style would not play well in the decade after the all-powerful Cubs announcer's death.

"At times, Harry showed he was a fan, and I'm not sure that style in today's world would work as well as Harry in his time," he said "I think now the fans want to form their own opinions."

But cookie-cutter announcers that don't stir any passion won't work well, either.

"If you're not yourself when you're behind the microphone and try to be someone else, it's when you get into trouble," Moreland said. "You've got to be you. I'm not critical. I don't think I'd ever have the critical style. But there is a place for it. In pro sports, you've got to call the kettle black."

Moreland's style no doubt will evolve if he ever gets a big-league analyst's job. He postponed such a quest until after Cole Moreland's 2005 high school graduation. The nearest big-league teams are in Houston and Dallas, but they are too far for Moreland to commute daily to work.

"We love Austin and would keep a presence in Austin," he said. "We've been out of the game at the pro level since 1989, and that is possibly a drawback. I have to be good at my craft when I do apply. A lot of ex-players are color analysts, but they played more recently. They can struggle a little while before they find themselves just because they know the teams."

Realizing the cagey entrepreneur keeps his fingers in several pies at the same time, Moreland has run his candy business since the early 1990s. With his father and wife, Cindy, as employees, Moreland's Munchies services small vending-machine operations in the Plains states. Competition from bigger operations will be a problem in upcoming years, but Moreland will ride it out as long as he can.

"It has a window of opportunity of probably eight to ten more years," he said. "I can already see the drop-off. But so far it's been very viable. It allows me the opportunity to stay involved in broadcasting."

At around the same time Moreland's Munchies began, Moreland founded the Baseball Academy of Texas. Working with former big-league pitcher Lee Tunnell, a Baylor product, Moreland's schedule of camps, clinics, and private lessons has morphed into a nonprofit operation.

"Anything left over the company's [operating budget] becomes traveling money for our teams," he said. "We've had 107 players go on to college baseball, 43 have signed pro contracts, and 5 have made it to the major leagues. We have a good setup. The weather is so good we don't need an indoor facility. In case of a heavy rain, we have Astroturf batting cages so we can keep working. It's fun to do."

Moreland can teach the proper hitting mechanics, other fundamentals, and how to react in different situations. But it's doubtful he can transfer the kind of internal fire and determination—a linebacker's attitude transferred to baseball—to his younger pupils.

"I didn't play with a chip on my shoulder, but my emotions were very visible," he said. "I was going to give everything I had.

I've never been afraid of going to work. As a player, I couldn't run, so I had to work at it. Broadcasting's the same way."

Another spur to Moreland's work ethic was his status as a hitter without a position for his first two and a half Cubs seasons. He moved from catcher to left to right. He'd go on to log considerable time at third and first base, too.

After playing part-time on the Phillies' 1980 World Series–winning team, Moreland had arrived in the mass emigration of Philadelphia players commissioned by their former manager Dallas Green, by now running the Cubs as GM. Moreland hit .302 as a 154-game regular in 1983. But when Bob Dernier was imported in the spring of 1984 from Philly to play center, incumbent Mel Hall, a left-handed hitter, moved to right in a platoon arrangement with the right-handed-hitting Moreland.

"I already established myself in '83, finishing sixth in the league in hitting," he said. "But I was platooned starting in '84. I was not a happy camper. We loved Chicago. We bought a home in [north suburban] Deerfield. I came home every day telling Cindy, 'I want to go.' I was in the prime of my career. I knew I could hit; I knew I could play. If I can't play here, I can help somebody."

Moreland ended up helping the Cubs more than even he could have projected. Hall was packaged with top prospect Joe Carter to Cleveland in the mid-June deal that netted Rick Sutcliffe. Moreland thus had right field all to himself and took full advantage. He was the Cubs' finest clutch hitter down the '84 stretch, finishing with sixteen homers and eighty RBIs in 495 at bats. In a prodigious run-producing lineup, he often batted cleanup.

August 1984 was Moreland's absolute peak. He had five homers and thirty-two RBIs with eight game-winning hits and a .360 batting average as the Cubs overtook the New York Mets in first place. He was named National League Player of the Month for his efforts. For good measure, he used his old Longhorns linebacking techniques by roll-blocking Mets hurler Ed Lynch on the mound in retaliation for a beanball episode as forty thousand Wrigley Field fans roared their approval.

And while many of his teammates' production dropped off due to slumps and injuries in 1985, Moreland stepped it up along with Ryne Sandberg. He drove in a team-leading 106 runs despite just fourteen homers while amassing career highs of 180 hits and a .307

average. Moreland batted .338 with runners in scoring position while racking up a career-high eighteen-game hitting streak near season's end.

"The emotional situation, I was not afraid of the pressure," Moreland said. "If you're afraid of failure, you're gonna fail. If I could get a pitcher in the stretch, he was thinking about the runner, he has more pressure to get me out than I had in hitting him.

"I understood it's a game of failure. Young players cannot understand that the best [hitters] in the game fail for their career seven out of ten times. The game is built around failure. The pitcher is the only person where success comes seven out of ten times. He has more pressure on his side. I'm not supposed to get it done."

And while his lack of speed was a handicap, Moreland got himself dirty diving all around right field. Runners hesitated to challenge his rifle arm. Moreland has thirteen assists playing right in 1986.

He also was willing to sacrifice his own style if called upon. In 1987, his homer output jumped to a career-high twenty-seven in a juiced-ball season. A line-drive, doubles-gap hitter by nature, he knew he had to provide some lift with the arrival of an MVP hitter in the lineup. As a result, his average dropped to .266, second lowest in his Cubs career.

"There were times, like in '87 when I was hitting behind Andre Dawson, when I was asked to hit the ball out of the ballpark. That cost me. I knew I had a responsibility in that spot hurting some people [to compensate for Dawson being walked intentionally]."

Despite his long-time production, Moreland was caught in the fallout from the quick deal of Lee Smith to the Boston Red Sox in the 1987 winter meetings. New GM Jim Frey desperately needed a closer when he discovered that Calvin Schiraldi, acquired for Smith, might not be up to the task. So Frey dealt Moreland to San Diego for the aging Goose Gossage. Moreland's numbers dropped in old Jack Murphy Stadium while Gossage was a total bust as a Cub.

Moreland moved on to a Detroit Tigers team on the decline in 1989. Hitting .299, he was attractive for other contenders. He finished up with a thirty-three-game stint on the Baltimore Orioles.

At thirty-five, it was time to quit moving his family around and head home to Austin.

Over the ensuing years, Moreland had time to think about his Cubs team's place in history—and that of the contender that GM Jim Hendry had assembled in 2003.

"Our '84 team, talentwise, we weren't that deep, especially on the mound," he said. "We were aging in the infield with Ron Cey at third and Larry Bowa at short. In the outfield, we weren't the greatest running outfield with me in right and Sarge Matthews in left. Take that team in '85, we would have still competed if it wasn't for all the injuries. We all had drive to get it done. We knew if we didn't get it done in '84–'85, it wouldn't get done with that group. Then, that '86 team was the team I thought we were short.

"But these [recent] Cubs, they have depth on the mound. I see this team competing for the next four, five years at a high level. Now you're finally seeing a good organization. It's a matter of time. It's so oriented around pitching. They're going to win some divisions. However, Atlanta proved it's still tough to get to the World Series."

Perhaps in this projected new, glorious Cubs era, Moreland will get a chance to do some broadcast-booth analyzing. If not, he'll continue bleeding orange, his love of the Longhorns showing through with almost every breath he takes on the air.

Keith Moreland and Jody Davis. Author photo.

Jody! Jody! Jody! The Manager?

O ne futurist who knew Jody Davis well had a prediction of what the noted outdoorsman turned Cubs folk hero's life might be like twenty years into the future:

"I think he'll disappear into the woods for awhile and not be seen for quite some time."

Nostradamus would have been proud. For the most part, Davis left the chants of "Jody! Jody! Jody!" and Harry Caray's broadcast-booth warbling about his feats behind in the memory banks. He'd do the odd card show here, the Cubs Convention there, but the former catcher's postbaseball life was a lot of hunting and fishing along with parenting of his three children, Josh, Ashley, and Jeremy. He threw in a little junior-varsity and American Legion baseball coaching for the kids.

Hanging around his native Gainesville, a short commute to Atlanta, Davis even passed up a chance to watch his old team battle the Braves at Turner Field in the 2003 National League Divisional Series. "It was too easy to turn the TV on," he said.

The vast majority of the time, Davis kept true to his own 1987 vintage proclamation. "I've never really wanted a career for myself," he said then. "Oh, maybe going into law school interested me at one time, but I don't think about that anymore. I enjoy being around the house. There's nothing more enjoyable than watching my family grow. I hear so many women say they can't stand to be at home so much with their kids. That's fine, but I'm different. I want to be here when they come home from school every day."

But not even determined homebody Davis could avoid being bitten by the baseball bug at some point. It's a powerful lure that could take Davis away from the man-made, fish-stocked lake by his house, along with the slower pace of down-home life. That bug bit him to the point that he'd travel to the Great White North to manage for the first time in his life.

At six feet four, lean and angular—seemingly more so than his playing days—Davis usually is happy in jeans and a checkered shirt. But he put a uniform back on in the spring of 2003 to manage in the short-lived Canadian Baseball League, running the Calgary team for a grand total of thirty-seven games before the league folded in midseason.

A big-name former Cubs batterymate lured Davis out of the woods into the dugout.

"I hooked up with Fergie Jenkins, who was the commissioner of the league, at a Randy Hundley [fantasy] camp," Davis said. "He offered me a job.

"The plan was for each team to have five Canadians on the twenty-three-man rosters. Games would be played Thursday through Sunday [to accommodate the long travel distances]. The season didn't start 'til the end of May."

In addition to Jenkins, the league had other ex-Cubs connections. Former outfielders Pete LaCock and Willie Wilson managed Niagara and London, Ontario, respectively.

But the plan seemed flawed from the start.

"For the most part, Canadians are not as hungry baseballwise as they are here," Davis said. "Eventually it ended up the downfall of the league. We couldn't get fans. There was nobody out in Calgary pushing ticket sales."

Like its big-league counterpart, the Montreal franchise spent 2003 wandering. The team could not locate a home ballpark and spent the truncated season entirely on the road.

Despite the abrupt ending, Davis can boast that he had Calgary in first place with a 24–13 record when the plug was pulled.

"I'm the winningest manager in Canadian baseball league history," he said. "I liked it a lot. The nine- and ten-hour bus rides, I wasn't crazy about. We had a good bunch of guys. It was really kind of amusing. I had three Japanese players, seven or eight American players, and seven or eight Dominican players. We had a couple of guys around to translate.

"The funny thing was, the Japanese and Dominican guys were trying to speak English to communicate with each other. The Dominicans couldn't speak Japanese, and the Japanese couldn't speak

Spanish. You get a bunch like that together, baseball's the international language. Get on the field, everyone pretty much knew what to do."

Davis would consider renewing a baseball role since Jeremy, his oldest child, has graduated high school.

"The baseball part of it I really enjoyed," he said. And he can tolerate the nongame part of managing, such as pre- and postgame media confabs and the politicking with upper management.

"It's just getting the right opportunity at the right spot," he said.

Back at home in Gainesville, Davis realizes at some point he'll need some regular work, just to avoid going batty with the kids gone. He made some money, but not the windfalls of later seasons. "I told my mom she had me ten years too early," Davis said of missing out on the multimillion-dollar payouts that became common in the 1990s.

At least he's got his Gainesville digs to enjoy while he searches for his next baseball incarnation.

As a young player, he loved the outdoors so much that he helped pay for the confluence of two small streams to be dammed up and create a two-acre man-made lake by his former house. On off days while the Cubs were in Atlanta, Davis would take his teammates for a fishing outing on the lake. Since then, he has sold his original house and the lake itself but has moved to the other side of the water.

"I was making $32,000 as a rookie," Davis said of his 1981 pay. "It didn't cost a whole lot [to dam up the streams]. We stocked it with bluegills, bass, and catfish. The game and fishing [state agency] gives you all the fish, so it didn't cost anything."

Davis's passion for hunting and fishing began in his youth in the hamlet of Oakwood, south of Gainesville. "It had one gas station and a post office," he said.

Like a lot of Georgia country youths, Davis learned how to use firearms early on hunting outings. But his specialty became the compound bow. "I became pretty accurate with it and I just fell in love with it," he said. "It's the challenge itself of getting close enough to shoot with a bow and arrow."

When certified Texan Keith Moreland joined the Cubs in 1982 after a trade from the Phillies, he immediately became a threat to

Davis's job. But instead of a rivalry, the pair became fast friends and hunting buddies.

"When two country boys are fighting for the same job and still hit it off, you know there's some chemistry there," Davis said. Eventually, he held on to his catcher's job while Moreland found a regular's role in right field. Now Davis's only complaint about Moreland is that he doesn't have enough time for the four-day hunting trips, with the crush of his University of Texas football radio work.

Like any hunter in the public eye, Davis had to face his share of antihunting activists. But he said many do not understand the benefits of wildlife conservation.

"Without question, that's close to my heart," he said. "In Georgia, we were overpopulated with white-tails [deer]. A lot of my good friends at home are game and fish wardens.

"I think that most of the 'antis' are misinformed. It really comes back to where you live. Where I grew up as a kid, there were hardly any deer at all. Hunting licenses go to restocking and conservation."

Davis dabbled for almost five years in the outdoors business. He owned Jody Davis' Sportsman, an outdoors store, in Gainesville.

"But if you like to hunt and fish, that's not the business you want to be in," he said. "You do not get to go hunting and fishing if you have a store to run. We did pretty well. It had been a store that had been pretty well-established in Gainesville for a long time that I bought."

Of course, Davis couldn't have indulged his outdoors passion if he hadn't made it in baseball. He grew into the sport after starting out favoring basketball. "But it just got to the point where I was a step too slow and a foot too short," he said. "I just loved competition."

Davis was signed by the New York Mets, then he moved on to the St. Louis Cardinals organization. Moving closer to a big-league call-up, his career almost ended before it started. In 1980, a blood vessel in his lower stomach ruptured. Davis's condition was touch-and-go before he recovered, and he feels forever fortunate.

"We went from wondering if I would make it through to climbing to the big leagues and playing ten years," he said.

The Cardinals let the weakened Davis go for $25,000 to the Cubs after the 1980 season. GM Bob Kennedy had been aware of Davis from his contacts in the St. Louis system he had once supervised. The acquisition turned out to be one of the better bargains in recent Cubs history.

In 1981, Davis eventually pushed Tim Blackwell out of the catching job, fought off Moreland in 1982, and really blossomed in 1983. The chants of "Jody! Jody! Jody!" and Caray's on-air promotion of the catcher reached a crescendo in a memorable June series against the Cardinals at Wrigley Field, which featured a Davis grand slam. He slugged twenty-four homers in 1983, the most by a Cubs catcher since Gabby Hartnett up to that point, while driving in eighty-four runs.

Davis's clutch hitting continued through 1984 as the Cubs charged into first place. He was named to the All-Star team for the first time. Along with buddy Moreland, Davis became known for his clutch hitting. His ninety-four RBIs, which into another century remained the season best for a Cubs catcher since Hartnett, included a crucial late-season grand slam that helped bury the competing New York Mets for good.

And he continued hitting at the right times in the National League Championship Series against the San Diego Padres. He had seven hits, six RBIs, and a .359 average.

"You think that the '69 group was closer than us, but I don't think that's possible," Davis said in a comparison of fabled Cubs teams.

"We came from everywhere, different walks of life. We came with a mission. Once we all got together, it was in all our hearts to win a game that day.

"We rolled through '84 with the feeling we couldn't be beat. We lost to San Diego, but we were still at the point where we could come back next year and do it again."

But a series of injuries to the entire starting rotation along with outfielders Gary Matthews and Bob Dernier sabotaged the repeat effort in 1985.

"Looking back, it's hard to imagine how good we could have been if those guys would have stayed healthy," Davis said. "If we had stayed healthy in '85, I think we could have won."

The Cubs might have been better off if they had given Davis more of a break from time to time. He played 151 games in 1983 and 150 more in 1984. He had to stay in the lineup the latter season not only for his offense but also for the lack of a healthy backup catcher much of the time. Frey did not want to press Moreland into service behind the plate again. At times, Davis's hitting slipped due to the exhaustion of catching.

"I really have no regrets," he said. "Maybe I would have played a couple of years longer [with a smaller workload]. But that was my makeup. When I got up in the morning, I wanted to go play. I felt that was the best way for our team to win. It was almost like I was more tired after a day off. Looking back now, I could have been a little better, statistics-wise, but I wasn't a Hall of Fame player."

Davis slugged fifty-seven more homers between 1985 and 1987 before his playing time began to tail off with the arrival of rookie Damon Berryhill in 1988. At the end of the season, he was traded to his hometown Braves, where he stuck around as a backup for two more seasons.

"When I retired, the actual thing between the lines and being with the guys was the only fun thing left anymore," he said. "The travel, the hotel rooms, the flights were so old at that point. I was at the point where my kids were ten, eleven. If you want to spend time with them, you have to be there."

Davis learned one other important lesson from baseball, one that was clarified when he witnessed the astounding collapse of his old team in the 2003 NLCS.

"The undescribable, sick feeling in 2003 was the same as '84," he said. "It was the first time I'd felt it since '84.

"Just five more wins [for a World Series title] in '84. Don't wait for next year to come around. You better grab it while you can."

All that time in the woods and on those Canadian bus rides gave Davis some extra clarity of thought. He sure would have liked to have heard "Jody! Jody! Jody!" chanted in a Fall Classic.

Big Lee the Coach

The temptation was always strong—and certainly often was acted upon—to refer in sports columns to Lee Arthur Smith as "Big Lee Smith."

Everything about this country-kid closer from northern Louisiana was outsized. He was once a power forward, but when he pitched, he started moving toward 1970s-style defensive-end size: six feet six and somewhere around 270 pounds. His production topped all other closers in history: 478 saves amassed from the Cubs to the Montreal Expos and a lot of stops in between. And his riotously funny clubhouse verbal and body English byplay was extra blue, at least triple X, stuff that can't be quoted or described even in the most candid book.

Now you run into Big Lee Smith and he hasn't gotten any smaller in his midforties. He still fills up a room, casts a giant shadow, and envelops your greeting with his own meaty hand. One thing never has changed since his mid-1980s Cubs prime, when he took the slowboat out to the mound to throw a heavy fastball that helped provoke a nickname, "Pea Shooter," from his teammates. Big Lee still speaks at a seventy-eight-RPM cadence.

"I was inducted into the Louisiana Sports Hall of Fame [in 2003]," he said, the words dashing by almost as fast as one of his former pitches. "Randy Hundley [Smith's Double-A manager back in 1979] is giving a speech. He said something about me at the end: 'Whatever you do, please don't ever grow up, because you're having fun.'"

You're used to the Smith style from bygone days. And the colorful persona that Smith carried through eighteen years in the majors is now being exposed to would-be closers and starters in the San Francisco Giants farm system he serves as roving pitching instructor. He has to grow up a bit in teaching the kids because not everyone can become another Lee Arthur Smith. Very few, indeed.

Two years after he retired in 1997, Big Lee started part-time advising the kids when the Giants' Double-A franchise was located in Shreveport, near his small-town home. But he had been in too many tight spots in the ninth to not share the wealth of his experience even more. Pretty soon the fella you thought never could be serious enough to be a full-time pitching instructor was put in charge of winning over young hearts and minds in which the Giants have invested megabucks in signing bonuses. Having former Cubs teammate Dick "Dirt" Tidrow and transplanted Chicagoan Ned Colletti—both of whom understand Big Lee better than most—working high up in the Giants front office is a big help.

"I go out there and they respect you," Smith said. "They remember when you played. I try not to get too serious about it. Guys we have now are so well-groomed out of college. They're a lot more advanced than we were because they have a helluva lot more coaches. When I was in the minor leagues, they had Jack Hiatt, the only coach we had."

"The kids I work with in Double-A and lower, I like to work with them. I get out there about three o'clock, try not to work them too hard. You get them to throw in between starts. They think they're tired, but that might be the day you have your best stuff."

Smith has to be committed these days, and not just doing it to keep a toe-dip in the game in Shreveport so he can take it easy while the team is out of town. The Double-A affiliate moved more than halfway across the country to Norwich, Connecticut, replaced by an independent team that was managed by former White Sox skipper Terry Bevington. So Smith has to wedge himself onto planes to work in Norwich, then dash down to Hagerstown, Maryland, a lower A-level club. Other assignments take him three thousand miles away to Fresno and San Jose, homes of the Giants' Triple-A and Class A California League affiliates.

No self-respecting pitching coach will try to change one of his charges' style if he's anywhere near successful. But Smith added to his repertoire throughout his career, a slider being employed liberally once he left the Cubs, then a forkball complementing his stuff at midcareer.

"If I get a guy that has control problems or is getting beat up a little, I try to teach him to move his hand on the ball, to get more movement," Smith said. "I worked with the forkball for our closers. But it's hard to teach guys to throw the cutter. You've got to control the strike zone with your fastball."

Actually, Smith has the best of both worlds. He's only gone eight to ten days a month, along with other scattered troubleshooting assignments. That way, he's not removed from the toddler twins he had with significant other Cheryl Radachowsky. And he can watch his three teenagers, the product of a former marriage, try to follow his path in his favorite sports. Oldest daughter Nikita was a star high school basketball player. Son Lee Arthur Jr. was a point guard and "thinks he's a shortstop," according to the old man.

Smith recommends basketball to help develop baseball skills.

"You play basketball to have some good peripheral vision, where you're working on seeing the guy who's open," he said. "But you also have to work at baseball itself. Down home, kids don't play enough baseball. Baseball's not a game you can just—boom—go out and play it. You have to play it year-round, to have agility, throw strikes, hit the ball, run bases, and slide. Basketball's a lot easier to play."

But not to coach at the youth level. "I would not coach anyone's girls basketball team," Smith said, rolling his eyes. "The attitudes they show. I've never seen so much equipment being thrown in high school. I coached bitty-ball, ages nine to twelve, and those kids are probably the worst."

Smith, the Cubs' number 2 pick in the 1975 draft, was coachable enough to get called up five years later. Originally a wild-high starter, he was converted to the bullpen by the time he got to Double-A, where Hundley managed him at Midland, Texas. Randy's ten-year-old son, Todd, visiting for the summer, learned how to conquer his fear of the baseball by catching the still-wandering pitches of Smith's in the bullpen. The younger Hundley went on to his own big-league catching career.

When Smith made his big-league debut in September 1980, the Cubs bullpen sported an astounding collection of names, once and future Cy Young and Fireman of the Year award winners. Top dog was Bruce Sutter, the savior who soon would be traded over a money dispute. Also in residence was Willie Hernandez, then an inconsistent left-hander whose great Detroit Tigers days were four years into the future. Bill Caudill, a fun-loving, night-crawling fireballer, was in and out of the bullpen flow. Tidrow was an accomplished setup man who was amassing the all-time record of games pitched (eighty-four) that season. The following season, another future stopper elsewhere, Jay Howell, joined the cast of characters.

Smith pitched in middle relief and even started several games before he was finally installed as stopper midway through the 1982 season. He often was unhittable with his blazing fastball, sporting a 1.65 ERA in 1983, but his efforts largely went to waste on mediocre Cubs teams.

One report had Smith's fastball clocked as high as 101 miles per hour. But from his present-day vantage point as a coach, he takes radar-gun readings with a grain of salt.

"A realistic gun reading for me was ninety-four, ninety-five miles per hour," he said. "The guns are not accurate. I don't think I threw consistently harder than Kerry Wood or Kyle Farnsworth. I was with Ugueth Urbina in 1997 in Montreal. Urbina threw a fastball. The gun reading flashed ninety-seven. The next pitch was a change—at ninety-six. What the hell are you timing, his arm speed or his pitch?"

Smith's fastball could be timed by some hitters like the New York Mets' Keith Hernandez or the San Francisco Giants' Jack Clark, two nemeses. He often had to pitch two or more innings for a save, setting up the chance he'd face a top hitter twice. And Cubs management, headed by GM Dallas Green, frowned on Smith's employing a sharp-breaking slider when he hung the pitch one day for a game-winning homer by the Giants' Candy Maldonado.

To this day, Smith wished he had been given the green light to throw another pitch as a Cub.

"I would have been a helluva lot better pitcher," he said. "If they had allowed me to throw the curveball that Fergie [Jenkins] taught me, it would have been great. He taught me a nasty curveball. But they said, 'You don't need another pitch.' Yeah, Dallas knew a lot about pitching. He won twenty games, but it took him eight years to do it."

Smith prepared himself in his own unique manner, be it walking at a snail's pace from the bullpen to the mound or getting extra rest in the clubhouse in the early innings.

"[Green] used to give me a hard time about how much time it took me to get to and from the mound," Big Lee said. "What am I, being paid by the hour? As a closer, you got to have a thick skin."

Not needed until the seventh inning, Smith sometimes took advantage of the trainer's table to take an early-game snooze. Nobody complained, which was why Smith laughed when informed Farnsworth had stirred up trouble in 2002 by being caught sleeping during a game in the clubhouse.

"They want to control shit," Big Lee said of modern baseball management. "You got guys who think they can run a team with a damn computer, and you can't do that. If Farnsworth's ERA is 7.00 and he's sleeping in the clubhouse, you got a problem [Farnsworth was suffering through an off-season at the time]. If it's 1.50, I don't give a damn if you wake up [an inning before you pitch]. If he's not going to pitch until the game's on the line, when he comes in, why the hell am I worried? You've got to govern some things so shit doesn't get out of hand over 162 games, but don't be ridiculous.

"I always gave myself enough time. A lot of people thought when they didn't see me, I was in the clubhouse sleeping. You don't last eighteen years in the big leagues sleeping in the clubhouse. I'd be in the clubhouse watching on TV the umpires, who's calling the inside corner, the outside corner, what they're calling in situations. I really learned a lot watching the monitor inside. Learning what Joe West will call on the outside corner with the game on the line. They complained in Boston about having a TV in the clubhouse, now they got it in the bullpen."

Smith certainly wasn't sleeping in the clubhouse before and after batting practice. His routines with buddy Leon "Bull" Durham were thoroughly hard-core in a less politically correct, sensitive era. Reminded today he was triple X and some of his routines are privately mimicked even today during idle Wrigley Field press box moments, Big Lee giggled with glee.

"He's the only guy I've ever been able to talk to like that, to be comfortable with," Smith said of Durham, now a fellow minor-league coach in the Tigers organization. "I was as close to Leon as my brother. I spent more time with him than anyone. The only time we were on the road when we weren't together was Cincinnati, where Bull lived.

"One day when everyone was into cowboy boots and polo shirts, I come out in a pair of stone-white jeans and red polo shirt, I walk to the lobby of the hotel and he's sitting with the same exact outfit. I say, somebody's got to go and change. We look like the fuckin' Bobsey Twins out there."

Outwardly, Smith did not have a vintage season in 1984, when the Cubs came out on top for their first title of any kind since 1945. He gave up almost a hit an inning, his strikeouts were down and he had a 3.65 ERA. But what was little known was that Smith pitched through an assortment of injuries to earn his thirty-three saves. That season, he was best known for two hard-hit balls against him. One was in August, when a liner deflected off his hip and caromed to shortstop Dave Owen, who threw to first to complete a game-ending double play. That prompted broadcaster Harry Caray to claim higher, heavenly powers wanted the Cubs to win. Caray made no such claim two months later when the San Diego Padres' Steve Garvey slugged a two-run, game-winning homer off Smith to win game 4 of the National League Championship Series.

Smith was more effective, saving a total of sixty-five games, for poor Cubs teams in 1985–1986. Then he established his Cubs high with thirty-six saves in 1987, but he was hit harder to go along with a 4–10 record. Smith was verbally unhappy around the clubhouse, a fact that still sticks in the craw of broadcaster Steve Stone and no doubt was noticed by then-broadcaster Jim Frey. A few years later, Smith said he was growing disenchanted by booing Cubs fans who seemed to blame him for their team's failures while anointing second baseman Ryne Sandberg the all-American hero.

When Frey succeeded Green as GM after the season, his first act in the 1987 winter meetings was to quickly bundle Smith and his 180 career saves off to the Boston Red Sox for lesser-light pitchers Calvin Schiraldi and Al Nipper.

"I have no idea," Smith said when asked why Frey was so quick to deal him. "Atlanta was looking at me for awhile. For the first two guys offered for me, they figured something's got to be wrong with me. Boston thought they got damaged goods."

Fresh from dissatisfaction in Chicago, Smith and Boston would have seemed a poor fit, given the Red Sox's and Boston's racial history. But Smith persevered with twenty-nine saves and a 2.80 ERA.

"I just got better," he said. "I never, ever had any racial issues. There was a lot of talk about that. Jim Rice was there, along with Ellis Burks and Oil Can Boyd. . . . I thought all that stuff was over. I told people that I come to play baseball, not to solve world peace. I come here to get an out. Then I give up a homer my first [Red Sox] game."

Smith moved on to the St. Louis Cardinals early in the 1990 season. With the Cubs' arch rivals, he hit his stride both emotionally and on the mound. Smith loved the slower pace of St. Louis life. Despite the intense interest of fans in Baseball Town USA, he liked the fact he could sit down with his family in a restaurant and not be bothered. Meanwhile, at Busch Stadium, he was reunited with former Cubs teammate Frank DiPino. The left-hander taught Smith a forkball that he began to use expertly as his fastball began to diminish in speed with age.

As with Sutter before him, the Cardinals benefited greatly from a homegrown Cubs stopper. Smith saved 160 games in the better part of four seasons in St. Louis, including a career-high forty-

Lee Smith and fiancée, Cheryl Radachowsky. Author photo.

seven in 1991. All the while, the Cubs scratched around for a closer, having only replaced Smith's production with one thirty-six-save season by the erratic Mitch "Wild Thing" Williams in 1989.

But when Smith was traded to the New York Yankees late in the 1993 season, he started to take on the veneer of a rent-a-closer. He moved on to the Baltimore Orioles for the strike-shortened 1994 season. Then he traveled cross-country for a season-plus stint with the Anaheim Angels before landing with the Cincinnati Reds early in the 1996 season. At thirty-eight, he suddenly was not a closer anymore. A twenty-five-game, five-save line for the Expos in '97 was his career wrap-up.

With the 478 saves in 1,022 games and a career 3.03 ERA, Smith would seem automatic Hall of Fame material. But when the Baseball Writers Association of America—some of whose members don't even cover baseball anymore—votes for Cooperstown inductees, there's always controversy. Smith was left far on the outside looking in, in his first two years eligible. Meanwhile, former Cubs teammate Dennis Eckersley, with 390 career saves, was voted in during his first year of eligibility in 2004.

Smith expressed no surprise he was not voted in quickly.

"It took a lot of players a long time to get in," he said. "Look at Bruce Sutter, it's going on twelve or thirteen years? When I played, I was not the flashy guy. Joe Torre said, 'Lee just goes out, does his job, and ambles off the field.' I don't know what the hell 'ambling' means. I'm not someone who produces commercials and didn't do appearances."

One theory on the writers' reticence regarding Smith is that he was a vagabond near the end of his career and did not get the kind of frequent high-profile postseason exposure that benefited Eckersley in the middle of his career.

"Did Ernie Banks ever play in a playoff game?" Smith wondered. "He's got the numbers."

But there's one drawback to the Hall of Fame. Inductees have to give a speech at Cooperstown. If Big Lee talked, he'd have to draw it out and keep it clean. Sitting near the podium, though, would not be a problem for his "ambling." He'd only have to walk a few feet.

Away from the lectern, in the Hall of Fame parties, the stories he could tell, the laughs he could evoke. Somebody's got to wake up and realize the Hall is big enough for Big Lee Smith.

Big Red's Live and in Color

Rick Sutcliffe knew all about the hazards of his old job. The wind might take a fly ball into the seats. A ball might take a bad hop. An umpire's strike zone might be floating all day.

But the lessons of all of those pitfalls from his pitching days couldn't help him when a switch meant to cut his microphone between innings wasn't thrown.

During the 2003 All-Star Game at U.S. Cellular Field, "Big Red" handled the color analysis for Major League Baseball International's English-language telecast. One commercial break began, but that familiar, slightly twangy voice kept talking, piped into the PA system of a party suite converted to an auxiliary press box down the left-field line.

So the assembled media could giggle a bit at Sutcliffe's offhand comments about the game and the broadcast, normally reserved only for his boothmate, assistant director, and any other hangers-on present. Luckily no zingers were being thrown at any of the assembled All-Stars, no inside information not meant for broadcast was disseminated.

But if the truth through an open mike or over the air to millions hurt anyone, so be it.

"It's no different than when I played," Sutcliffe said. "I really don't give a shit whether anybody likes me or not. I'm all about respect. I didn't care as a teammate whether you liked me or not. I wanted you to respect me, and in turn I hope to respect you.

"The same thing works for me as a broadcaster now. I'm in every clubhouse before every game, and I'm in the winning clubhouse after every game. You can always find me. If I say something you don't like, I'm accountable. I'm there. Once every two weeks, somebody's upset with something I said, and we figure it out. Either

I'm telling the truth and you have to deal with it, or wait a minute, I got it wrong. And if I did, I'll more than compensate for it."

Rick Sutcliffe is now everybody's guest all over baseball. He's climbing the status ladder as a national color analyst, seemingly on every ESPN telecast not aired on the trademark Wednesday and Sunday nights. He transcends the roles of media person and former player expertly. A sign in the Cubs player lounge warns that no media are allowed past that point, but Sutcliffe strolls into the cramped area as if he had never retired from his ace's status at Wrigley Field.

Oh, how his former teammates will give him hell about being a TV glamour boy now. "He's got a face made for radio, but he's on TV now," said old batterymate Jody Davis. Sutcliffe, nearing fifty, has made one concession to the slickness that TV requires: he has shaved his legendary mountain-man red full beard. Only a goatee remains. But the persona is still the same, his stature in Cubs history as the 1984 Cy Young Award winner for his 16–1 record secure as ever.

Sutcliffe has imparted the wisdom of his fifteen years on the mound to droves of Padres minor-league pitchers. But far more than that have access to his pitching mind-set via his baseball-announcing assignments.

Sutcliffe first hooked up with TV when the San Diego Padres—those dastardly conquerors of him and his merry band of Chicagoans in game 5 of the 1984 National League Championship Series—again beat out the Cubs, this time for his services as a pitching coach a year after his 1994 retirement.

With the endorsement of Padres president Larry Lucchino, who knew Sutcliffe from their Baltimore days, he developed a routine of splitting time between the minors and the broadcast booth.

"He liked some of the things I did with the younger pitchers, [Mike] Mussina and [Ben] McDonald," Sutcliffe said of Lucchino. "I told him, thanks, I wasn't sure, I'd get back to him.

"Then I called the Cubs. I tried for a week to get ahold of [general manager] Ed Lynch, and he wouldn't return my calls. Finally I got ahold of him and said, 'Ed, I'm thinking about getting back into the game as a pitching coach. Is there anything that I can do?' He said no, absolutely nothing.

"Then I called Lucchino back the next day. He said, 'If you want the big-league [pitching coach's] job, it's yours.' I said, 'No, I'm not ready for that.' I started my playing career at the rookie level. If I wanted to be a big-league pitching coach, I would start at that level, too. I agreed to go to the rookie league with the Padres.

"It was in the paper three days later, in *USA Today*. Ed Lynch called back. Ed says, 'Sut, something opened up.' I said, 'Ed, do you guys get *USA Today* in Chicago?' Then he got quiet. I figure [many years] later, I can tell the rest of the story."

The rest of the story is that Sutcliffe is happy bopping around the majors, but not committed as yet to a 162-game grind of working as one team's primary color analyst. He'll flit across the country going from one ESPN early-week telecast to another, then to a Padres game, but never a block of five to seven games in a row.

"I really like where I'm at right now," Sutcliffe said. "I got an opportunity to do the All-Star Game and the World Series for Major League Baseball International. It's televised to all the foreign countries and, more important, to all our armed forces. I've got a brother who's a marine.

"As far as moving on, going to another level with other employers, that doesn't interest me now. ESPN's been great."

Sutcliffe long has been linked to coming back to the Cubs in the broadcast booth. But the desire for some family time each week probably has quashed several logical entry points back to Wrigley Field. He thinks the door is still "open" to an eventual return.

"My priority is my family and especially my daughter [Shelby]," Sutcliffe said. Shelby, often seen as a cute toddler in celebratory scenes back in 1984, is now "five foot eight, blonde and blue-eyed," according to Dad. "She got her good looks from her mom [Robin]." The old man was most proud of Shelby's academic prowess as a premed student at Texas Christian University.

But when the younger Sutcliffe finally flees the nest for good, the pitcher turned broadcaster will alter the strategy. "At some point I'll either become a full-time commentator or put the uniform back on in some sort of capacity," he said.

Many pundits say former players won't come down hard on their present-day brethren. Sutcliffe brushes back that accusation.

Sutcliffe enjoyed a toe-dip into winning as the pitching mainstay on the Cubs' 1984 and 1989 NL East title winners. But he believes a new, permanent Cubs winning era is at hand.

"They're going to straighten things out because of one guy," Sutcliffe said. "Dusty Baker would not have come on board if there weren't certain things that are important that he has control of. He's been around winners. The Cubs, at times, the past few years have gone out hoping to win. But they didn't expect to win. Dusty Baker always expects to win.

"Dusty was like an older brother to me, as teammates when I first came up with the Dodgers. I've seen him coach. I've seen him manage. He taught me a lot about the game as a young kid. He's going to do the same thing with the [Mark] Priors and the [Carlos] Zambranos and the [Kerry] Woods."

Sutcliffe even provided instant karma to the 1984 Cubs. His mid-June arrival via trade from the Cleveland Indians was the watershed event of that season. A competitive Cubs team that was batting rich and pitching poor before he burst on the scene was transformed into a mound monster. A six-feet-seven Sutcliffe towered over all hitters with his near-corkscrew delivery that resulted in that 16–1 record, a strikeout an inning, a 2.69 ERA, and signs bearing red beards instead of *K*s denoting each whiff. The Cubs' team ERA, hovering around 4.00 in early June, was cut to 3.75 by season's end due to the superb starting work of Sutcliffe, fellow late-spring pickup Dennis Eckersley, and lefty Steve Trout.

Cubs fans, scarred by deals that dispatched the likes of Lou Brock, Rafael Palmeiro, Lee Smith, and others fated to achieve elsewhere, still debate the merits of the June 13, 1984, Sutcliffe trade in which top prospect Joe Carter was sent to Cleveland. It's true Carter carved out a spectacular career, culminating in his World Series–winning homer in 1993 with Toronto. But if the truth be known, the Cubs wouldn't have won the NL East in either 1984 or 1989, breaking the never-ending first-place drought, if Sutcliffe hadn't steadied the pitching staff with sixteen victories in each season.

The Cubs got Sutcliffe on his ascendancy. He had been NL Rookie of the Year with a 17–10 record as a Dodger in 1979 but somehow fell out of favor with Los Angeles. Two years later, he was banished to Cleveland, baseball's Siberia of the time.

"It felt pretty good in Cleveland," he said. "I had an opportunity to pitch in LA the first year. Then, for whatever reason, Tommy Lasorda didn't think that I belonged in the big leagues. In '82, I got a chance to pitch for Cleveland, got back in the rotation, and got lucky to win the American League ERA title [2.96].

"In '83, I got to go to the All-Star Game. In '84 I got off to a slow start [4–5, 5.15 ERA]. I had a dental problem, which set me back a couple of weeks. I was a free agent at the end of the year. Cleveland didn't think they could sign me, and fortunately Dallas Green had his arms wide open."

Sutcliffe's potential was transformed into reality by his new teammates.

"It's a real easy answer," he said. "Position by position, I had an opportunity to play for a better team. Anytime you get the defense of Bobby Dernier and [Ryne] Sandberg, the offense of Sarge [Matthews] and Jody Davis, it has a tendency to make everyone look better."

The '84 Cubs seemed to be one of the last of the old-school, old-fashioned teams crowded with distinctive players who had fun playing on the field and had a good time after hours.

"I think more than anything it was the personalities on that team," Sutcliffe said. "You had a little bit of everything with the enthusiasm of Sarge, the speed of Dernier, the toughness of [Keith] Moreland, the power of [Leon] Durham, the all-around game of Sandberg, the fieriness of [Larry] Bowa, the quiet confidence of Ron Cey, the energy of Jody Davis.

"You had the security blanket in Lee Smith. [Tim] Stoddard, [George] Frazier, Dennis Eckersley, the cover boy in Scott Sanderson, the total left-hander in Steve Trout. These people genuinely loved this city. More than anything, that's what got them and the fans together."

Even though the Cubs tripped up in San Diego in October '84, the future seemed ensured after Green re-signed Sutcliffe, Trout, Eckersley, and Sanderson to lucrative contracts after the season. That strategy appeared to work when the Cubs got off to a good start in 1985.

Then came a fateful Sunday afternoon, May 19, in Atlanta, with Sutcliffe off to a 5–3 start that included two shutouts, a 2.11 ERA, and four complete games. Trying to beat out a double-play grounder, Sutcliffe tore his left hamstring.

"Hustling is part of the game, including going down the line trying to beat out a double play," Sutcliffe said. "The problem was,

Rick Sutcliffe at Wrigley Field. Author photo.

I didn't listen to the doctors. I had some internal pressure to get back out there. I was supposed to be out six to eight weeks."

Instead, Sutcliffe limped back to the mound at Wrigley Field on June 7. He shut out the Pirates 1–0 on two hits. He paid a big price for hurrying back.

"I spent the next two days in the hospital," he said. "I had bled all the way down into both feet, you could see the purple. I was in intensive care. I was on fluids."

Despite being waylaid, Sutcliffe bounced back on the mound to take his turn. He made four more starts, pitching well statistically, before going on the disabled list with a strained muscle on July 8. He came back again on July 23, beating the Padres 8–1. He couldn't get past two-thirds of an inning in his next start on July 28 in Los Angeles. His season ended the next day with an 8–8 record. Sutcliffe had done serious damage to his shoulder by coming back too fast, in the same manner Dizzy Dean had altered his career by rushing back after suffering a broken toe in the 1937 All-Star Game.

"I did something really stupid," he said of the June 7 return. "But along with doing that, I initially tore the labrum in my shoulder because I didn't have a leg to land on. I had to use all arms to do it with. It was a mistake. That was the point where Rick Sutcliffe the power pitcher had to become Rick Sutcliffe, the control and finesse guy."

Within three weeks of Sutcliffe's final 1985 start, the remaining four regular rotation starters—Eckersley, Trout, Sanderson, and Dick Ruthven—joined him on the disabled list. That unprecedented string of bad luck doomed the '84 winners to being a one-year wonder—and started team architect Green on the slippery slope out of the Cubs organization.

Sutcliffe struggled through a 5–14 season with a bad Cubs team in 1986, rebounded to win eighteen games in 1987 and held the pitching staff together for much of the 1989 NL East title season before more arm miseries overwhelmed him again. He rehabbed again and pitched decently the last two months of the 1991 season but was let go by Larry Himes's first moves as general manager. Like other players, Sutcliffe was furious for years afterward at Himes.

He would go on to finish up in Baltimore and St. Louis before calling it quits. But only physically. You see, Big Red is the eternal ace. He seemed to want to bite off Jim Frey's head whenever he came to the mound threatening to pull Sutcliffe out. The competitive spirit will always be there.

"I'll never lose my desire to play," he said. "I just lost my ability to play, but that doesn't mean my mentality as a player will change."

Now, the camera's red light has to fill in for the umpire's cry of "Play ball!" Rick Sutcliffe will again put in a full nine innings' effort thinking along with the pitcher, because he can easily put himself in the pitcher's shoes.

An Agent of Principles

Supersized homes are the rage at the dawn of a new century. Situated on some prime land in the tony Chicago suburb of Lake Forest, Scott Sanderson's house goes a bit further. The structure, one of a series of similar big homes with a lot of surrounding grounds, ranges somewhere between supersized and an outright mansion.

Well, what do you want the man to live in? Sanderson spent the better part of nineteen seasons pitching in the major leagues from the late 1970s to the mid-1990s. Multimillion-dollar contracts permitted lifetime security for the savers and maybe even for the spenders, too.

Sanderson was a saver during his big-league days. So he can afford the house, just a few miles north of his longtime residence in Northbrook, where he grew up following a Cubs team for which he eventually pitched from 1984 to 1989.

"I'm conservative by nature," said the six-feet-five Sanderson, middle-aged but still trim, a gentleman who could pass for ten years younger.

He traveled enough in his day. He has not set up a separate office elsewhere. Sanderson's joined tens of millions of Americans whose morning commute is no longer than their bedroom to an office in another part of the house. And since he pays the bills, Sanderson staked out a prime corner part of the residence for the office, which opens out to the surrounding landscape through large windows. Even a top Tribune Company executive would like the spaciousness and décor of Sanderson's neat office, which has some sports memorabilia but doesn't overwhelm visitors with such souvenirs.

"This is definitely my style here," Sanderson said as he leaned back in a black leather chair, letting the phone go to voice mail as he developed his train of thought.

And definitely the career for which he pined midway through his baseball career. Sanderson is one of a handful of players who have become agents, representing both former teammates and newcomer achievers to the game. Self-taught in the arts of negotiating, a natural at player relations, Sanderson can pursue his preferred postbaseball life while still keeping wife Kathleen and teenage children Patrick and Erica rooted in familiar surroundings.

Sanderson is knowledgeable enough to have gone into managing, coaching, and the front office. He's handsome and articulate enough to have been a good broadcaster. But, always a man of firm and well-thought-out beliefs and principles, Sanderson went where he felt the need was greatest for his talents.

"I thought about it halfway through my career," he said. "I began to recognize there was a place in baseball for players once they got out of the game to continue serving the game of baseball, helping the game of baseball. Obviously that takes place in the management side of baseball and takes place in the broadcast booth. I looked at the other side of the table and didn't see too many players who had gone into this who had been successful. I care so much about the game of baseball. One way you can influence the game of baseball is to influence the players of the game, because that will have a domino effect on other players."

Sanderson simply went a different direction in his desire to serve.

"I looked at [management and broadcasting] and saw that was well covered," he said. "There are plenty of players who have gone in that direction. Former players are well represented in that area. It was in this area that I didn't see many former players, especially not major-league players. I do think there's a difference between having a career in the major leagues as opposed to a career in the minor leagues, as far as the experiences you have and the advice you have."

Starting in 1996, Sanderson first went out on his own in representing players. But by 2000, he partnered with experienced agent Mike Moy. Their firm, now based in Sanderson's home and Moy's office in Atlanta, now has twenty-eight clients, led by Todd Helton, Josh Beckett, and Lance Berkman.

Sanderson first learned negotiations in a real trial by fire—on the players' negotiating team that represented all major leaguers in

talks with owners, including the Armageddon situation that resulted in the debilitating 1994–1995 strike.

"I thought it was important in talking with owners as a player,
to let them understand the tremendous amount of respect we had
for them as owners and give them the credit due that they were
owners of individual teams," he said. "They had a right to do
whatever they wanted to do with their own money. But as players,
we collectively had the right to stick together. There's a right way
and a wrong way to go about negotiations."

The strike damaged baseball, and recovery did not begin in ear-
nest until the Mark McGwire–Sammy Sosa home-run race of 1998.
Sanderson insisted that the players never had any intention of hurting baseball.

"I know the players care very much about the game," he said.
"A lot of times, you take a stand not just for yourself. There's an
awful lot of players that gave up a lot of money at the end of their
careers [during the strike] that they personally would not be able
to recover. A lot of people who have stood up not only for their
own rights, but so playing conditions would be good in the future.

"We came about it with respect and integrity. I know the hundreds of hours we put in as players to get this settlement done. You
can't tell how disappointed we were when the commissioner called
off the remainder of the season and postseason. At that point, you
don't turn back the clock but move forward as best you can."

Sanderson took from labor talks not only much of his own negotiating philosophy but also a desire for conciliation at all levels of
baseball.

"I very dearly wanted it to become a partnership," he said. "I
didn't understand why the players and owners had to be at such
odds when we, in essence, wanted the same thing—the success of
the game of baseball. I wanted to have the players and owners fit
more like hand and glove than like battering rams going at each
other. It's still a goal of mine, to have the players and owners understand that the game works best when everyone wins."

Sanderson also learned about the art of the deal from Dick Moss,
his agent during the 1980's. Moss also represented Andre Dawson,
Sanderson's teammate with the Cubs and Montreal Expos. But as
the 1990s dawned, the idea that had been kicking around in his

mind came to fruition. Sanderson would use himself as his own training ground as an agent.

"For the last six years, I represented myself," he said. "I had already reached my peak and was on the backside. I did that in preparation for what I'm doing today. I didn't want whoever my first client was going to be to be my training ground. I used myself as my training ground."

Sanderson certainly got to know a whole host of general managers on the back nine of his career. After an 11–9 season for the Cubs' 1989 NL East titlists, he moved on to the World Series–bound Oakland Athletics, for whom he won a career-high seventeen games. Then he signed a multiyear deal with the New York Yankees in 1991, winning sixteen his first season. By 1993, he had moved on to the Anaheim Angels but was picked up by the San Francisco Giants and rookie manager Dusty Baker for the pennant stretch. The following year, Sanderson came back home for the strike-shortened season with the White Sox. He finished up, pitching almost to his fortieth birthday, with two injury-plagued seasons with the Angels in 1995–1996.

Wasn't there an old saying that a person who represents himself has a fool for a client? Sanderson disagreed.

"My [later] contracts were pretty straightforward contracts," he said. "I had watched contract negotiations. I understood negotiations. I figured I was at least capable of entering into negotiations for myself. I might have left some money out on the table.

"I learned a lot. I'm sure there were some mistakes made along the lines. I was going to be the only one to pay for my mistakes. It's a different dynamic when you go into representing yourself. In a normal business flow of baseball negotiations, when an agent calls a general manager on behalf of a player, it's business as normal. When a player calls a general manager on behalf of himself, there are times when that can come across as, 'Oh, this player is desperate.' This business dynamic shifts a little."

Several years before the Angels released him midway through the 1996 season, Sanderson began talking to a slew of players, to find out their experiences with agents—good and bad.

"I wanted to hear from them to see if it was different from my experiences," he said. "Playing for as long as I did, I developed wonderful relationships all across baseball—players in the American League and National League, management. When I decided that I wanted to represent players, that was pretty good news to a lot of people. There were some players ready to have me represent them right away. I took three weeks off after I got released."

Sanderson's first client was Yankees utility player Andy Stankiewicz. He also handled some minor leaguers who would not be fated to head to the big leagues but who would provide the new agent a wealth of experience.

He started out from a good base of relationships to tap into contract talks.

"Even now there's not a single organization where I don't have a wonderful relationship with someone, somewhere in that organization, whether it's a general manager, assistant general manager, manager, coach, equipment manager," he said. "I know a ton of owners. There were relationships forged during the time I was on the players' negotiating committee. When you treat people with respect, I don't believe that's lost on people."

Sanderson also knew his income would drop precipitously as he tried to build his client basis up from the lower-salaried players. But he had saved his money and could ride it out.

"We've been married twenty-five years," he said of his wife. "Kathleen knows how passionate I feel about the game of baseball. If I were going to stay in the game of baseball after my playing days were over, it would only be in the capacity of serving the game.

"I knew going into representing players that I didn't need the income from a second job to support my family. But I needed to work. A man works to support his family for a living. I thought it was important [for my children] to see me working so that their expectations and their life experiences would be more realistic with what they probably would face."

While Sanderson signed his first clients, he also began three years' worth of conversations with Moy, who at the time headed the baseball and football divisions of Orlando-based Leader Enterprises. Big-time agent Robert Fraley, who later was killed in a plane crash along with golfer Payne Stewart, headed the firm. White Sox slugger Frank Thomas was one of their top clients.

At first Sanderson rejected Moy's suggestion to move his family to Atlanta to form a new agent's firm together. The two continued talking while Sanderson continued learning the business.

"Intuitively, he knew I'd have to learn lessons the hard way," Sanderson said of Moy. "I'd be banging my head against the wall and stubbing my toe in ways he could have saved me from."

But by 2000, Sanderson and Moy finally joined forces, agreeing to have dual offices in their respective home areas. E-mail and other technology eased the separation. Sanderson will defer to his partner any day in pure negotiating ability.

"I happen to think Mike is the single best negotiator in major league baseball," he said. "There's a talent he has that's incredible. You'd like the negotiations to end with both parties satisfied. There doesn't always need to be blood in the wake. But you also want your clients to know you fought as hard as you can to get them the contract they deserved. Those are interesting dynamics to put together."

The partnership works, Sanderson said, because of his complementary skills with Moy, as a kind of Mr. Inside, Mr. Outside. Moy is the skilled dealmaker; Sanderson is the relationship guy at the ballpark.

"My experience is inside the locker room and on the field, where you don't get to go if you're not a player," he said. "It's the insight behind the scenes, in the bowels of the stadium, the inner sanctum where nobody's allowed."

In addition to contract counsel, Sanderson will talk about the mental aspect of pitching with clients like Beckett. But he leaves the mechanical end of mound work to the client's pitching coach.

Sanderson's firm is almost maxed out in the number of clients. Generally, he and Moy will work in newcomers when other players they represent retire.

"There is a saturation point," he said. "It's one of the luxuries we have. One of the things players love about us is there's not layers and layers they have to go through to find us. There are two people, that's it. If you allow the growth to get away from you, there's still only twenty-four hours in a day and two people.

"We're a smaller firm with a very strong reputation in the game. We're small enough to where we can spend a lot of time with the players. We're extremely picky about who we take on as clients now. I don't want to spend my time managing office personnel. If you continue to take on more and more players, you have to continue to take on staff or else the service will suffer. And we don't ever want the service to suffer."

Although Sanderson and Moy crafted one of the game's megabucks contracts with Helton and the Colorado Rockies, Sanderson will not be surprised if such a deal is not duplicated by another client.

"Whoever has the pen in their hand has the right to say, 'I'll write the check,'" he said. "It's been my contention all along that owners set the salaries. There's also a marketplace out there. Owners have a right to spend money and decide how to spend it. I never want to take that power away from the owners.

"It's a real simple economic equation. It works just about everywhere in the world. When revenues go up, salaries go up. When revenues fall, salaries go down. People ask me all the time: 'Where will these salaries stop?' There's a real simple answer: They will stop when revenues stop. I've never begrudged an owner of a baseball team the right to stop wherever he wants to stop on spending."

Surprisingly, Sanderson's opposition to a salary cap is based on the concept of a restraint of trade on the owners' part.

"That takes away from ownership's right to spend money when they want to," he said. Especially Yankees owner George Steinbrenner.

"He has the right to spend it the way he wants to," Sanderson said. "When he writes a luxury tax check for $60 million to $70 million, it's spread throughout the game. There was a period of fifteen years from the early 1980s to the mid-1990s where the Yankees spent an awful lot of money but never got into postseason. No one was crying that they were spending too much money then."

Sanderson was beneficiary of a Cubs franchise that spent money after the 1984 NL East title season. Along with Rick Sutcliffe, Steve Trout, and Dennis Eckersley, he was tendered a lucrative multiyear deal by GM Dallas Green following a respectable injury-shortened season of an 8–5 record and a 3.14 ERA.

After spending his first six seasons with the Expos, including a sixteen-win season in 1980, Sanderson had a "dream come true" playing in his hometown, coming over in a three-way deal with involving the San Diego Padres prior to '84. Two decades later, he hasn't altered his feelings despite representing players all over baseball. "I have a fierce loyalty to the Cubs," he said.

But Sanderson was never all he could have been in blue pinstripes. Pain was his constant companion due to back problems that eventually resulted in two surgeries. As a result, he never started more than twenty-eight games in a season. He missed almost all of the 1988 season after one operation. When he did take the mound, he often was crimped. He ended up shuttling between the bullpen and rotation when he was able to pitch.

He has no regrets, though.

"My time here with the Cubs was physically hard," he said. "I was hurt. Yet I did everything I could to get out there on the mound. I made a ton more starts than maybe I should have.

"As an athlete, it's not our job to let people know that you're hurting while you're playing. You go out and do the best you can. There were plenty of days I left the house, Kathleen was looking at me and she said, 'How are you going to do it?' I said, 'I don't know, but I'm going to do it.'

"I don't know anyone who pitched for any length of time who didn't go through some degree of pain. We all inside the locker room understand that. It's part of the game."

While reliever Lee Smith will forever have to live down Steve Garvey's game-winning ninth-inning homer that boosted the Padres to victory in game 4 of the 1984 National League Championship Series, Sanderson has a good reason for replaying that game. He started it for the Cubs, allowing three runs in four and two-thirds innings.

"I think back about that game all the time and the hitters that I faced," Sanderson said. "I know full well I started that game. I also know everything that was going on. Physically, I couldn't have done more than I tried to do."

As long as mentally and physically Sanderson was in the game, he would not look back and second-guess himself.

"Regrets? No," he said. "The only way you can have regrets is if you feel you came up short on effort. Not just effort in a game but effort in off-season [preparations]. I don't have any regrets, but it doesn't prevent me from feeling badly that we didn't close the deal [in both the 1984 and 1989 postseasons]. I wanted to do that for the city of Chicago.

"What comes to mind is all the great times I had in baseball and all the wonderful relationships that were formed."

Sounds like the first and last lesson about baseball Sanderson will provide for his clients.

Golfing, Card Playing, and Remembering

A lot of guys in Jim Frey's position would still be haunting ballparks or amateur diamonds. Even at a seventy-some-thing stage of life, they cannot cut the cords to baseball. They'd have "special assistant" or "consultant" titles; they'd be kept on the payroll in a minor way and have the privilege of hanging around the game that has nurtured them for their entire lives.

But old-hitter Frey threw a changeup. Barely past his sixtieth birthday, he decided he wouldn't wear out his welcome, pulling the plug on his active career in the early 1990s, a little too early instead of way too late. And when he made his opinions known to his Tribune Company bosses, his retirement pace was stepped up even further.

You'd figure the only man to ever manage a Cubs first-place team while serving as general manager for another division winner would just continue scouting, evaluating, and teaching as long as he had his wits. Yet Frey and wife Joan are now content to split time between Baltimore in the summer and a golf community half-way between Fort Myers and Naples, Florida, when the weather turns cold.

"I play golf, and I play cards, and we take a few trips," Frey said. "We visit our kids and our grandchildren, spend the summer in Baltimore with them. We just take it easy. At our age, there isn't a hell of a lot else we can do."

Frey eschewed baseball hanger-on status.

"A lot of people just can't walk away [from baseball]," he said. "My time had come. I was very lucky, very fortunate. Some people cannot walk away. Some guys love having that microphone and camera on them."

Frey had last worked for a major-league organization in 1992, serving out the last year of his Cubs general manager's contract filing occasional scouting reports to the office of successor Larry Himes. A few years later, he briefly sported a fancy title of "vice chairman of baseball operations" for the Somerset Patriots of the independent Atlantic League. The reality was just some consulting and talent evaluation. Now he's a certified old-timer, following the game from a distance.

"I was comparatively young when I decided to go home," Frey said. "The only thing I really miss is putting a team together and watching the guys develop. The thrill for me was watching the team come together. I had a couple of teams [that I managed] win. Both years didn't start out all that well, but then they caught fire. It was quite a thrill here when they came together.

"August and September of 1984 [as Cubs manager] was probably the highlight of my life. It was quite exciting. In 1980, going to the World Series in my first year as manager [of the Kansas City Royals] was quite exciting. But if I had to weigh one against the other, it would be the time I spent in Chicago."

Frey had the ultimate of highs and some depressing lows as skipper in '84 and general manager of the 1989 NL East titlists. Mostly the good times were remembered when Frey was reunited with eighteen of the '84 players at the Cub Convention in 2004.

Time healed most old wounds. There was little talk of the subsequent disintegration of the '84 team or the disgruntlement players felt toward Frey by 1986. Fans asked Frey for far many more autographs than they had questions about his trades of Lee Smith and Rafael Palmeiro in the first year of his GM's tenure. And there will always be questions with Smith drawing Hall of Fame votes for his record 478 saves and Palmeiro celebrating his five hundredth career homer in 2003.

Rather, there was time to talk about glory days with Ryne Sandberg, about how Frey adjusted his batting style to drive the ball, just in time for Sandberg's Most Valuable Player season in '84. Frey had been a longtime hitting coach, but Sandberg was his greatest success story, coming after he assumed a manager's job.

He never gets tired of talking about getting Sandberg going. An interview with Frey in 1990 about Sandberg, then the NL's leading home-run hitter, featured Frey telling the questioner to "shut up and keep on writing" when a follow-up query was attempted. He was just as enthused years later.

"When I said he was an MVP-type player, there were people in the organization who alerted me that it might cost me my job if I changed his style," Frey said. "The safest thing in the world is never to go out on a limb and never say a guy's going to be a good player.

"That's the thrill of managing or coaching—working with young players, watching them develop," he said. "As batting coach, it's satisfying watching some young players develop, but it doesn't pay as much as the other [manager and GM] jobs."

Frey had been a baseball lifer who paid his dues as a minor-league batting champ who narrowly missed a big-league call-up with the St. Louis Cardinals in the late 1950s. He later was re-nowned as Baltimore Orioles' batting coach during the Birds' glory years of the late 1960s and early 1970s. But in 1984, he came within three innings of possessing the most desirable manager's role in modern Cubs history.

Frey piloted the strongest post–World War II team, a ninety-six-victory powerhouse possessed of six players with eighty or more RBIs and the NL's best pitching staff in the second half of 1984. He repeatedly railed profanely against references to past Cubs failures and the supposed inability to win amid an all-daytime home schedule. "Fuck 1969," said the man who never self-censored his language when cameras and mikes were not present.

After two impressive victories in the best-of-five matchup to open the NLCS against the San Diego Padres at Wrigley Field, a World Series entrée seemed ensured. Some players admittedly thought they had it won on the plane out to San Diego.

But when the Padres romped in game 3, pulled out a memorable victory on Steve Garvey's walk-off homer off Lee Smith in game 4, and used a couple of well-placed ground balls to come from be-hind to steal game 5, the second-guessing began and followed Frey around for the next two decades. Most of his players believed Frey should have started game 1–winner Rick Sutcliffe in game 4 and game 2–winner Steve Trout in game 5. The three days' rest outings, in theory, could have applied the chokehold to the Padres instead of saving Trout to open game 1 of the World Series against the

Detroit Tigers. Instead, Scott Sanderson worked game 4 and Sutcliffe started game 5.

"I still do think about it," Frey said. "There are times when things flash back to me, and I do think about San Diego. We thought we kind of got screwed because we only got two home games [attributed to the lack of lights in Wrigley Field]. We were in the sixth inning [of game 5] with a three-run lead and the seventh inning with a one-run lead, and Sutcliffe hadn't lost a game since the middle of June or around that time.

"It just didn't work out. When it happened again [in 2003], you do get reminders. Too often, I must add. If you know anything about baseball, the last three outs are the toughest. You have the best hitters and the best pitchers going at each other. Some guys have a great stomach for the first six, seven innings but don't have the stomach or heart for the last three, especially in a playoff or World Series situation.

"We just didn't hold them. I don't know what to say. It was unfortunate."

Even more unfortunate was an injury-prompted thirteen-game winning streak that wrecked a 34–19 first-place start in 1985. The entire rotation of Sutcliffe, Trout, Sanderson, Dennis Eckersley, and Dick Ruthven were on the disabled list together at one point in August of that season, while losing additional time before and after that point.

"If those pitchers had stayed healthy, the Cubs would have been a contender the rest of the decade," Frey said. "We ended up winning seventy-seven games losing five starting pitchers."

The inevitable grumbling began, and it heightened going into 1986. Frey told beat writers privately that he questioned whether several veterans were undermining his managing. In turn, players whispered dissatisfaction with Frey's choice of lineups. With the Cubs just 23–33 on June 12, Cubs GM Dallas Green fired Frey.

But he did not stay away for long. Tribune Company was growing more restive about Green's stewardship. A curious move then ensued—Frey was hired after the 1986 as WGN-Radio color analyst, pushing the popular Lou Boudreau to part-time status. Frey had not expressed previous interest in a radio gig. A long process that would end up affecting Cubs fortunes all the way to the turn of the millennium had begun.

"Bringing Jimmy Frey back was the start," Green said in 1999 of the process of greasing the skids under him. "They asked me if I minded Jimmy coming back to do radio. That probably was their preparation to replace me. There was really no one who could take my place from within. When I did get fired and he immediately was named GM, two and two gets to be four."

On November 11, 1987, less than two weeks after Green was cashiered, Frey—possessing no high-level front-office experience—was named GM. Almost immediately he named lifelong friend Don Zimmer as manager. And within a month, he ran Lee Smith out of town as fast as he could get the first offer from the Boston Red Sox.

Frey had seen Smith close-up traveling with the Cubs throughout 1987. The stopper was not a happy camper, often expressing his feelings in the most profane way. So Frey and Zimmer concluded the deal with the Red Sox in "half an hour," according to the late Gordon Goldsberry, then Cubs scouting director and one of baseball's most respected front-office types at the time. All the while, teams like the Los Angeles Dodgers were ready to bargain for Smith. The Cubs got easy-to-hit starter Al Nipper and nervous-Nellie fireballer Calvin Schiraldi. Frey was warned by a colleague that Schiraldi was sweating bullets on a thirty-seven-degree night in New York during the late-inning drama in the 1986 World Series. Originally projected as Smith's successor as closer, Schiraldi was put into the rotation the following spring.

Although Frey made several moves to ensure an NL East title in 1989 while taking advantage of a bumper crop of homegrown Green/Goldsberry products, the move that brought Mitch "Wild Thing" Williams to the Cubs at the 1988 winter meetings would haunt Frey the most. To get Williams, he dispatched left fielder Palmeiro, a .308 hitter with forty doubles but just eight homers in '88, a season when the baseball apparently had been "dejuiced" compared to power-happy 1987. Also moving to Texas was young lefty Jamie Moyer, who had somehow gotten on Zimmer's bad side. More than a decade later, baseball graybeard Moyer was winning twenty games with the Seattle Mariners as one of the game's classiest mound acts.

"I was always impatient for players to expand their ability, to be as good as they possibly could be," Frey said.

Jim Frey. Author photo.

But his impatience, which prevented an auction to the highest bidder for Smith, turned into severe imprudence with Palmeiro. Frey craved power that Palmeiro would not be fated to supply for a few years. However, one stereotype has stuck through the years—that Frey had a choice of keeping either Palmeiro or Mark Grace to play first base. In reality, Palmeiro had never played first as a Cub and said he was prepared to learn to play a decent defensive left field. The Rangers eventually moved Palmeiro to first but had not gone into the deal with that intention.

Frey did admit he considered trading either Palmeiro or Grace to Texas. Tom Grieve, then GM of the George W. Bush–owned Rangers, said later he thought Palmeiro had twenty-five-homer potential.

"It was pretty well agreed—and I didn't make any of those decisions solely—that we all thought [Palmeiro'd] hit fifteen to twenty homers a year," Frey said. "We didn't think Grace would hit that many. We had a choice. I actually offered Grace to Texas, but they wanted Palmeiro. We thought they'd be similar-type players. Grace would be a consistent hitter and an excellent fielder. We needed the help from Texas. The people now forget we won our division again in 1989 and had a chance to get to the World Series.

"When he hit five hundred, you have to be happy for him. He's had a great career. We knew he was going to be a good hitter. I don't think he knew he was going to hit five hundred. He's been a big RBI man and good, strong power man. I have no regrets. They hadn't won here in forty years. We were trying to win a division and a World Series. Our number 1 goal was not to keep individual players. Our number 1 goal was to put a team in the playoffs and World Series."

Palmeiro refused to complete the circle, rejecting a trade back to the pennant-contending Cubs from the Rangers in August 2003. Gaining notoriety as a Viagara spokesman before he was forty, Palmeiro spent his post-Chicago days through 2004 shuttling between the Rangers and Baltimore Orioles.

After the Cubs' pitching collapsed in 1990, Frey went on a free-agent spending splurge in the following off-season, landing slugger George Bell, starter Danny Jackson, and reliever Dave Smith. The signings were a near disaster. Bell underproduced and was a clubhouse detriment; Jackson was hurt; and Smith was washed up. The Cubs' fortunes sagged once again. And the farm system, which had revived under Green and Goldsberry, was sliding backward again since Frey had fired Goldsberry following the 1988 season.

But Frey began to feel eggshells under his feet when Cubs president Don Grenesko, a Tribune Company–trained financial guy, stepped in to fire Zimmer a month into the 1991 season.

"I was told I had to fire Zimmer," Frey said. "And if I was not going to fire Zimmer, he'd go down there and fire Don himself. I felt as if that was possibly the beginning of mistrust. I found it hard to go to the ballpark with the same resolve, without the same respect."

Frey had planned to retire at the expiration of his contract following the 1992 season. At one point, he was offered a three-year extension by Cubs chairman Stanton Cook, another Tribune Company suit who was meddling too deeply in baseball operations. Frey told Cook he'd mull it over.

All the while, Cook cast around for a new team president to replace Grenesko, who was returning to Tribune Tower. He was rejected by Blue Jays GM Pat Gillick. Then Cook switched gears, listening to pitches from Larry Himes, in baseball purgatory for a year after being fired as White Sox GM late in the 1990 season. On November 13, 1991, Frey was informed he'd be put out to pasture in Baltimore for the final year of his contract in favor of Himes.

At the press conference to introduce Himes, Cook and Grenesko nervously eyed Frey. "Cook said to Grenesko, 'Don't let Frey talk today. Don't let Frey grab that microphone,'" Frey said. "Despite that, I grabbed the mike. I thanked everybody for eight great years. [Cook and Grenesko] were greatly relieved."

So was Frey, in a way. He had survived a brush with a corporate culture that he described as "very secretive . . . a CIA mentality."

Frey was sincere in his farewell speech. Shuttling between Baltimore and southwest Florida, he realizes he'll always have Chicago in his heart. Don't begrudge a longtime baseball man such joyous thoughts, even if he had been the first of three successive Cubs GMs who had been promoted one or two notches beyond their true level of capability.

From Hell-Raiser to Man of Salvation

" I feel most people choose failure without really knowing it. I'm going to teach somebody about succeeding."

Dickie Noles can't sum up his mission in any better combination of phrases. Where there are tripwires and temptations, Noles believes he can point to a better way. His strategy is part "been there, done that" draw on personal experiences, part plain ol' common sense and part fierce adherence to a faith that insists the best is always ahead.

Combative as ever but channeling that emotion in a different manner, Noles could go through middle age ruing his bad luck. He still wonders who his biological father is, and probably will never know, but won't let that huge hole in his personal game deter him. He looks back at a career split among the Phillies, Cubs, and cameo bits with other teams as potential unfulfilled, yet not one "What if?" emerges in a conversation with Noles.

He can't afford to look back in anger or distress, can't afford to be less than strong. Noles realizes he's up against a modern societal style of easy self-indulgence that might make the so-called counterculture of the 1960s and early 1970s blush with embarrassment. Be it the thirteen-year-old kid battling the change of life or the twenty-one-year-old Phillies prospect struggling to climb the ladder through the minors, Noles will be there to attempt the salvation effort, like the burglar who becomes the security expert.

"I still fear no man," Noles said. "I fight for the Lord now, but I won't back down in my belief system."

His days of battling alcoholism and assorted personal demons, of being arrested four consecutive seasons in the minors, of fighting with a police officer, of a baseball career almost gone to waste, seem at once so distant and so close they could still smack some sense into Noles. He'll never let himself feel too comfortable. Otherwise the former pitcher with the curly hair who had two tours of duty with the Dallas Green–run Cubs in the 1980s wouldn't be as effective in steering others away from disaster.

Phillies owner David Montgomery let Noles run with his program of character building in the mid-1990s, and he hasn't stopped ever since.

Noles will go outside the cloistered world of baseball to operate his three-part SAVES program, the acronym standing for Students Attitudes Values Education and Substance Abuse.

"Geared toward high school and college students, it starts with making the right choices," Noles said. "It's how to become the best person you can be. Why some choose success while others choose failure without knowing it.

"The second part is about decisions and dreams. It's more geared toward middle school students. And the second part is aimed at athletes, about how to get natural highs, how dedication and discipline are needed to reach the top, about trying to get the most out of your ability."

His official Phillies title is "employee assistance professional." With baseball players needing every edge imaginable to succeed, with any distraction ready to pull them down, Noles keeps busy with the full support of top management, flying to the far-flung outposts of the farm system as needed from his Philadelphia-area home. But each January, he'll put the players through a program as comprehensive as any spring-training drills, including substance-abuse education, media training, and life experiences, including one very basic skill—how to treat a woman.

"The uniqueness of this is we get down and dirty from the beginning of the player's career," Noles said. "It's preventative medicine. It's five to seven days of training. We teach that leading with power is not always the best example. Instead, lead with influence. We emphasize words like 'honesty' and 'character.' 'Integrity' is a great word to use."

In an introductory phase, Noles will have the players introduce each other and switch seats to become the other person. "We want to make them tell something about each other without an athletic reference. They struggle with it about who they really are. We tell them you are someone other than a baseball player. You will always be known as a baseball player, but you won't be lost in that."

In a real role change, Noles will play a media member as mock interviews are conducted to teach the players how to handle the media even when times are tough. "I tell them no matter what kind of day they had, they should be honored that they're being interviewed," he said.

The session about dealing with women is something that would not have played in baseball ten or twenty years ago.

"There's a portrayal that ballplayers all screw around," he said. "We teach good family men to be good family men. Sure, there are a lot of women out there. If you love the woman you married, why would you want all these other women? Why would you be willing to give up your family for a one-night stand? Be a warrior instead of a wimp to battle through temptation, to not get laid that night."

Noles has the players "rolling and laughing" when he describes to them what happens to a man's penis when he catches sight of a woman wearing a short skirt in a bar. Then he'll bring in a real live subject.

"I've brought in knockout girls wearing short skirts, and I'll ask the players what color eyes or hair they had. Most of the time they didn't notice because they weren't focusing on those features. But it's a way of making them understand [there's] a quality human being [beyond the sexually attractive features]."

Noles has even worked with two gay players. He made an impact with one, who contacts Noles on holidays.

During the program, he sets aside an entire day to deal with substance abuse. Although he'll acknowledge some genetic predisposition to use drugs or alcohol, Noles assures the players that does not mean they, too, will become addicted as the second or third generation.

"Don't get hung up on genetics," he said. "The environmental risk of marijuana use is huge. We're smoking more marijuana than at any time in history. Rap music glorifies it. Snoop Doggy Dog does a mainstream commercial. We live in a disgusting time for music. All sports does is mimic society."

Steroids will increasingly occupy a larger part of the substance abuse time. The strength enhancers have been insidiously creeping into baseball since Noles's playing days.

"We heard in '86 and '87 there were players using them," he said. "We heard about [Jose] Canseco. By the early nineties, I heard a lot of rumors. I worked with several players who admitted using it. The addiction is psychological. They like the way their bodies look. Doctors have been supplying the steroids."

On his trips through the Phillies farm system, Noles has had to deal with players with some surprisingly tragic backgrounds. One strapping six-feet-six, 225-pound prospect absolutely smoked an opposing first baseman with five or six punches after he was tagged hard on the same spot where the prospect had just been hit by the pitcher. Investigating the situation later, Noles found out the player was literally averse to human touch. He had been the product of an environment in which his mother was a crack cocaine–addicted prostitute.

Noles was never going to back away from this player when warned not to touch him. He'd keep moving forward because he knew that turnarounds were possible. It's possible to climb out of a hole so deep that daylight can scarcely be glimpsed.

Noles's mother was an unwed teenager when he was born in Charlotte, North Carolina on November 19, 1956. Ken Noles eventually was presented as a father figure to Dickie, but he was hardly a role model. The elder Noles and other members of his family had severe drinking and drug problems.

"I know I was damaged goods coming into baseball," he said of being drafted in the fourth round in 1975 by the Phillies. "I think baseball saved my life. I was a street person who was mean. My upbringing did not have a great family background. Baseball was the only thing I enjoyed doing. As a kid, I wasn't honest, wasn't caring. When I got into baseball, I realized if I didn't change direction, I would end up exactly where I was heading—to jail."

Disputes were settled with fists or worse. "The way you learned to be accepted was to fight," he said. "I never really enjoyed fighting, but not many people could last as long as me."

Managers such as Lee Elia tried to straighten Noles out in the Phillies farm system. The effort was a real struggle with Noles's quartet of arrests, fights with police officers in and outside the United States, and substance abuse.

Somehow, he clawed his way into the majors, serving as a major contributor out of the bullpen to the Phillies' 1980 world championship team. But he was hardly a media relations role model as is his generation-later alter ego.

"I absolutely hated the writers in Philly, because Lefty [Carlton] said not to talk to the writers, and I wanted to be like Steve Carlton," Noles said.

Two years later, taking a flier on his potential, new Cubs GM Dallas Green imported him, along with other Phillies products he had formerly managed, to Chicago.

"Everyone in baseball knew that if I stayed focused on the sixty feet, six inches, and didn't listen to the dugout chatter [about my personality], I could do well," Noles said.

In his straight and sober moments, he flashed tantalizing potential. On April 28, 1982, Noles one-hit the Cincinnati Reds at Wrigley Field.

"When that game was over, I realized it had been such an easy game," he said. "I was 0-and-2 on almost every batter. It could have been a no-hitter. The only hit was a little flare by Eddie Milner that Steve Henderson let drop in. Fergie [Jenkins] told me, 'If you do that all the time, there's no stopping you.'

"But the next time I wasn't focused. I got angry. I tried to muscle the ball. I confused that with being aggressive."

Counsel was again offered and rejected. "[Cubs pitching coach] Billy Connors said if I came up with a changeup, I would win twenty games," he said. "But I thought the changeup was a wussy pitch."

Noles was 10–13 in 1982. But the following season, he was hardly worth the five-and-dime quality his 5–10 record suggested. He tussled with a Cincinnati police officer in a bar fight, suffering torn knee ligaments in the process. Noles was fined, sentenced to six months in jail, and was sued. Green had seen enough. He entered Noles into a substance-abuse rehab center in Chicago.

"I'm really a Cub at heart," Noles said. "Bob Dernier considers me a Cubbie. Chicago is where I changed my life. The guy who really forced the issue was Dallas Green."

Trouble is, his career was drying up just as he was drying out. Noles was just a mop-up guy on the 1984 Cubs and was dealt away to the Texas Rangers at midseason. He bounced to the Cleveland

Dickie Noles assisting a beneficiary of the Sunshine Foundation. Photo courtesy of Dickie Noles.

Indians in 1986, then came back begging for a job with the Cubs in spring training 1987. Although Green offered him just the minimum $67,000, somehow Noles held out and got $150,000. He pitched decently in middle relief with a 4–2 record and 3.50 ERA before being traded with a week to go in the season to the pennant-panting Detroit Tigers. Noles picked up two crucial stretch-drive saves in the four games he pitched.

"I felt like I was on my way back," he said.

The official tag of the deal with the Tigers was Noles for a player to be named later. On October 23, 1987, that player turned out to be . . . Noles himself.

But the humor in the loan-a-player situation was short-lived. Whatever further plans Green had for Noles were never known. A week after getting Noles back in what turned out to be his final Cubs trade, Green was fired by Tribune Company honcho John Madigan. Successor Jim Frey, with whom Noles was on the outs during the former manager's tenure in 1984, did not re-sign him. Noles went back to the minors, pitched in three more games for the Baltimore Orioles and Phillies in 1988 and 1990, respectively, and finally called it quits before he found his new calling.

Years later, he allowed himself only a short few seconds for regrets. In his late thirties, messing around on minor-league fields with the Phillies farmhands, he could still throw eighty-six to eighty-seven miles per hour.

"I am convinced that if it wasn't for my alcohol problems, I could have still been pitching [through the mid-1990s]."

But he is what he is now. And he hopes the players he advises won't have it half as tough.

"Human beings evolve rather than change," Noles said. "It's about becoming the most well-rounded individual you can be. Think positive, have humor, have some fun with life, and be realistic."

Tug's Old Friend

Cubs fans of any seniority and possessing good recall are not going to look back with fondness at the memories of Tug McGraw.

A colorful lefty reliever in his heyday between 1969 and 1980, McGraw was a member of the fabled '69 Mets club that rushed past the stunned Cubs in September and didn't stop 'til they won the World Series. Eleven years later, McGraw was thrusting his fist in the air, helping win another Fall Classic, this time for a Phillies team that had continually humiliated the Cubs. All along, McGraw boasted of his good fortune, bellowing "You Gotta Believe" as a cheerleading cry and flashing the "choke" sign at Wrigley Field bleacher fans as he stood shagging fly balls in the outfield.

Tug McGraw, enjoying a late-in-life image revival at the turn of the millennium as father of country music superstar Tim McGraw, died of a brain tumor at fifty-nine on January 5, 2004. And while the old-time Cubs fan may have been ambivalent at best about McGraw, at least one former Cubs pitcher was particularly moved by the ex-pitcher's ten-month-long terminal battle with cancer.

Warren Brusstar, an unsung hero of the 1984 National League East champion team, and McGraw went way back, to their high school days, when Brusstar grew up in Napa, California, while McGraw hailed from neighboring Vallejo. Brusstar and McGraw were teammates on the '80 Phillies. And when McGraw got sick, Brusstar was there for him.

But there was more. Brusstar's wife, Jennifer, became McGraw's caregiver in the last months of his life. Jennifer Brusstar and Tim McGraw also cooperated to write a book adopting the elder McGraw's catchphrase. *You Gotta Believe* was a chronicle of McGraw's life, coming out in the spring of 2004 and going further than his 1974 tome *Screwball*, cowritten with Joseph Durso.

While Brusstar had his mind and body helping green Phillies farmhands as pitching coach of Class A Batavia of the New York–Penn League in the summer of 2003, his heart was with McGraw a few hundred miles away in Philadelphia.

He had been with McGraw the previous spring training when he was first diagnosed.

"People started to notice that there was something wrong with him, that he wasn't making a lot of sense when they were talking to him," Brusstar said. "They started getting worried about him.

"Tug couldn't talk at the end. He couldn't communicate. He could answer you, but he couldn't ask you a question. With our long relationship, we could communicate. My wife would get upset with him, because he wouldn't ask her things. He would to me. A couple of times we went out to lunch together, went to the movies together [less than a month before McGraw died].

"They thought they got 99 percent [of the tumor]. But he had a grade 4 tumor that was regenerating at 40 percent a day. They tried everything with Tug. They put wafers in his head." Jennifer Brusstar took McGraw to cancer specialist Harvey Friedman at Duke University.

Jennifer had worked in a store owned by McGraw's cousin. With McGraw going through a divorce, he was living alone. With help from Tim McGraw, coming in when his concert schedule permitted, Jennifer supervised Tug's care and began working on the book.

"She and Tim came up with the idea of writing the book," Brusstar said. "It covers his life in general. She gave him his meds every day and helped coordinate his care. One day he might have needed more pain medication. It was day by day. He was fine [other than the tumor], even gained weight. He weighed 230, 240 pounds. He was huge." The Brusstars took McGraw to see his son's Las Vegas concert as a kind of farewell trip.

Once the minor-league season ended, Brusstar returned to Napa to take care of his children while his wife was three thousand miles away in Philadelphia with McGraw. "My biggest concern was how she handled it emotionally," he said. "But she handled it fine.

"With her writing the book, she finally realized what an icon he was," Brusstar said. "She didn't know who Tug was because my wife wasn't into baseball. She realized what a good person he was, all the good things he did in the community."

Warren Brusstar. Author photo.

Helping chronicle his friend's end game was the latest in a long series of baseball-oriented journeys for Brusstar, who pitched in 340 games, all as a reliever, for the Phillies and Cubs.

After his big-league days ended in 1986, he worked in a series of coaching jobs starting at the University of California–San Diego. Then he moved back to Napa after his father died. Brusstar coached junior college baseball before he started tutoring pitchers with the independent San Bernardino Spirit.

"The players kept coming and going," he said. "It was quite an experience. We had fifty-something pitchers [trying out] from 9 AM to 6 PM on Easter Sunday." Brusstar then worked in the independent Atlantic League for one season before he returned to the Phillies organization as a minor-league coach in 1999.

"The biggest thing for these kids is they're not used to throwing on a daily basis," he said. "We have a fifteen-minute program where the kids throw every day."

Along with relievers like Tim Stoddard, George Frazier, and Rich Bordi, Brusstar was part of a cadre of unsung bullpen heroes on the '84 Cubs. Whenever a starter did not go at least seven innings to directly hand the ball off to closer Lee Smith, these setup and middle-inning relievers held off opponents until Smith's entrance. And they were all right-handed; the only lefty on the entire '84 Cubs pitching staff was starter Steve Trout.

"I got left-handers out as good as I did right-handers, if not better," Brusstar said. "Hard sliders down and in. I could get away with them."

Brusstar had a 3.11 ERA in forty-one games in 1984. He was hardly chopped liver. The previous season, after GM Dallas Green had brought him over as part of a huge migration of ex-Phillies to Chicago, he was 3–1 with a 2.35 ERA. He ran up a scoreless streak of thirty and one-third innings, exceeded by one-third of an inning by reliever Les Lancaster in 1989.

"It went from the end of May to the middle of July," he said. "I finally got aware of it after six weeks. What was really ironic was when it was broken, that morning I was doing a weight program and [Bill] Buckner was sitting on the training table, icing and doing what he had to to get ready. He said, 'Y'know, you haven't given up a run for a while. You haven't given up a home run this year.' That day, I got behind Kenny Landreaux 3-and-1. I threw him what I thought was a sinker away, and it ran right over the middle of the plate. He hit it into the first row. It was the only home run I gave up the whole year."

Buckner had jinxed Brusstar, but the latter couldn't rip him too badly. The two had gone to Napa High School together.

Those old central California connections were hard to break. Near the end, Tug McGraw couldn't fully express his thanks for such links. But in the biggest jam of his life, the equivalent of a tie game, bases loaded, nobody out and a 3-and-0 count on the hitter, his old friend Brusstar came through for him.

Author! Author! (Retired)

Why Jim Brosnan hasn't turned his home into a for-profit museum, heaven only knows.

With the exception of twenty-first-century cars on the street in Morton Grove, eighteen miles northwest of downtown Chicago, the surroundings might as well be in the prime of fifties' suburban culture. When a visitor enters Brosnan's home through the basement garage, he immediately sees wife Anne's 1964 white Chevy convertible taking up half of the area, resting on the concrete like a beached whale. The original tires are flat, but the body is in good shape. All the antique job needs is a buyer. In the meantime, Brosnan provides a hint of what's to come by cleaning out five years' worth of old *Sports Illustrated*s from the back seat.

Moving through the door into the house, you go into Brosnan's "hole," in his own words. When Jim and Anne moved into the split-level home in 1957 while he wore the baggy pinstriped flannels of the Cubs, the basement would have been called a "rumpus room." But since Brosnan never adhered to convention, the basement became anything but Eisenhower-era kitsch. He turned it into an author's redoubt.

Now the author's retired, his last copy for hire churned out in the late 1980s. But he's left behind all the tools of his former trade.

Only a Singer sewing machine interrupts the literary train of thought. The bookshelves are crammed with titles, while classics like *Tropic of Cancer* and *The Thin Red Line* interrupt the published volumes of jockocracy. On another bookshelf are periodicals ranging from a 1976 *Playboy* to a similar-vintage *Boys' Life*, a former staple for Brosnan's work. An original Apple computer waits in vain by a wall for a user, while two portable manual typewriters are retired behind the bar. One is an Olympia model, now busted, on which Brosnan pounded out his two seminal works, *The Long*

Season and *Pennant Race*, that ranked as the first realistic chronicles of everyday baseball life.

Brosnan's hole is now his library, but he does not require church-like silence. He can read with noise in the background or with memories dancing about his fertile mind.

"I broke my typewriter," he said. "I did it deliberately. I slammed it down behind the bar. I was pissed off at something. I had written what I had it in me to write. The kids came up to show me how to use a computer. I forgot the next day.

"My story is I have twenty thousand books I've got to read before I die. If you can be a professional reader, that's what I do. The only thing I missed were rare times I turned a good passage in a paragraph or chapter, where it came out exactly the way I wanted to say it."

Brosnan will continue to whittle down his massive reading list in the same house. He has no plans to move, even though he could fetch at least ten times the original sales price of $32,500, a handsome rate back in 1957. Almost all his old neighbors have moved away, replaced by a United Nations crew of residents from Vietnam, Korea, and Pakistan. Retirement villas in Arizona or Florida do not yet beckon the septuagenarian Brosnans.

"I don't mind it," he said of the harsh winters. In fact, when he tires of reading, Brosnan will open up the garage door beyond the antique Chevy and start chipping ice in the driveway.

He has been a rare bird, a ballplayer turned professional writer.

"You don't make enough money for the hours you put in compared to the baseball business," Brosnan said of the lack of athletes following in his wake. "As a baseball player, you put in three, four hours a day. And you're making a helluva lot more money than doing anything else."

But Brosnan was fated to be the eleven-year Cub turned pennant-winning Reds closer who would take the vow of poverty as a writer.

Growing up in Cincinnati, he read the glossed-over, antiseptic books on baseball. And when he became a player himself, he saw the difference.

"The books I read as a kid did not reflect what it was really like in the big leagues," Brosnan said. "I said, 'I could do better than this.'"

During an army stint that interrupted his minor-league career, he took aptitude tests. "They said I would be good as an accountant or writer," he said.

Kicking around book ideas and dabbling in journal writing during the 154-game campaigns as a journeyman Cubs starter eventually resulted in *The Long Season*, a chronicle of the 1958 season in which newly promoted starter Brosnan was traded to the Cardinals a month into the campaign for third baseman Alvin Dark. With the book proceeds due, Brosnan must have felt he was in the pink. Eccentric Cubs owner Phil Wrigley had bumped his salary up to $15,000 when he became a starter. Wrigley apparently felt starting pitchers should command a specific pay scale, hence the $15K. Cards GM Bing Devine, riding herd on beer-baron owner Gussie Busch's millions, was shocked when he saw Wrigley's largesse written into Brosnan's contract.

Brosnan's first book, preceding *Ball Four* by more than a decade, eschewed the lurid and prurient aspects of baseball life. *The Long Season* simply portrayed the on-field rhythms of baseball in a realistic light in a style that all ages could read. Brosnan was bespectacled and pipe-smoking, but he was neither highbrow intellectual nor profane guttersnipe.

"I did not put in foul language," he said. "There was never any doubt my books were written by me. It was a personal language. I never had any sense of cleaning things up. It never would have occurred to me, writing phrases with 'shit' and 'fuck.'"

Fellow author Leonard Schecter, one of the iconoclastic "chipmunk" sportswriters in New York in the early 1960s, ripped *The Long Season* and *Pennant Race*, a similarly styled chronicle of the 1961 Reds' National League title season that Brosnan helped fuel with his best-ever season out of the bullpen.

"He said I should have put eyeglasses on hotel rooms to see who's fuckin' who," Brosnan said of Schecter. "Why? 'Because that's the way they [ballplayers] are,' he said. I said, 'What the hell do you know?'"

Oddly enough, Brosnan was initially discouraged from authorship by adman Arthur Meyerhoff, for whom the pitcher worked in the off-season handling audience research projects. Certainly a Brosnan Cubs-oriented book might have made things sticky for Meyerhoff, who handled the Wrigley Gum Company and Cubs accounts for Phil Wrigley. Meyerhoff's office was in the Wrigley Building, a few floors below the gum magnate's.

Oddly enough, years later—after Brosnan built up a reputation as an author—Meyerhoff suggested he write a biography of Wrigley. Brosnan never undertook the project. If he could have had that decision over again . . .

"I would have been able to find out how much he knew about baseball," Brosnan said of Wrigley. "I would have found out whether he cared one way or another about the game. As a former Cub, I would have asked him key questions."

Soon after his career ended with the White Sox in 1963, Brosnan expanded his media work onto the airwaves. Having liked his books, Howard Cosell invited Brosnan to air some commentaries on the ABC Radio Network. Soon after, Tom Miller, the general manager of ABC-owned WBKB-TV in Chicago, recruited Brosnan to be his main sports anchor for the princely sum of $45,000 a year. Brosnan's top baseball salary was $33,000. "I had made more than Frank Robinson, because I had a better year than he had," Brosnan said with a chuckle.

Teaming with news anchor Frank Reynolds, later headed for ABC network anchor fame, Brosnan dutifully read the scores in black and white telecasts at dinnertime and at 10 PM, only occasionally getting out of the office. On August 19, 1965, he and a film crew raced at midafternoon to Wrigley Field trying to interview Reds pitcher Jim Maloney, who had just no-hit the Cubs in the first game of a doubleheader. Maloney wanted $25 to do the interview, then relented. Brosnan also alighted a jogging cart in a celebrity race on the harness track. With his cameras whirring, Brosnan drove his horse past a cart bearing the rotund figure of *Chicago Tribune* sports columnist David Condon.

Brosnan's TV gig only lasted a couple of years. Going back to writing, he limited his broadcast work in later years to filling in on sportscasts for Red Mottlow, dean of Chicago sportscasters and a pioneer in tape-recording athletes' pre- and postgame locker-room interviews.

Brosnan soon developed a sideline as a reviewer of sports books. He still has strong opinions.

"Roger Angell can't write a bad book; he can't write a bad story," he said. "If you have Roger Angell writing a book, you can rest assured you're going to find something different, something new about the game as he saw it. He would listen to people talk about baseball."

He has very mixed opinions about another famed baseball book author named Roger.

"Roger Kahn's *Boys of Summer* was good," Brosnan said. "For a news reporter who had been hearing a lot of this stuff but didn't put it in the paper, it was good.

"But he's written a couple of bad books, especially one on Pete Rose. I thought he was conned by one of the great con men in the game. I couldn't believe that Roger would fall so low as to believe a guy who from the time I knew him, at age fifteen, I knew he was a con artist from the start. He simply bought what people said, not even questioned it. He had the resources to find out; he could have learned everything."

Brosnan also avidly read Dick Schaap's prolific works but wanted more.

"Dick also was a better reporter in the sense he got the story from people who had the story," he said. "Whether he could turn it into personal prose, his own particular style, where you would have looked at this as written by Dick Schaap, was something else. I don't think he was very good at that. It could have been better if he would have taken some more time. But the guy worked so damned hard about everything and knew everybody or wanted to know everybody."

Two of Brosnan's favorites were Lawrence Ritter's *The Glory of Their Times* ("He has the feel of the old-time players, had their language down") and Luke Saulisbury's *The Answer Is Baseball* ("It's a fan writing about his feelings on baseball"). He also liked *Squeeze Play* by Jane Leavy, later renowned for her Sandy Koufax biography.

Brosnan's favorite pure writer was Red Smith.

"Nobody in the business ever wrote as good as he did," he said. One big seller was merely a compilation of Smith's columns. "But he also wrote a book on fishing," Brosnan said. "If you know fishing, this is one thing that he wasn't going to be able to sell to a magazine or newspaper. It was a very good book about fishing."

So what makes a good writing style for Brosnan the reviewer?

"The writer of a book, if not having done it himself, has to un-

Jim Brosnan. His groundbreaking baseball books flank the typewriter he wrote them on. Author photo.

derstand how it was done," he said. "You don't have to have done it to understand it. Passion is absolutely necessary if you're going to be a memorable writer. You can't knock it out, type it out, without having a feeling for it."

Brosnan had an excess of feeling for baseball, having clawed his way to the majors through a decrepit Cubs farm system starting in 1947. Signing out of high school in Cincinnati, he made a grand total of $125 a month for four months pitching in Class D. "But I got a $2,500 bonus to sign," he said with mock pride. "The next year I made $150 a month, a raise of $25 a month for winning seventeen games."

Brosnan wasn't going anywhere fast by 1953, when he was 4–17 for the Springfield (Massachusetts) Cubs of the International League. But the parent club was so strapped for pitching that he got a spring training invitation. He pitched well and made the club but also saw manager Phil Cavarretta fired before opening day for telling Wrigley he had another lousy club. "I was there in the din-ing room in Dallas where Cavarretta got the news and was fired," Brosnan said.

He was belted around in eighteen games in relief in 1954, went back to the minors, then stuck in the majors for good in 1956. Brosnan pitched decently as a swingman in the rotation and bullpen for a couple of the worst Cubs teams of the fifties before being put in the rotation out of spring training in 1958. He was 3–4 in eight starts with a 3.14 ERA. Soon Brosnan made his escape from Wrigley Field via the Alvin Dark trade. Making too much money for the Cardinals' tastes, he moved on to Cincinnati in 1959, where he was shifted to the bullpen full time. Brosnan was 10–4 with sixteen saves for the '61 pennant winners, providing more grist for his books.

So from the inside out, why was the Cubs organization so putrid at the time?

"They picked the wrong people to teach," Brosnan said. "They had Charlie Root and Morrie Arnovich as minor-league managers. Root was a good pitcher but a terrible manager. Wrigley did not have good people running the ball club and farm system. They were people who needed a job.

"Wrigley had so many other interests. Baseball was something he promised his daddy he'd do. I heard that from Bill Veeck. Wrigley was too willing to listen to his betters, those who had been in baseball, like [Walter] O'Malley. I know this for a fact. Meyerhoff was ready to sell the angle, 'Have a Picnic at Wrigley Field,' as a major point for watching a ballgame. Well, every other ball club in NL is going to have a laugh. They feel they'll have a three-day picnic coming into Wrigley Field. Meyerhoff did not like it.

"'Relax with Wrigley Spearmint gum' was perfect. One, it was good gum. Two, it would make you feel better while you chewed it. That was a great ad campaign for gum. But I don't think Wrigley knew what a quality product on a baseball field was."

"He was a nice man. He could get along with anybody. Max, his chauffeur, would describe him as his best friend. Max would invite him to help him with that big car he drove him in. They'd work on the car together."

At least the Cubs of those dark ages were good for a few laughs. All-time Chicago columnist Mike Royko included Brosnan in his hilarious Cubs quizzes. The question: Which pitcher injured himself warming up and had to leave the game when his uniform shirt got caught in his zipper?

Well, Brosnan did hurt himself just coming into a game, but his fly was not involved.

"I had some worn-down spikes that caught on the rubber," he said. "Royko knew the real story, but the zipper made for a better story."

And as the pitcher turned author, who was Brosnan to argue with a good yarn?

A Lifelong Practitioner of *Wa*

Out in O'Fallon, Missouri, a far northwest suburb of St. Louis, George Altman is a Chicagoan out of place.

To be sure, he's got family in nearby Ballwin. He and his wife, Etta, moved to O'Fallon from the center of the state, in the capital of Jefferson City, a few years back after Etta's mother passed away. But if the truth be known, Altman was out of his realm in his previous go-around in St. Louis, back in 1963, and he always came back to Chicago, where he had served two tours of duty with the Cubs, no matter where he went in the world.

"Eventually I'd like to get back to Chicago," said Altman, still as courteous as ever in his early seventies, the same guy as when he was a hard-hitting outfielder at the dawn of the 1960s.

But what about the infamous winters? Didn't Altman get enough of the windchill and snow when he'd leave the house at dawn to trudge down to the trading pits at the Chicago Board of Trade?

Well, yeah, but now Altman dabbles in the markets on the computer in the warmth—or in the blast of air-conditioning amid a Missouri summer—in the comfort of home. He's always ridden the cutting edge of technology, even fiddling around with electronic chess on his computer.

"I don't have to be outside," he said of returning home and living out the cold.

Big George Altman never has changed. He always knows how to get by and get along. That's the only way he's gotten to where he is, as he always was.

"Adversity sometimes can't be helped, so you go on and do the best you can," he said. "My philosophy is you do what you have to do. Tomorrow is going to be a better day."

Such a stance helped Altman survive Jim Crow in college, the

Negro Leagues, and his early pro baseball career with the Cubs. It helped him through a wacky change in his batting style mandated by the then-senile mahatma Branch Rickey. It kept him going through a whole string of injuries that hurt his career and a bout with colon cancer that threatened his overall health. And it provided him a basis to survive the culture shock of playing in Japanese baseball, where foreigners were tolerated but not welcomed.

Altman learned about the Japanese concept of *wa*, a sense of harmony. The Japanese applied a solitary mind-set of community to the masses, but Altman possesses a certain kind of singular harmony. He should have been a star after hitting .303 and .318 with forty-nine total homers in his two best Cubs seasons. But if life did not turn out the way Altman dreamed, well, you just keep on going and enjoy what you do have.

He certainly did not have peace of mind every day trading bonds and soybeans from 1976 to 1989, in a continuation of the business career he had established in the off-season when he first came to the Cubs in 1959. He had to get out of his soft-spoken persona to survive in the maelstrom of screaming, gesturing traders. "I always did what I had to do," he said.

Altman's six-feet-four frame bailed him out many times. "It helps to see and be seen," he recalled. Old teammate Glenn Beckert made a good buck in the pits, while former Bear George Seals could outphysical Altman with an old defensive lineman's build.

Eventually Altman had to seek out a more peaceful way to move money. He moved to Jefferson City and began trading over the Internet.

"My body can't take the wear and tear of the pits anymore," he said at the time. "It's a mental weardown. It's a frustrating business even in the best of times. With the pushing and shoving, with all the losses you know you will take, you reach a point where you have to get away."

The Altmans found their more peaceful life in Jefferson City. Etta returned to school at Lincoln University, while her husband served as a volunteer hitting coach for the school's baseball team. George traded over the Internet while running a home-based business involved with selling legal services. Active in helping troubled youth back in Chicago, he became a mentor at a local high school and helped in a youth program at his church. Frustrated because

George Altman as a Cub. Photo courtesy of George Altman.

he felt he couldn't make a dent in youth problems in the big-city ghetto back in Chicago, Altman felt he made a modest impact in the smaller city.

Altman just can't forget Chicago. The city was his launching pad to whatever he has done in his life.

He was intertwined with some of the most distinctive names in Cubs history. Signing with the Negro League Kansas City Monarchs when he graduated from Tennessee A&I University in 1955, Altman soon moved into the Cubs organization at the behest of Monarchs manager Buck O'Neil, who was switching to what turned out to be a three-decade-long scouting gig in Chicago. Altman joined Monarchs teammates Lou Johnson, eventually a two-time Cub, and J. C. Hartman.

A stint in military service took two years out of Altman's pro career. But he finally managed to make it to the Cubs in 1959. Altman showed flashes of power, even hitting a crucial homer that knocked the Giants out of the pennant race late in the '59 season. He also made a key catch at the right-field wall in the ninth inning of Don Cardwell's 1960 no-hitter against the Cardinals. But the first of a series of injuries slowed his progress.

"I had never gotten the proper instruction in how to slide," he said. "I used to jam my wrist all the time."

All the while Altman tried to hone his skills in winter ball in Cuba just as Fidel Castro came to power.

"It was a beautiful place," he said. "After games, there'd be dancing in the streets. Castro was at some of the games. Other times he'd give speeches on the radio. We'd go to the game at four, five, six in the afternoon, Castro would be on the radio. After the game he'd still be talking, continuing the same speech."

In 1961, Altman was still a semiregular. After one month, he was thrown into the lineup in Los Angeles against a hard-throwing left-hander: Sandy Koufax. As a minority player in a less-enlightened era, he had to go along even though the strategy seemed wrong.

"I don't know whether it was a case of throwing me to the dogs," Altman said. "But I got lucky. I hit two home runs off Koufax. I stayed in the lineup and was in the groove all season."

Altman was the Cubs' leading run producer in 1961, slugging twenty-seven homers, driving in ninety-six runs, and batting .303. Named to the All-Star team, he slugged a homer off Mike Fornieles in the National League's 5–4 victory at San Francisco.

"Just to be on the field with Willie Mays, Hank Aaron, and Mickey Mantle was a thrill for me," he said. "You're hitting against the best. In those circumstances, you'd be a little nervous and kind of lose your concentration. I was lucky I didn't."

Altman looked to repeat his power numbers in 1962, but his power was curtailed somewhat by the wrist injuries from sliding. Still, he hit twenty-two homers while batting a robust .318. He was the right fielder in a lineup that baseball observers would have stated was a dream order of Hall of Fame–caliber players: Billy Williams in left, Lou Brock in center, Ron Santo at third, and Ernie Banks at first. Kenny Hubbs was NL Rookie of the Year at second base. Problem was, the pitching totally collapsed, and the Cubs had their worst-ever season at 59–103, in ninth place behind the expansion Houston Colt .45s.

Even amid the losing, Altman earned admiration for his production and personality. When the Cubs' player representative job came open, Altman bid for the role and thought he had a majority of support from his teammates. However, word filtered up to the front office. No African American was going to be player rep at this juncture in Cubs history. The edict came back down: white outfielder Bob Will would get the job.

Altman's first Cubs tenure ended soon after the 1962 season. He was dealt to the Cardinals along with pitcher Don Cardwell, with the Cubs getting pitchers Larry Jackson and Lindy McDaniel in return. Altman was welcomed by a Cardinals fandom and management that already was accustomed to African American producers such as Bill White, Curt Flood, and Bob Gibson. With Stan Musial on his last legs, Altman was expected to be the left-handed power bat to fill the gap.

But Branch Rickey, then a meddling senior advisor to Cards owner Gussie Busch, came up with the idea that Altman should change his batting stroke to pull the ball to right, over the short porch into the old Busch Stadium pavilion. Altman had possessed a kind of inside-out hitting style that enabled him to stroke homers into the left- and center-field bleachers at Wrigley Field, a direction always more favorable to power hitters than bucking frequent in-blowing winds in right.

"At first, I ignored it [the pavilion] and hit something like .356," Altman recalled. "Then someone came from the front office and told me to pull to take advantage of the short porch. They told me Mr. Rickey had come up with that idea.

"I started stepping in the bucket. Things fell apart. I regret letting someone talk me [into] something I wasn't capable of doing."

His big-league career was forever changed. Altman dropped to nine homers, forty-seven RBIs, and a .274 average and was shipped off to the woeful New York Mets for 1964. But manager Casey Stengel prematurely put Altman back in the lineup after he suffered a dislocated shoulder on the last day of spring training. Again, he had a subpar year.

But John Holland was persuaded to reacquire Altman. He traded center fielder Billy Cowan to the Mets for Altman. To accommodate the old favorite in left field, Billy Williams was moved out of position to center field for opening day 1965. But the experiment did not last long. Cubs coach Alvin Dark had suggested Altman try to drag bunt. He did one day but tore a hamstring in the process. Thus Altman played only part-time the rest of 1965 and through 1966. He made a few pinch-hitting appearances for the Cubs in 1967 before an unexpected opportunity revived his career, thousands of miles away.

At thirty-four, Altman was offered a spot on the Lotte Orions, a Japanese big-league team. The game was almost the same, by the rules, but he experienced culture shock in and outside the game. It was bad enough trying to squeeze his tall frame into Japanese-style hotels at first. But the very nature of foreigners in the Japanese game was nearly warped. Their numbers were rationed on each team and could not equal or exceed Japanese players' achievements.

"It would be OK for you to be fair," Altman said. "They would walk you. One time I was going for the batting title in August, and the guy behind me was top competition. He was a left-handed hitter. They took the second baseman and put him on the shortstop's side of second base. He went 4-for-4.

"I went along with it. A lot of American players were pampered, used to being number 1, and had a hard time handling this. But dealing with segregation helped me in Japan."

George Altman today at his home in O'Fallon, Missouri. Photo courtesy of George Altman.

"They believe in the *wa*, harmony. I made up my mind—it's their game, their country. You go along with it."

Realizing the proverb that when in Rome, do as the Romans do, Altman learned both batting discipline and physical conditioning in Japan. He practiced swings by using a mirror on his side, to learn not to move his head just before he made contact. And the grueling pregame workouts typical of Japanese big-league teams, then and now, allowed Altman to tune himself up into the best shape of his life as age forty approached. He would end up playing eight seasons and ranking as the top American home-run hitter of the 1970s with 211.

Altman credited the intense physical conditioning with perhaps saving his life when he contracted colon cancer at age forty-three, at the end of his Japanese baseball tenure.

"We had a kamikaze manager who had us doing things physically that seemed ridiculous," he said. "We'd get up in the morning to run. We'd take about half an hour to get ready—in order to get ready to practice. If I had not been doing that strenuous exercise, I might not have been as healthy to handle the cancer."

Altman only wishes he had better conditioned himself earlier in his career. He reasoned he might have avoided some of the debilitating injuries.

"I wish I knew what I know now," he said.

Altman won't complain about any glory being sidetracked. And he won't hang crepe over past health problems. All he had to do was remember the sight of ol' teammate Santo, with whom he met at midseason 2004 while the Cubs visited Busch Stadium. He marveled at how Santo was getting along and going along as Cubs radio color analyst despite losing both legs to diabetes and his bladder to a cancer operation.

"I indicated to him that he's a real bulldog, a fighter," Altman said. "He was that way on the field. The average person would have given up a long time ago. I love Ronnie's attitude. He lives for the Cubs. He loves the Cubs."

So does Altman, despite a career track that should have had more justice to it. But that sense of inner harmony has compensated for any wrongs. Life is on the plus side for Big George.

Selling a Few Fords in His Time

Don Cardwell won't give you the hard sell.
"You tell it like it is and try to be nice to people," he said.

Cardwell prefers to cultivate your long-term relationship, so you come back to him through even economic downturns to buy your company cars.

And you can have any model you want as long as it's a Ford. Cardwell may have moved around from the Phillies to the Cubs to the Cardinals to the Pirates to the Mets and finally the Braves during a fourteen-year pitching career that included an astounding no-hitter in 1960 at Wrigley Field. But once he put on a suit, he was loyal to one brand. He worked for one Ford dealer for the better part of a decade. He's worked for another ever since. Cardwell was good in his no-hitter against the Cardinals, but he's even better as fleet manager of Parkway Ford in Winston-Salem, North Carolina.

And in his line of business, he claims he mainly has to worry about General Motors and not every Japanese import. That's just the way the fleet end of the job, serving businesses, goes.

"It's long established," Cardwell said. "Foreign cars don't get into fleet work. People associate foreign cars with their personal car."

Cardwell has to depend on relationships to carry him through. Layoffs hit North Carolina industries hard since 2000. Companies may not buy as many cars. The area is truly Tobacco Road. R. J. Reynolds, a giant area company, used to buy several thousand cars nationwide before they whacked thousands of employees.

Cardwell can be creative in his dealings, but even a savvy salesman such as himself has limits. He can't allow his dealership to take a bath on fleet sales.

"We know how far we can go [in discounting] not to lose

money," he said. "You look after your people as best you can." And if he can't move his cars to businesses, he'll go the auction route.

The Taurus has been Cardwell's best seller for a long time. But the salesman drives a Winstar. He's also liked the Crown Victoria and LTD station wagon. Any model was fine for him, wife Sylvia, and their three children, now grown. Cardwell now has to figure out enough room in the car to pick up any of his five grandchildren.

He's also glad he's not in the main showroom. Cardwell's been with Ford so long he has the right of free speech.

"I can't get in the new Thunderbird," he said. "It's too small. It's a toy. The old T-Bird was good. It's just a change. Now they've got a Mustang coming out with five hundred horsepower. How many people need five hundred horsepower?"

Cardwell alighted with Ford when Jack Smith, owner of the former Cloverdale Ford dealership, recruited him, Clete Boyer, and basketball player Joe Cunningham to work as salesmen at the dawn of the 1970s. Smith was a big sports fan.

Cardwell liked the work, getting into the fleet end of the business. When Smith left Cloverdale Ford, he gravitated toward the Parkway dealership in 1981.

All throughout his salesman's tenure, he's had to duel forces out of his control. He was peddling land boats when the first gas crisis hit in 1973. Then there were interest rates in the middle and upper teens as 1979 melted into 1980. And the inevitable downturns where a new car was a luxury to most consumers.

But Cardwell always was undaunted. Remember, he used to face the bases loaded, nobody out in a tie game. He couldn't give up then, and won't in the dealership.

"You just make adjustments," he said. "It's not like the world is going to end. Remember, when you leave baseball, a game you've been playing most of your life, your income is zero."

The impact of his baseball background in moving cars isn't as great in Winston-Salem as, say, Chicago. Along with tobacco, the area is a college basketball hotbed. However, there are a few suggestions of a Cubs connection. Cardwell has an old poster of Wrigley Field in his office. Duke coach Mike Krzyzewski is North

Carolina's most famous Chicago expatriate, always wearing his Cubs partisanship on his sleeve.

It's doubtful, though, that most North Carolinians have seen the black and white videotape of Cardwell's no-hitter in the second game of a doubleheader on May 15, 1960. They'd scarcely believe that this mild-mannered salesman was the tough, nearly sidearming right-hander effortlessly mowing down the Cardinals in the gathering shadows of a late Sunday afternoon.

If Cardwell's postbaseball life in Winston-Salem has been solid and steady, the pinnacle of his pitching days was truly sensational. He became the first pitcher to hurl a no-hitter in his first start after being traded to a new team. And he was enveloped in the greatest on-field celebration of fans seen at Wrigley Field since Garry Hartnett's "homer in the gloamin'" in 1938.

Cardwell was a twenty-four-year-old pitcher of some promise in his fourth big-league season when the Cubs, desperately in need of effective starters, traded starting second baseman Tony Taylor and backup catcher Cal Neeman to the Phillies on May 13, 1960. First baseman Ed Bouchee accompanied Cardwell in the deal to Chicago.

He hardly had time to catch his breath coming off the plane from Philadelphia when manager Lou Boudreau told him he'd start against the Cardinals in the nightcap of the doubleheader on May 15. Meanwhile, Sylvia and the couple's young children were left behind in Philadelphia. They had just moved up to the City of Brotherly Love from North Carolina, expecting to spend the summer.

Of course, Cardwell wanted to make a good first impression.

"You get a little nervous since it was your first start," he recalled. "Warming up in Wrigley Field, you're awfully close to the stands. You can almost reach over and shake hands with the fans. You get a little nervous. You want to make sure you don't throw one wild and hit somebody in the stands. You get a little edgy."

Cardwell ran into National League president Warren Giles while both sat on the bench just before he took the mound in the first inning.

"Don and I were there all alone," Giles told Cubs announcer Jack Brickhouse after the game. "I told him, 'You're pitching in a good ballpark, and the wind is for you.' I asked him if he felt strong. He said, 'Yeah, but I've never felt so nervous before. . . . I wish I was out there this minute.' "

Nobody could forecast anything more than a quality performance. A no-hitter, let alone in a new pitcher's first start, sounded preposterous, with doppelganger odds against it.

"The odds were unreal," Cardwell said. "But it's unpredictable with the stuff you have. Sometimes I left the bullpen, you didn't feel great, and I told them, 'You guys hang loose.' Other times, you had great stuff in the bullpen, and you don't do anything in the game."

Cardwell left nothing in the bullpen. He walked Alex Grammas in the first inning. Then he retired the Cardinals the rest of the way as the Cubs staked him to a 4–0 lead against St. Louis starter Lindy McDaniel. Included in the dramatics was a strikeout of pinch hitter Stan Musial to conclude the eighth inning. By now the WGN-TV broadcast crew had requested that the videotape machine back at the Tribune Tower studios be turned on. History was being recorded.

Cardwell lost just a little bit in the ninth, heightening the tension. Pinch hitter Carl Sawatski, leading off the ninth, belted a long drive to right field. George Altman backed up into the vines to make the catch.

"I knew it wasn't going to make it," Cardwell said with a laugh. "A lot of times as a pitcher, you can tell how well a ball was hit. The ball didn't sound like it had enough carry to it. George Altman got back to the warning track, and I said, 'OK, that man's out.' "

George Crowe, another pinch hitter, then flied to Richie Ashburn in center field. That brought up slash-hitting left-handed batter Joe Cunningham. He worked the count to 3-and-1, then thought he drew ball four on a borderline pitch. But it was called a strike. Cunningham squawked briefly, then set himself again in the batter's box. Cardwell delivered, and Cunningham sent a sinking liner toward left field.

"I made a good pitch," Cardwell said. "The ball was sinking, going down and away from Joe. He went right out after it, made contact. Moose, bless his heart, made a great catch coming in. He got a good jump on the ball."

Lumbering left fielder Walt "Moose" Moryn somehow beat the liner to a blade of grass, making a dip-glove catch to complete the no-hitter as he ambled into the infield. Immediately, Cardwell was mobbed by his teammates. Right behind the Cubs players were thousands of delirious fans, having little to celebrate in this dark age of continual losing seasons, swarming onto the field from the box seats or lowering themselves from the bleachers onto the warning track.

Within seconds, Cardwell was being ushered over to the third-base box seats to be interviewed by WGN's Vince Lloyd. However, the happy mob closed in, with only a handful of Andy Frain ushers and WGN-TV assistant director Arne Harris to hold the fans back.

Even from the vantage point of four-plus decades later, the videotape—the oldest of a sports event known to exist—is riveting to watch. Harris, suffering from premature male pattern baldness at twenty-six and with his hairpiece still a few pay raises into the future, yelled at the rooters: "Get out of here. Let him get on the air!" Lloyd, wearing sunglasses, tries to get something out of an obviously stunned Cardwell. "I don't know what to say. I'm just lucky," the crew-cut pitcher had said, out of breath.

Lloyd asked him about facing Musial in the eighth. "I was scared. He's always hit me so good," Cardwell said.

What about Cunningham? "He's too tough to pitch to. He's rough."

How did his fielders help him? "They came up with four good plays on me. They saved me."

When did he know he was throwing a no-hitter? "Some kids [near the dugout] kept telling me I had retired so many in a row."

Cardwell was worried about the jostling he was receiving and wanted to leave. "I tell you, it's getting a little rough," he said to Lloyd. "I don't know what to say. I'm glad the Lord was with me today."

Then he was hustled down the left-field line with a cordon of ushers paving the way. The fans surged toward the corner, where the clubhouse entrance was located, to get a final look at Cardwell.

Up in the broadcast booth, Giles told Brickhouse that the on-field celebration was the best he had seen.

"I have never seen such a demonstration of enthusiasm at a base-ball park, whether it was at a World Series or winning a pennant, than on this field today," he said.

Immediately following Giles on the air was Cubs general man-

Don Cardwell and wife, Sylvia. Author photo.

ager John Holland, doing a rare broadcast interview. Having just traded for Cardwell, the overcoat-and-fedora-clad Holland was beaming. He bragged how Cardwell fit into his "program" of young pitchers that also included Glen Hobbie and Bob Anderson.

Amid the maelstrom of whooping-it-up people, the game ball that Moryn caught was retrieved for Cardwell. He keeps it in a glass case at home today.

Cardwell posed for photos with his teammates in the clubhouse after he was rescued from the fans. But without his family, his celebration away from the ballpark was muted. He simply settled into a rotation slot on a team that was going nowhere. For the rest of the season, Cardwell was 7–14, distinguishing himself only at the plate with five home runs.

He made a decent comeback in 1961. On a team that was 64–90, Cardwell was 15–14 with a 3.82 ERA. But in 1962, he fell back into the losing rut with the rest of the Cubs, chafing under the crazy "college of coaches" scheme, going 7–16 with a 4.92 ERA. This time, the clubhouse was in near mutiny under the martinet rule of head coach Charlie Metro, who ran the team the final two-thirds of the '62 season.

"There's a day off after the All-Star game," Cardwell said. "The whole pitching staff rebelled because the acting manager ran us to death [in a Wrigley Field workout] that day. He ran us foul line to foul line. But we just kept running, and we were determined to outlast him. We were out there forever. He finally told us to go back to the clubhouse." To this day, Cardwell refuses to confirm that acting manager was Metro.

Cardwell can't explain why the Cubs did not develop into a contender with great arms such as himself, Hobbie, Anderson, Dick Ellsworth, and others, along with homegrown players like Altman, Ron Santo, Billy Williams, Kenny Hubbs, and Lou Brock.

"Why didn't we do more?" he said. "It just didn't work out. "I don't know how you can explain it. Pitching in that ballpark in summertime is tough."

Cardwell was packaged with Altman in a deal to the Cardinals on October 17, 1962. Oddly enough, McDaniel, the losing pitcher in the '60 no-hitter, came over from St. Louis along with starter Larry Jackson and catcher Jimmie Schaffer. Cardwell was a Cardinal in name only. A month later, he was relayed to Pittsburgh in yet another deal, this one for shortstop Dick Groat.

He became a journeyman pitcher for both the Pirates and Mets through 1970. As a spot starter with an 8–10 record in '69, Cardwell had a front-row seat for the Mets' amazing late-season charge that swiped the National League East away from a Cubs team that had seemingly escaped the losing doldrums.

"By the first of July, definitely after the All-Star Game, it seemed like everything started to jell," he said of the Mets. "We didn't lose games by errors. We just hung in there and got great pitching. We had Tom Seaver, Jerry Koosman, Gary Gentry, but didn't use Nolan Ryan that much. He had military duty."

Cardwell liked Ron Santo as a teammate and all-around player. But from an opposing player's viewpoint, Santo's postvictory heel-clicking in 1969 was considered a breach of baseball etiquette. Ditto was pitcher Dick Selma's cheerleading of the left-field bleacher bums from the bullpen. Those actions became a motivating factor for Cubs foes.

"The only thing I didn't like was the jumping up in air, clicking heels, and the circuslike thing in the bullpen," he said. "You don't do that." In the end, the Mets finished with a 38–11 kick. The Cubs were 8–18 down the stretch from their season high point. Cardwell does not know if the vanquished team panicked under the pennant pressure.

Cardwell savored his World Series ring but in recent years seems to have regained his Cubs identity. He's been invited back to Wrigley Field for special events and has attended several Cubs conventions. Hey, at the very least, it's a nice short vacation for Sylvia and himself.

"What draws me back?" he said. "Just knowing to myself that I played there. I didn't have a good record, but I enjoyed Chicago. I enjoyed playing those day games."

Walking on the field in recent years, right where he was mobbed in 1960 while talking to Lloyd, Cardwell loved the atmosphere.

"There's a lot of excitement," he said. "They took us on a tour of the ballpark. Our family went up into the center-field bleachers. I'd never done that. It was really something. It was surprising how popular those rooftops were."

The early-twenty-first-century crowds dwarf those of the 1960 season. But on one special day, Don Cardwell prompted a World Series–style celebration in the Friendly Confines. More so than just pitching a no-hitter, he gave Cubs fans a chance to really let loose and experience the kind of joy usually limited to those teams that seem to specialize in postseason success.

An Ol' Lefty's Business-Minded Viewpoint

You'd figure that you'd have an eternal thirst for baseball once you win twenty-two games and sport an ERA of 2.10 during your peak season of pitching for the Cubs.

And even a couple of twenty-loss seasons before and after logically couldn't dampen that kind of sparkle.

Yet once Dick Ellsworth made the clean break from the game at the tender age of thirty-one, he did not look back or long for a comeback or coaching position. He went back home to Fresno, California, and got on with the rest of his life.

Sometimes Ellsworth's still-unmatched numbers as the last Cubs left-hander to win twenty games with the lowest starter's ERA in any season since World War II might come up in conversation. But the flow of words and deeds around Ellsworth is more likely to center on land values around Fresno, the migration of folks from the overcrowded California coastal megalopolises, and wild state politics that now center on a former Terminator.

These days, Ellsworth, senior vice president of the land division of Pearson Realty in Fresno, is part demographics analyzer, part hometown promoter and part middle-American businessman.

"Our area will continue to grow," he said. "The central San Joaquin Valley is projected to be the growth area in all of California for the next ten to fifteen years. The reason is available land and relatively inexpensive land costs. That of itself will generate a lot of housing construction and will promote a migration into the great valley area from other areas of California, where people have realized large equity positions in their homes.

"The baby boom generation is coming into the fold. That segment of society has a lot of spendable income. They are looking for a place to transfer their money. We're experiencing a real migration [from Los Angeles and San Francisco]."

But wasn't the big migration from California *out of state*—to Arizona, Nevada, and other places a few hundred miles or more away from overcrowded freeways, high crime rates, high taxes, earthquakes, and political turmoil? Ellsworth said that population outflow did take place due to "political issues" but that a stabilization is starting to take hold.

How Arnold Schwarzenegger tackles the myriad problems as California governor is not going to alter Ellsworth's decision to come back home to what was in the early 1970s just a smallish agriculture-oriented city off the beaten path.

"As I look back, I made the right decision," he said. "Since moving back to California, I've never been more than seven minutes from my office. I live on a large lot with a big house. We've got great weather, and we're relatively close to major amenities. You've got Yosemite National Park; we are two and a half hours from the ocean, and three and a half hours from LA or San Francisco. And we have an economy that's not dictated by shocking national government mandates or trends.

"Fresno has improved for the better. We've improved in that we're becoming a more diverse society, more diverse economy. We're not so much reliant on the agriculture industry. We're a major health care center and a major business center for central California. Conversely, as a result of that, we've taken on some [urban] problems such as air quality, crime, and [how to house and employ] large numbers of immigrants here because of California's favorable social programs."

Ellsworth's own migration into the business world started long before his career ended.

"In 1966 and 1967, I invested some money in land in the Fresno area," he said. "In one case, I made a handsome profit through use of a broker. But another property developed problems through lack of management and leadership.

"When I moved back to Fresno, my main concern was paying attention to my investment. I kind of got the bug, hanging around with real estate people and attorneys. I enjoyed some memorable experiences in the game. But I made up my mind that if I was going to be successful in anything else, I'd have to play 110 percent into it. I didn't have a college education to fall back on. I entered the real world at thirty-one, when my contemporaries had established themselves in business. I couldn't look back and hang onto something that had passed."

Ellsworth had enjoyed a decade-long career. His son Steve, a six-foot-eight right hander, was 1–6 in seven starts for the 1988 Boston Red Sox.

"He and I made a pact when he was a junior in high school that he would do whatever he wanted—without being in my shadow," Ellsworth said. "I didn't want him to be known as Dick Ellsworth's kid. He wasn't expected to strike everybody out. It took the pressure off him."

But other than following his son's career and applauding the Cubs "because I'm interested and encouraged that they have a front office that is creative enough and committed enough to actually put a good product on the field," Ellsworth's interest in big-league baseball today is, well, tepid.

"My interest in baseball in general, major-league baseball, has waned for the simple reason that to this day, I have a hard understanding why baseball should be show business rather than an extension of the game kids grow up believing in," he said.

But Ellsworth is a supporter of the presence of Triple-A baseball in Fresno.

"My interest in baseball in Fresno doesn't really hinge on the simple fact of the game of baseball but what it does for the community," he said. "A professional baseball team, if delivered correctly to the public and not losing sight of the fact it's a game, can be a major asset to the community."

He wishes former Cubs owner Phil Wrigley had truly realized the impact of a winning Cubs team on the community of fans in Chicago. Ellsworth had to endure some of the darkest seasons in team history, made worse by incompetent management and the chaotic "college of coaches" program. He was one of a slew of Cubs called up at a too-young age with a lack of experience, who then left to try to find their way on the job in the majors.

Ellsworth had been signed out of Fresno High School in 1958. One of his prep teammates was future Cincinnati Reds fireballer Jim Maloney, then mainly a shortstop. "Jim would pitch on the side, pitch in games when we ran out of pitchers," Ellsworth recalled.

Directly out of high school, Ellsworth, whose specialty was a sinking fastball, was called up to the Cubs to pitch in the annual Boys Benefit exhibition game against the White Sox at Comiskey Park. Activated briefly on an injury-riddled staff, Ellsworth made one 1958 start, going just two and one-third innings and allowing four runs before being sent back to the minors.

Still only twenty, Ellsworth joined the rotation in 1960, going 7–13. He was 10–11 in 1961, then a horrible 9–20 with the losingest Cubs team in history in 1962.

"In 1962, when I was 9–20, I reminded everyone it was a team sport," he said. "As I looked at my stats for that year, it was hard for me to understand how I lost twenty games."

But suddenly the 103-loss stumblebums of '62 perked up. The Cubs were like an entirely different team in 1963, actually playing spirited, fundamentally sound baseball. Their only drawback was a slew of offensive holes in the lineup after third baseman Ron Santo, an early Ellsworth road roommate, and left fielder Billy Williams. Ernie Banks was ineffective or inactive most of the second half due to illness, helping drop the team batting average to .238.

A final 82–80 record could have been eight to ten games better with even an average lineup. The Cubs still managed to contend until mid-August. The pitching staff's ERA was 3.08, second in the National League to the vaunted Dodgers of Sandy Koufax and Don Drysdale. No Cubs staff since had such a low ERA.

Helped by a high mound and the more generous strike zone of the time, Ellsworth was the major beneficiary of the 1963 upsurge. Employing a newly developed slider to go along with his sinker, he amassed a 22–10 mark that included one of the best innings-pitched-to-hits ratios in modern Cubs history—290 2/3 innings, 223 hits. Most astounding was his 2.10 ERA. Among Cubs starters in the ensuing four-plus decades, only Greg Maddux in 1992 has come close to that mark with 2.18 during his Cy Young Award season. Next were Mark Prior with 2.43 in 2003 and Bill Hands with 2.49 in 1969.

Ellsworth once again emphasized teamwork for his success in '63. He was close to fellow top starters Larry Jackson and Bob Buhl.

"I don't think a day went by in Wrigley Field that I and at least four other pitchers, along with the catcher and Ron Santo, sat in the clubhouse for an hour after the game," he said. "Win or lose, we talked about the game, critiqued what happened. And on the road, the pitchers were together—we sat in the lobby together and had dinner together. On off days, we'd charter fishing boats.

"It was invaluable to me, coming off a bad, losing season. My mind was wide open. Everyone was sincere in helping each other. I sense there isn't that togetherness today. The last thing in the world we talked about was salaries."

For one of the few times in postwar Cubs history, the team had the right pitching coach and manager for the right group of players. Fred Martin, who a decade later taught the split-finger fastball in the minors to a struggling Bruce Sutter, was the staff's guru.

"Fred Martin constantly talked about how important it was to change speeds and have a good change-up," Ellsworth said. "Bob Kennedy [then labeled "head coach"] demonstrated he was going to be a players' manager. We knew he was going to be there all year after all the problems with the rotating coaches. He was a competitor, thought pitching was important, and I think he elevated the pitching staff's self-esteem."

By now Ellsworth and his young family had settled down in north suburban Morton Grove, just a couple of blocks from pitcher–author Jim Brosnan, whose daughter baby-sat for the Ellsworths. During the off-season he handled public relations and promotions for the Serta Mattress Company, a Cubs broadcast sponsor. Ellsworth's Cubs salary soon would top out at $32,000, decent money for the mid-1960s. The future seemed bright.

But by midseason 1964, the outlook dimmed again. In the previous off-season, promising second baseman Kenny Hubbs was killed in the crash of his private plane. Lou Brock was traded on June 15 for pitcher Ernie Broglio, whose elbow was about to blow up. And Ellsworth's 10–6 start in '64 was about to turn around quickly. He developed tendinitis in his elbow. With the exception of Jackson's twenty-four-win season, the Cubs' pitching went south in the second half. Ellsworth finished 14–18 with a 3.75 ERA.

He suffered a repeat in '65. Starting off 12–6, he again was afflicted with tendinitis but continued to make his starts. Ellsworth ended up '65 with a 14–15 mark.

"I was disappointed that I couldn't put together a full year of

Dick Ellsworth. Photo courtesy of Dick Ellsworth.

quality pitching. The slider caused tendinitis. When I quit throwing the slider, the problems went away. I'd get off to good starts, then it would hurt. But you kept on pitching—you didn't go on the disabled list. You weren't guaranteed anything then."

Some of Ellsworth's best efforts went unrewarded. On May 15, 1965, Ellsworth took a no-hitter into the bottom of the eighth against the Dodgers in Los Angeles. Leading 1–0, with two runners on base, Al Ferrara slugged a three-run pinch homer for the only hit off Ellsworth in the eventual 3–1 loss. The tough-luck loss took place on the Cubs' first trip to Dodger Stadium. During their third visit—September 9—fellow Cubs lefty Bob Hendley also allowed just one hit but lost 1–0 when Sandy Koufax threw a perfect game.

His pitching life only got worse in Leo Durocher's first year as manager in 1966. With the Cubs headed for another 103-loss season, Ellsworth never had a first-half surge. He was 5–18 and hopeless, ending up with a postwar-worst 8–22 record, 3.98 ERA, and 321 hits allowed in 269 1/3 innings. He endured two pitching coaches, Durocher warhorse "Fat Freddie" Fitzsimmons, who was replaced midway by veteran Robin Roberts, doubling as a coach in the last season of his career.

"Leo intimidated a lot of everyday players," Ellsworth said. "The wheels fell off the wagon that year. It was a big transition year. If you were a pitcher on the ball club, you weren't going to benefit. It wasn't the focus. It was trying to get people together again."

Few left-handers ever followed Ellsworth long-term into the Cubs rotation. Ken Holtzman and Rich Nye held forth in 1967–1968. Steve Trout was 13–7 for the 1984 NL East champions, while soft-tossing Greg Hibbard surprisingly won fifteen games in 1993. Terry Mulholland pitched competitively in 1997–1999. But the Cubs simply have not had any tradition of effective left-handed starters since Ellsworth's best year and Holtzman's back-to-back seventeen-win seasons in 1969–1970.

Former Cubs official Blake Cullen studied the issue when he served as assistant general manager in the early 1970s. Cullen believed lefties were far more hittable in Wrigley Field in the way they came off the mound in their deliveries, permitting a good hitting background.

"My theory doesn't relate to background as much as weather," Ellsworth said. "The weather runs in cycles. I firmly believe in the years I pitched in Wrigley Field, the wind was more of a negative factor. It blew out more to left or left-center."

The ballpark could not have been the deciding factor in the end. After spending the 1967 season in Philadelphia following a trade for right-hander Ray Culp, Ellsworth had proof in 1968. He moved on to the Boston Red Sox and should have been battered in Fenway Park, a graveyard for left-handed pitchers. But he had a revival season in '68 with a 16–7 record and 3.03 ERA.

"The year I spent in Boston with the Green Monster over my shoulder, I broke more bats because right-handed hitters were leaning out over the plate to jerk the ball over the monster.

"When you play in Wrigley Field, the other team has to play there, too. I figure when you walk out there, it's even. If you play on grass, it doesn't matter if the fences are three-hundred- or five-hundred-feet deep. If you keep the ball on the ground, you'll win the majority of your games."

Oddly enough, Culp, who quickly fell out of favor with Durocher in less than a full season in 1967, joined Ellsworth as a Red Sox teammate in 1968. Culp was 16–6 that season, then went on to rack up back-to-back seventeen-victory seasons in 1969–1970.

Ellsworth's career petered out as a reliever with the Cleveland Indians and Milwaukee Brewers between 1969 and 1971. It was time to find another career and decompress from a baseball life.

Yet the ol' lefty cannot forget two fellow pitchers, one during his time and another from the viewpoint of televised games.

"The greatest ballplayer I have seen in my life was Sandy Koufax," Ellsworth said. "He had a greater impact of any player, pitcher or anyone, that I ever saw. It was a thrill to pitch against him."

Fast forward to a control-maniac right-hander and fellow homegrown Cub.

"People asked me, 'How do you relate to today's pitchers, guys who throw five hundred miles per hour?'" Ellsworth said. "I've told them consistently over the years that the guy who gives you the greatest value for your ticket is Greg Maddux. He's a pitcher, not a thrower. He truly matched his intellect with the game of baseball."

Like Maddux, Ellsworth signed right out of high school and did not have a college education but possessed much of the same baseball intellect. The difference was the support system. He's made up for what he didn't get in baseball in the eternal value of land in the big valley.

A Transition from Hard Work

Y ou can easily forgive Glen Hobbie if he spends a month in spring training in Mesa, Arizona, lounging around his motel swimming pool before he ambles out to watch the Cubs play at nearby HoHoKam Park.

"That breaks up the monotony of winter," Hobbie said. He's put in his time on the job, be it baseball or business, surviving all the physical and emotional stresses that finally ended in his retirement as a factory manager in 1996.

And when Hobbie gets back home to a farm in Ramsey, Illinois, near downstate Vandalia, don't push him to get in his car to make the nearly hour drive to St. Louis to watch big-league games. Been there, done that from the inside out. Hobbie likes his present-day vantage point just fine. Remember, he doesn't really care for big urban centers after growing up in the hamlet of Witt, population eleven hundred, and then residing in the bigger town of Hillsboro, with forty-five hundred souls, while he was in business.

"Some people couldn't stand being out of the city," Hobbie said. "I'm one who didn't like being in the city. I don't go to St. Louis for games, and I haven't been back to Chicago for years. I can sit in the living room and watch my sixty-inch TV set in my big chair and not fight any crowd and not worry about beer spilling. The ballpark's not as comfortable as that air-conditioned house.

"If I was twenty years younger, I'd like to go there [Busch Stadium]. But I don't live in a traffic environment. I don't enjoy driving in a traffic environment. Around here, if I see five cars in ten miles, that's traffic."

The home stand now is rural and quiet for Hobbie and wife Sharon.

"We bought a 288-acre farm," he said. "We have six acres of yard. We rent out the farm ground. I usually get a few head of cattle each spring, and I also have a thirty-acre hayfield I mess with."

Life now is the antithesis of his baseball days, when Hobbie was one of the most tireless Cubs pitchers in history. You want a workhorse who could make thirty-three starts and thirteen relief appearances all in the same 1959 season? Hobbie raised his arm to answer the call, albeit sometimes reluctantly and with the attendant aches and pains. And he kept pitching even after that arm and back had given out, his busy big-league career finally flaming out at age twenty-eight.

That meant Hobbie spent far many more years of his life in business than baseball. That business fortunately at the start was close to his native stomping grounds halfway between St. Louis and Springfield, Illinois. His job as manager of the Roller Derby Skate Corporation, quartered in Litchfield, Illinois, was both a blessing and something else. He'd help midwife the rise of in-line skating while later on he'd be in the unenviable position of telling many of his neighbors they no longer had jobs.

Hobbie's postbaseball journey began through a relationship with a former minor-league teammate who headed up Roller Derby Skate Corporation in Litchfield, population sixty-five hundred. The factory was Litchfield's bellwether employer, with 750 workers on the payroll at its peak. More jobs existed in the factory than at the Allis Chalmers plant to the north in Springfield. Hobbie became plant manager.

"We made roller skates, roller blades, hockey skates, and one time even baseball spikes—Stan Musial brand spikes," Hobbie said. "They were cheapies, low end."

The boom on Hobbie's watch took place a decade after he started. Roller-skate wheels had long been made with a clay compound, then a rubber-clay compound. At some point the designers thought of constructing wheels with a eurothane compound.

"The eurothane acted as a shock absorber, but you still have the speed," he said. "It has a tremendous grip on asphalt and concrete. Between the eurothane wheel and the molded upper, it made roller-blading practical. Otherwise, not too many people could stand the stress on the ankles. It's like having your ankle in a cast once you're laced up."

Roller Derby Skate Corporation rode the boom of in-line skating throughout the 1980s. Then came globalizations, and a slew of foreign countries were able to manufacture goods at the same quality but with much cheaper labor costs. The 1990s may have been good economically in many places but not to the workers in Litchfield.

"We went from a manufacturing to an import–export company," Hobbie said. "All of our lines became manufactured in Taiwan, then shipped to our warehouses. We broke orders down to ship to Wal-Mart, KMart, and Sears, wherever."

The wave of layoffs was steady and nearly complete. Plant employment eventually dropped to just twenty. As management, Hobbie survived but also had to deliver the bad news.

"Some were your neighbors," Hobbie said. "You're talking about foreign workers making about $1 or $2 a day versus our crew making $14 an hour in a unionized operation. What's the solution? If I knew the long-term solution, I'd be in Washington, D.C. Many of your competitive companies do the same thing. They're forced to. If you're charging $4, $5, $6 more for your product than your competitor, you're not going to make many sales."

"It was very rough. The layoffs went in stages, by seniority and divisions. You'd post the list of names, that two weeks from today

Glen Hobbie. Author photo.

will be their last day. It's a job you have to do. Of course you have to worry about it. I got several people hired [elsewhere]. The good workers I had, I said, 'If you need a recommendation, have them call me.'"

There were some silver linings for the unemployed in Litchfield. Hobbie said several other smaller companies' employment rolls increased, absorbing some of his factory's laid-off workers. One was Shutt, a manufacturer of NFL player helmets. A brake-parts manufacturer also stepped up hiring.

Hobbie could not have related his baseball experiences to those of business. He did not experience that sense of rejection felt by many of his old teammates at some point in their baseball careers. He had a good, long run with the Cubs in an unstable era from 1957 to 1964 after being purchased for $85,000 from Double-A Memphis in 1957. Only after he was traded to the St. Louis Cardinals two weeks before the infamous Lou Brock deal, then optioned down to the minors before the Cards' memorable '64 pennant drive, did Hobbie see the dark side of the baseball merry-go-round.

Possessed of a hard, sinking fastball, Hobbie was one of the quartet of good arms the Cubs brought up in the second Eisenhower administration. By 1958, all four were on the parent club. Joining him were Dick Drott, Moe Drabowsky, and Bob Anderson. Problem was, all broke down physically at young ages. The quartet's members were not healthy at the same time. Of the group, which broadcaster Jack Brickhouse called "our horses," only Hobbie had the only truly long run as a Cub—the better part of eight seasons.

Hobbie's rubber arm was one good reason why old Cubs management warhorse Clarence "Pants" Rowland signed him after watching him pitch at Memphis. With Rowland in the stands, Hobbie started game 1 of a doubleheader, then relieved in the nightcap. Cubs manager Bob Scheffing figured he could get more of the same double-duty from Hobbie once he came to the Cubs. In 1958, his first full Cubs season, he appeared in relief thirty-nine times, made sixteen starts to fill in for an injured Drott and Drabowsky, and came away with a 10–6 record and 3.74 ERA. That earned him a rotation spot—and more—in 1959.

Hobbie estimated his hard sinker was between ninety and ninety-five miles per hour. Scheffing and successors Charlie Grimm and Lou Boudreau desired too much of a good thing. In

1959, Hobbie made thirty-three starts and was 16–13 overall. He also came in relief thirteen times, recording one of his baker's dozen of defeats. Then, in 1960, Hobbie started thirty-six times while relieving on ten more occasions. He was 16–20 overall, his loss total leading the National League. In relief, Hobbie was 2–3 with one save. In the two seasons, he totaled twenty-six complete games.

"I actually thought I pitched better baseball in 1960 than the year before," he said. "I had all the pitches working—fastball, curve, changeup."

He turned in macho performances in an even more macho game than today.

"I remember one game in Milwaukee. I was told to knock Henry Aaron down," Hobbie said. "That was the last thing I wanted to do. He was hitting .120. We woke him up, and it was a much harder out."

At first, Hobbie found out he actually was better throwing in relief appearance between starts.

"I would find games where I pitched in relief after I started, I had better stuff than the game I [started]," he said. "But it wouldn't last long. For thirty, forty, fifty pitches, I had better stuff. The next start, I was fine. You didn't tell them when you pitched; they told you what you'd do.

"I pitched against St. Louis on a Friday, went eight innings and got beat 2–1. Then I came back on Sunday and shut them out 1–0. That's a lot of pitches in three days. The Sunday game, I walked into the ballpark, and Scheffing threw me the ball and said, 'You're pitching.' I said fine. Somebody was probably hurt. I wanted to get on the mound any time I could."

"What it does is it burns you out on the game. You're better off getting away from it."

Recalling his annual workload, Hobbie said today's pitchers can display their best stuff in shorter bursts.

"These kids today don't have to pitch more than six or seven innings," he said. "They turn everything loose for six or seven innings and don't have to pace themselves. They come to the big leagues prepared as well as anyone. We were exposed to throwing hard, and that was it."

Watching his old team blow the 2003 National League Championship Series to the Florida Marlins, Hobbie had some sharp flashbacks watching young Marlins ace Josh Beckett stifle the Cubs. Beckett spun a complete-game two-hit shutout in game 5, then came back with two days' rest to throw four innings in relief in the clinching game 7.

"It scared me when I knew Beckett was going to pitch," Hobbie said. "He reminded me so much of the old pitchers because he'd come back with better stuff [in relief]. He was on a roll and throwing the ball so smooth he could have thrown the ball forever. It was a reminder. Take a guy like Warren Spahn. He was so smooth throwing the ball—look at his career, he never got injured."

Eventually the starting–relieving load took its toll on Hobbie. Though he believed he'd soon be the "best right-handed starter in the league" after his 1960 season, such a goal was postponed forever when his body began breaking down in 1961. He experienced lower-back pain, above his right hip. He could not properly follow through in his delivery to keep his sinker down in Wrigley Field.

On a West Coast road trip, Hobbie visited Dr. Robert Kerlan, the Dodgers' team physician and a pioneer in modern sports medicine. Kerlan suggested he lay off pitching for awhile to rest the back. But when he returned home, Hobbie instead got a cortisone injection in his back from the Cubs' team physician.

The cortisone did not last his entire start. To compensate for the pain, Hobbie changed his delivery. He injured his shoulder. "It hurt like a toothache," he said.

But, like most of his teammates, he continued to pitch through pain and declining effectiveness. The alternative was to not pitch at all, a hazard in an era of one-year contracts.

"After the first few years I had in Chicago, you'd figure they'd be concerned," Hobbie said. "But they thought of me like a piece of meat. Today, they would have had enough money invested in me to have not taken those kind of chances. If I'd have been on the disabled list for fifteen days, I'd have been fine. But then, the credo was to pitch. You felt you were going to lose your spot.

"Then, you had to play through injuries. Now they take care of injured players much better."

Gradually moving out of the front of the rotation and finding himself with even more bullpen duty, Hobbie declined to 7–13 with a 4.26 ERA in 1961 and 5–14 with a 5.22 ERA in 1962. He had a minor uptick at 7–10 and a 3.92 ERA in 1963, but his days in Wrigley Field were numbered. An 0–3 mark in eight games (four starts) in 1964 led to his trade to St. Louis.

Despite his injury track, Hobbie enjoyed his time in the majors, even if he had to battle that Chicago traffic in the rush hour going to and from Wrigley Field. Now, from the comfort of his easy chair in front of that giant-screen TV, he's a happy armchair analyst. That back and shoulder pain is consigned to another era.

"Most of the fun is thinking along with the pitchers," Hobbie said. "I loved watching [Greg] Maddux and [Mark] Prior, who pitches like a twenty-year veteran.

"If the pitching staff the Cubs assembled today lives up to their potential, it could be one of the best pitching staffs of the last twenty years."

They might have said similar things way back when about Hobbie, Drott, Drabowsky, and Anderson. Their arms were ahead of their time and way ahead of the team's Dr. Sawbones medical care of the day.

Plastics Is the Way to Go

Surely, Bob Anderson didn't take his hint from the movies. But he could have.

In *It's a Wonderful Life*, Jimmy Stewart, in the guise of George Bailey, is happy his brother is bringing home a new bride—and chagrined that Harry Bailey has also been offered a job in the booming plastics industry by his new father-in-law. Yeah, plastics, the way to go in the 1930s to beat a job at the Bailey Building & Loan.

Move the clock forward about thirty-five years. Dustin Hoffman, playing a Benjamin Braddock getting an advanced degree in life in *The Graduate*, is told that plastics is the future; plastics is a great career.

Now, in real life early in the twenty-first century, Anderson knows that plastics is his path to a good day's work at an age when others are counting minutes to the "early bird special." His blue-collar roots in Hammond, Indiana, and remembrances of long outings on the mound both in the rotation and bullpen at Wrigley Field between 1957 and 1962 have molded him in his present direction.

By no means a retiring guy with his seventieth birthday rushing up fast, Anderson is general manager of sales of Insul-vest, a manufacturer of insulation for the plastics industry. A twenty-nine-year tenure in sales of steel products for autos, railroad cars, construction, and hardware for Inland Steel in Tulsa, Oklahoma, followed by dabbling in sales of nutritional supplements did not provide an entrée to later-in-life idleness. And when you played before the real big jackpot in pensions, drawing around $1,100 a month, you want to keep working as long as possible.

"I tried retiring [for a year and a half]," Anderson said. "But I like to keep busy. It's a heck of a lot more fun being busy. I can't see myself playing golf every day. I would like to work well into my seventies. I'll work 'til my wife [Sherry] says it's time to stop."

The process of networking brought him in touch with his present gig. He has to learn a whole new mind-set compared to his steel-industry days. And it's just as hot.

"We're injection-molding magnesium, at temperatures of eleven hundred degrees," he said. "It's ever evolving. Plastics has replaced a lot of steel [in manufacturing]. And there is increasing foreign competition. There is a lot in China."

Having worked for several decades in the now-battered domestic manufacturing sector, Anderson sees the United States becoming "more and more a service country. The U.S. is paying the price of being the fastest-growing industrial nation in the world. We now have Third World industrial nations going through the agony of growth.

"The World Bank funds the building of steel mills in these countries. We're being penalized for being leaders of the world, inventing everything."

So where is U.S. industry going?

"You will see specialized trends in manufacturing," Anderson said. "But the thing that frightens me is the wage scale overseas. Prices in China are so extremely cheap."

Anderson first settled in Kansas City after his career ended, then moved down to Tulsa while working for Inland Steel.

"I've grown to love Tulsa," he said. "It's a really clean city. We've got a lot of friends in the area. It's not nearly as busy as Chicago."

Anderson knows all about the pace of life in Chicago, having spent all but one of his baseball seasons as a Cub as one of a well-rated group of hard-throwing pitchers coming up in between 1956 and 1958. Announcer Jack Brickhouse had called Anderson, Glen Hobbie, Dick Drott, and Moe Drabowsky "our horses." But they were horses that all came up lame. All developed arm trouble, their potential never fully realized in Wrigley Field.

But the future still seemed bright for Anderson in 1959. In his first full year in the Cubs rotation, he had the pleasure of playing just thirty miles from his native Hammond, just across the state line from Chicago. He thus earned the nickname "Hammond Hummer" after his birthplace and crackling fastball. When he did not feel like driving in those more innocent days, Anderson would hop the South Shore interurban train into the Loop, walk two blocks to the subway, and catch the "L" to Wrigley Field.

Anderson's most high-profile moment came in a "baseball is a funny game" moment on June 30, 1959. In an otherwise humdrum Cardinals' 4–1 victory over the Cubs, he triggered the comic side-show by inadvertently putting a second ball into play. It was the only time two baseballs were seen on the field in memory.

With one out in the fourth inning, Anderson threw an inside pitch to Stan Musial on a 3-and-1 count. The ball bounced away from catcher Sammy Taylor toward the screen.

"The way Stan batted, it looked like he was peeking around a corner," Anderson said. "It looked like he was nearly checking his swing all the time, his bat was moving so much."

Musial started trotting to first base with his walk. But Taylor and Anderson began disputing with plate umpire Vic Delmore that the ball had ticked Musial's bat. Nobody called time. At the urging of the Cardinals' bench, Musial rounded first and headed for second.

Absentmindedly losing track of the original ball, Delmore pulled a ball from his pocket and flipped it to Anderson. Catching sight of Musial's dash for second, the pitcher wheeled and threw, but the ball flew over Cubs second baseman Tony Taylor's head.

"It was just a reaction," Anderson recalled. "I threw the ball toward second. Then I saw another ball coming over our heads from behind the plate."

The original ball was touched by both public address announcer Pat Pieper and batboy Bob Schoenfeldt before Cubs third baseman Alvin Dark picked it up. Dark fired it on one hop to shortstop Ernie Banks, covering second as Musial slid in. Seeing the wild first ball sail into center, Musial picked himself up to head for third but was tagged out by Banks.

Cardinals manager Solly Hemus and Cubs manager Bob Scheffing argued for twenty minutes with the umpiring crew headed by Al Barlick. When play resumed with Musial ruled out, Hemus charged out of the dugout to announce he was playing the game under protest. WGN-TV taped the Keystone Kops affair for replay on their late news, but the video record soon disappeared. Too bad.

"A comedy of errors," Anderson said. "Only with the Cubs at that time could something like that happen."

The defeat proved the difference in reaching a .500 season for Anderson. He was 12–13 finishing 1959, then was 9–11 in 1960 for a 60–94 Cubs team.

He was hearty on both the mound and at the dinner table.

"Bob was something," teammate Jerry Kindall said. "He could eat. We'd go out to dinner, and he'd have three milkshakes at one sitting."

In 1961, Anderson was moved to the bullpen.

"I already had two years' worth of starting," he said. "They had pitched Don Elston every day, practically three innings at a time, and he couldn't do it anymore. They asked me to relieve, and I did it.

"I wanted to pitch, sure. But in those days if they asked you to do something, it was like telling you. The worst decision I made was to pitch in relief."

Managers, or in this case the head coach in the crazy "college of coaches" Cubs scheme, sure knew how to abuse their pitchers then. In one stretch, Anderson went three innings for a save, four innings for a win, and three innings for another save.

They were asking for trouble. Anderson had cortisone shots in his elbow after the 1959 season.

In one August 1961 series in Pittsburgh, Anderson thought he had Roberto Clemente struck out on a 1-and-2 pitch that Clemente had taken. But the umpire missed the pitch.

"I had to throw another pitch," Anderson said. "It was a fastball on the inside of the plate. I jammed him and got Roberto out. I felt something in my shoulder, a sensation, not pain. I think the handwriting was on the wall."

Two days later, while Anderson warmed up, he felt like "someone had jabbed a hot poker" in his shoulder. After another three-inning stint, he did not pitch for several weeks. Cubs management told him a visit to the doctor wasn't needed.

Every time he pitched from that point forward, Anderson felt a "tug" in his shoulder. The life in his fastball was gone. He finished 1961 at 7–10 with a 4.26 ERA, then was ineffective in 1962 with a 2–7 mark and 5.02 ERA. Traded to the Tigers, he was finished at twenty-eight in 1963.

Since he didn't exercise his shoulder, the old injury did not hurt him—until he was examined by a doctor for a strained left shoulder suffered while golfing thirty years later. Mentioning the old injury, the doctor pushed at the area, driving Anderson to the floor.

"It was my rotator cuff," he said. "That's what I had hurt in 1961."

But with sports medicine not even in its infancy, while a macho attitude toward pain prevailed among both players and management, such an injury was career ending.

No matter. Anderson left baseball happy for the experience, possessing few regrets, and went to work. And still works, an enthusiastic plastics man who will always remember baseball.

"I still have fondness for Wrigley Field and the Cubs," he said. "Everywhere I went, there were Cubs fans. It's absolutely amazing. There's not a ball club around, except maybe the Yankees, that has that many fans."

Life after Infamy

E rnie Broglio isn't alone in his scapegoat status.

He knows all about a good soul named Steve Bartman, a fan doing the right thing but in the wrong place at the wrong time. Longtime Cubs rooters figure Broglio and Bartman are "Killer Bs"—infamous names in Cubs history who helped steer their beloved team way offtrack.

Bartman expected to attend game 6 of the 2003 National League Championship Series to cheer on his Cubs and have a good time. But his life changed forever with an inopportune deflection of a foul ball. Similarly, Broglio expected to round out a quality Cubs rotation and push the North Siders toward contention when he was traded from St. Louis on June 15, 1964. Yet his right elbow soon turned to mush. Meanwhile, the man for whom he was traded, Lou Brock, sparked the Cardinals to a World Series triumph, did not stop running and hitting for another fifteen years, and punched an express ticket to the Hall of Fame.

"I don't think anything will ever take me off the hook for that deal," Broglio said. "As long as Lou and I are alive, they'll always make that comparison."

Even with the pall of being a scapegoat—as unfair as it is—hanging over your head, you have to go on with your life. Broglio's big-league career ended two years after the Brock deal, his surgery-scarred elbow never totally bouncing back. He did not continue in baseball as a coach or manager. But even as he worked unloading kegs in a beer distributor's warehouse near his San Jose, California, home, Broglio began giving back to a game that had given him both fame and infamy.

Broglio knew how to pitch, knew how to snap off one of base-ball's best curveballs in the early 1960s before his career went bad all at once in Cubs pinstripes. So he began coaching kids, first as an assistant baseball coach at Saratoga High School in San Jose. Lately, he's gone out on his own, conducting private lessons and teaching at baseball camps.

But Broglio didn't stop there. Putting on an inventor's cap for the first time in his life, he tinkered with materials to come up with a "throwers' arc" to aid in teaching proper mechanics.

"It's two [plastic] PVC pipes, with a thirty-degree and twenty-degree bent," Broglio said. "You set it on a tripod, and you can raise the arms up and down depending on the pitcher's height. His arm comes through the arc. The goal is to keep weight back and keep the arm in an L-position as it comes up through the arc.

"I got tired about preaching about how to throw the ball. So I had to come up with something [three dimensional]. It's a five-lesson program."

Broglio tried to work the throwers' arc into his circuit of youth instruction. Most of the camps are indoors and are run with former pro pitcher Roger Samuels. Camp size ranges from as few as twelve students all the way to between forty and sixty.

"I teach the change-up and the cutter," Broglio said. "The slider causes damage to the elbow, and the splitter is tough to master. I got into it because I got tired of kids getting hurt in Little League. And I got tired of looking at coaches who did not know how to instruct."

Raised in the old school, Broglio does not like the twin features of early-twenty-first-century pitching: pitch counts and the radar gun.

"It puts a lot of thoughts in kids' minds about throwing hard [at the expense of proper mechanics]," he said. "It's made worse because you've got parents and coaches who don't understand the correct procedure of throwing the ball."

"Years ago, the philosophy was 'the more you throw, the stronger you get.' You never heard of some of those injuries they have now. Why do they preach long toss to strengthen your arm? Nothing strengthens your arm as much as throwing the ball off a mound. I watched Barry Zito's workout, and it's not good. He starts out in center field. He starts off wrong, and it gets worse."

Broglio's model pitcher is Cubs ace Mark Prior. "He throws the ball exactly the way I taught," he said. "It's not herky-jerky. It's a great mechanical delivery."

Broglio does not like to attend games at the two Bay Area ball-parks in San Francisco and Oakland. The center-field camera gives him a better view of the pitchers. And he has long written off the idea of getting up close and personal with pro pitchers.

"The major-league teams have their own people," he said. "I've been out of the [organized] game too long. Their philosophy is not the same as mine. Pitching [instruction] is done from the front offices, where they map out the program for the minor-league kids. I had talked to some of the San Jose Giants pitchers and expressed my thoughts, but they had never heard of them."

If only Broglio knew then what he knows now.

Pitchers of the early postwar era commonly worked through pain. They were under pressure to maintain their rotation spots, with eager minor leaguers hoping to grab an $8,000 or $10,000 salary—a bump up from bush-league paydays—to take their place. Sports medicine also was far more primitive. A pitcher commonly worked 'til he totally broke down. Surgeons would then do as much damage as they purportedly were correcting when they'd cut open an elbow or shoulder; arthroscopic surgeries were still a distance in the future.

"You always tried to hide everything you could, because you never knew who was waiting to take your position," Broglio said. "You didn't do it to jeopardize your career. You did it to get that ball every fourth day as a starting pitcher."

Broglio's career no doubt took this path of cumulative injuries and a pitcher's macho denial. An original San Francisco Giants product, he was dealt to the Cardinals on October 8, 1958. Snapping off that curve with brutal efficiency, he was 21–9 with a 2.74 ERA in 1960 in St. Louis. A dip to 9–12 the next season was followed by a 12–9 mark in 1962. Broglio took twenty-one cortisone shots in his right shoulder in '62.

He rebounded in '63 with an 18–8 mark and 2.99 ERA as the Cards made an ultimately unsuccessful September charge at the front-running Dodgers.

"When I was a teenager, I used to watch him pitch," said future Broglio Cubs teammate Ken Holtzman of his youthful days growing up in University City, Missouri. "He was one of the best pitchers in the National League."

As the '63 pennant race heated up, so did the pain in Broglio's elbow. But he insisted he was fine by the following spring training and returned to the Cards' rotation. He was 3–5 with a 3.50 ERA in eleven starts.

Broglio was not Cubs GM John Holland's first choice as he tried to peddle Brock. He had first eyed young lefty Ray Sadecki, who eventually would come to the Cubs—though twenty-five years later as a minor-league pitching coach. Right-hander Ray Washburn also was high on Holland's wish list.

"We gave them a list of pitchers with three names on it" was the recollection of Cards GM Bing Devine, with whom Holland frequently made trades. "Broglio was one of them, but I don't recall the other two."

As the June 15 trading deadline rushed up on Holland and Devine, the eventual Broglio-for-Brock swap was agreed upon.

Holland could not have helped picking up on rumors that Broglio had some arm problems. Veteran pitcher Lew Burdette, traded from the Cards to the Cubs almost two weeks previously, told his new employers he had heard Broglio had taken the cortisone shots.

Broglio also had fallen in the esteem of the Cards' front office.

Ernie Broglio and student with the pitcher's arc.
Photo courtesy of Ernie Broglio.

The honchos did not like him taking up residence in Gaslight Square, a kind of bohemian St. Louis neighborhood. He had locked horns with Cards manager Johnny Keane, who liked to call pitches from the bench. Keane and Devine also were aggravated by Broglio's missing several starts with a groin injury that required treatment from the Cubs' team physician during a swing through Chicago two weeks before the deal.

Former Broglio St. Louis teammate Lindy McDaniel, by then the Cubs' closer, almost immediately noticed that Broglio had lost steam on his fastball. "He had a great fastball that set up the curve, but I thought he didn't have enough speed," McDaniel said.

Broglio had several decent Cubs starts, but his overall effectiveness continued downhill. In his first start against his old team on July 28, 1964, at Wrigley Field, Broglio yielded six runs and eight hits in six-plus innings. His elbow was a time bomb ready to go off.

On Sunday, August 23, 1964, with a 4–5 record as a Cub, Broglio woke up in a New York hotel room with his elbow in a locked position. It had ballooned in size to that of a cantaloupe. He complained to roommate Joey Amalfitano that the elbow had locked up. "He throws the hotel room key to me and says, 'Here, unlock it,'" Broglio recalled. The pitcher was sent home to Chicago while lefty John Flavin was called up from the minors to take his place on the roster.

Broglio finished up 1964 at 4–7 with a 4.04 ERA in sixteen Cubs starts, allowing 111 hits in one hundred and one-third innings. Brock hit .348 with thirty-three stolen bases the rest of the season with the Cardinals, happily collecting a World Series ring.

At least his old Cardinals teammates did not forget Broglio.

"I won three games for the Cardinals in 1964 before the trade," he said. "That helped them get into the World Series; they only won the pennant by one game. The whole ball club called me from a pay phone at Stan Musial's restaurant after they won in '64. That showed what they thought of me."

Very soon after the Cards' triumph, Broglio and the Cubs would get the worst possible news. His elbow maladies were diagnosed as a frayed ulna nerve and bone chips. He underwent surgery.

Privately, the trade was regarded as so much a fiasco, factoring in Broglio's breakdown, that the lords of the game mandated that medical information about players be made available to teams consummating trades.

Brock-for-Broglio is still looked at as a negative role model for baseball transactions.

"It never ceases to amaze me that whenever trades that don't look good are made," Broglio said, "they're always using this trade as an example of the worst. Never any other trade."

Broglio was barely a batting-practice pitcher, dragging himself to the mound in 1965 with a zigzag scar on his elbow. He was 1–6 with a 6.93 ERA, making only six starts out of twenty-six appearances. Then the Cubs gave him a second chance at a comeback under new manager Leo Durocher in spring training 1966. Broglio spun off a sixteen-inning scoreless streak, earning a spot in the rotation.

But that effectiveness disappeared once the season began. In Broglio's first start, he was wild, throwing eighty pitches in the first four innings and walking seven in the eventual seven-inning stint. He quickly got on Durocher's bad side, amassing a 2–6 record, 6.35 ERA, walking thirty-eight, and fanning just thirty-four in sixty-two and one-third innings. On July 5, 1966, Durocher backed up his proverbial truck by releasing him outright to Triple-A Tacoma.

Broglio's Cubs tenure did not go to total waste, though. Holtzman credited Broglio's veteran presence on the roster in '66 as helpful to fledgling hurlers such as himself, Fergie Jenkins, and Bill Hands.

"You just can't measure what a guy like that means to your career, to be able to talk to him about the game," Holtzman said. "I learned more in the first three weeks from these guys like Ernie than I did all my previous playing career. Certainly, Ernie made a difference in all three of our careers."

Despite that clubhouse and bullpen counsel, Broglio's name continued to reverberate as a scapegoat throughout Cubs history, even providing grist for a line in a play that eventually would run all over the world for decades.

"I saw the play *Bleacher Bums* on TV," he said. "After Brock's name was announced in the lineup [the play originally was set in 1977], one of the characters says, 'I wonder where that bum Broglio is?'"

Brock and Broglio were reunited twice, at an old-timers game in Wrigley Field in 1990 and at the 1995 Cubs Convention. The reaction at the old-timers game was predictable.

"They introduced me next to last, and Lou Brock was last," Broglio said. "As I was introduced, I came out and took my hat off. Everyone stood up and gave me a great ovation of boos. I started laughing and took a bow. Then they introduced Lou Brock and, my God, I thought Wrigley Field was going to collapse the way they cheered him.

"I'm so happy Lou made the Hall of Fame."

He should wish for some long-term happiness for Bartman, who also became a punch line for comedy writers. The very first Second City revue after the 2003 NLCS featured a Zelig-like Bartman messing up everyday situations for others.

Bartman ought to ask Broglio how to handle infamy that was not one's fault. Broglio could not have changed the way the Cardinals medical staff treated him or Holland's shoddy general managing. And Bartman did not force Mark Prior to walk Luis Castillo on the next pitch after the deflection and throw a bad pitch that Ivan Rodriguez slashed for an RBI single, could not force Cubs manager Dusty Baker to bring in a reliever to spell a tiring Prior, and could not field an easy grounder that Alex Gonzalez booted.

"Looking at it from every angle, he did not get his hands over the railing," Broglio said. "How can they put blame on the guy when the ball is in the stands? He did not go out of his way to take the ball out of [Moises] Alou's glove.

"The only thing I can say is forty years later, I'm recognized. I felt sorry because it was not his fault. He's in the stands, and he has a right to the ball."

And a right to a life after infamy. Ernie Broglio can show him the way.

Bob Hendley and Chris Krug

Life Is Good for a Tough-Luck Battery

A Lefty–Lefty Conversation

"I was laid-back and low-key. I never was a star."

You'll never get Bob Hendley to toot his own horn. He could if he wanted to, having overcome shoulder problems for more than a decade-long pro baseball career and three decades of successful high school baseball coaching in his native Macon, Georgia.

Hendley would never seek out publicity. But his connection to one of baseball's greatest-ever pitching duels would envelop him with notoriety, cut up into two increments thirty-seven years apart.

His name rings a bell to anyone who followed the better-than-big-league career of Hall of Famer Sandy Koufax. On September 9, 1965, Koufax hurled the fourth and last of his career no-hitters, a perfect game against the Cubs, at Dodger Stadium. He won 1–0 as losing pitcher Hendley allowed just one hit, a seventh-inning bloop double by ex-Cub Lou Johnson, that had nothing to do with the sole unearned run resulting from batterymate Chris Krug's throwing error on a Johnson steal attempt two innings previously.

The one hit in the game for both sides set a record for fewest hits ever in a major-league game, thanks to southpaws Koufax and Hendley each pitching the game of their lives. But Hendley ended up with the toughest-luck loss in Cubs history this side of game 6 of the 2003 National League Championship Series.

Koufax expressed empathy for Hendley's unrewarded stellar effort afterward, and he never forgot his formidable foe. Those memories for both Koufax and Hendley came alive when author Jane Leavy penned *Sandy Koufax: A Lefty's Legacy*, a best-selling 2002 book that tapped into the public's continuing fascination with the aura of Koufax.

Leavy tracked down Hendley and a host of players, executives, and media types who were present for the perfect game. Hendley's reaction to being a tough-luck loser and his postbaseball life, centered on coaching in private high schools in Macon, were chronicled.

Koufax already had sent a memento to Hendley.

"A number of years ago, when my youngest son [Bart] was young, our local newspaper wrote an article about my career," Hendley said. "Bart took the article and sent this to Sandy. He asked Sandy if he would sign the article, which he did. Sandy also put a message to Bart on an index card, to say hello to your father."

Soon after *A Lefty's Legacy* was published, a package arrived at Hendley's home. He was taken aback by its contents.

Inside was an authentic 1965 baseball autographed by Koufax with the inscription "What a game!" Included was a note, short, sweet, and on target, like its author: "We had a moment, a night, and a career. I hope life has been good to you—Sandy."

Hendley always had admired both Koufax the pitcher and the person. Now the kudos would go through the roof.

"I would never write to him and ask him for a baseball," Hendley said. "When this baseball came, I couldn't believe it.

"I've taken a fair number of things away from baseball as memorabilia. A lot of people talk in terms of what they're worth monetarily. To me, this is the best thing that I have ever taken away from baseball, regardless of what it is worth. It will never leave me; that's how much it means to me."

But Koufax wasn't done acknowledging Hendley in the afterglow of the book.

"Jane Leavy said Sandy said a lot of good things about me," Hendley said. "I had said good things about him when I talked to her. I told Jane in one of my last conversations that I'd like to talk to him. He had also said he'd like to talk to me. I said I would like to talk to him for what he did for my son. Jane said she'd have him call me. I just passed it off; I didn't think it would happen.

"About a week later, the phone rang. My wife picked it up and said it was for me. I picked it up. He said, 'Hello it's Sandy.' I thanked him about what he had done for Bart. We talked in general about what we were doing, for about twenty to twenty-five minutes. The conversation was like he and I had known each other for years. It says volumes about the person."

In retirement, Hendley's name had come to the forefront in a manner he had not experienced in his entire life. He appeared on a National Public Radio program with Leavy. The *Macon Telegraph* did a huge feature spread on his connection with Koufax, including photos of the autographed baseball.

"It's a thing that has kind of brought my name out as far as playing baseball," Hendley said. "I was born and raised in Macon, played pro baseball twelve years, then coached thirty years. People didn't seem to relate to it. But since this came out, people said, 'I didn't know you played.' A lot of people are younger and could not have remembered. I do see a fair number of people who bring things up."

And to think that Hendley was perfectly content coaching and teaching in Macon, the perfect-game experience filed far away in his own memory bank. He had been thankful for a journeyman player's career, but life was supposed to go on beyond baseball from Day One.

"I had given up a baseball scholarship at the University of Georgia [to sign with the old Milwaukee Braves]," he said. "I enrolled in Mercer University here after I signed in 1957 and started the fall quarter. I'd get one quarter in here, one there. I had to really work the university to allow me to leave early or come back late [from baseball seasons]. I assured them I'd do the work.

"I played winter baseball two years, and one winter I was on active [military] duty. Finally, in 1970, I got my degree, a bachelor of arts with a major in English and minor in sociology. When I left baseball, I went into PE and coaching. I enjoyed that more than I did the classroom. I coached a little football, but primarily I coached baseball, girls' softball, and basketball."

Hendley could not land a teaching position at Macon's public schools, so he embarked on a long career in area private high schools. He started at Tattnall Academy, then moved on to River North Academy, where Hendley's baseball teams won four Georgia state titles at the class AA level. After River North closed, he moved on to Stratford Academy, spending nineteen years as assistant head baseball coach through his retirement in 2001. Stratford won five state class AAA titles with Hendley helping out.

"Stratford is one of the elite schools in the area," he said. "It will compare with a lot of schools academically in any part of the country. The average SAT score is 1,000. A lot of kids go to college as sophomores, after taking advance-placement courses. They want to be in an atmosphere of learning. The kids work hard."

Hendley never had to break down the curveball scientifically at Stratford. He also did not have to bring up his baseball career. Had he done so, he would have given a lesson in perseverance.

A prime left-handed prospect coming up at the tail end of the Braves' Milwaukee glory years, Hendley had to learn how to craftily spot the ball after an elbow injury robbed him of his best fastball. He was just under a .500 pitcher in three Braves seasons, moved on to the San Francisco Giants in 1964, and then finally was traded to the Cubs along with catcher Ed Bailey in the spring of 1965.

After a short stay in the minors, Hendley was called up in the second half and put into the rotation. He drew the short straw on that memorable Thursday night at Dodger Stadium, although Hendley already had some success in head-to-head duels against Koufax. The newly signed Ken Holtzman, just nineteen, was used in batting practice early that evening to simulate a hard-throwing left-hander for the Cubs hitters.

But all the preparation did not do the Cubs—fielding one of the weakest lineups in their history outside of Billy Williams, Ron Santo, and Ernie Banks—any good against Koufax. The Cubs had been no-hit by the Reds' Jim Maloney, who had issued ten walks in his ten-inning stint, only three weeks previously. And master-of-control Koufax only grew stronger in the late innings. He struck out the last six hitters, totaling fourteen for the game.

Hendley issued one walk in his outing, and it cost him. He walked Johnson leading off the fifth. He was sacrificed to second. Then he took off on a steal attempt to third. Krug threw the ball into left field as Johnson scored. To this day, Hendley blames himself for walking Johnson and allowing him to take a big lead off second.

The Johnson double parachuted softly into right field. The hardest-hit drive was a long liner by Koufax batterymate Jeff Torborg that was nabbed in front of the Dodgers bullpen gate in left field by Byron Browne. Overall, he struck out just three but retired the Dodgers in order in six different innings.

Hendley recalled for interviewers after the game how another game had meant more to him than the tough-luck loss. As a Brave, he once had gone eight and one-third hitless innings before giving up four hits. The Braves won, too.

When he woke up the next morning in San Francisco, Hendley finally realized the magnitude of the game in which he'd played a crucial part.

"Although it hurts to know you lost, I still had a good feeling about it," Hendley said. "You knew you were a part of something special. The hurt was probably a little lessened."

And it was lessened even further on September 14, 1965, at Wrigley Field, when Hendley was matched up again with Koufax. This time, Williams, practically the only Cub to hit Koufax competitively in his career, slugged a two-run homer that was just enough for Hendley to nurse to the finish. He finished with a four-hitter as the Cubs won 2–1. That lifted Hendley's record to 3–1 in six outings against Koufax.

"I don't think as a player you look at [revenge] as a personal thing," Hendley said. "When you face Sandy Koufax again, you've got to be at your best to compete. As a player, you have a job to do. You concentrate and put your effort into the job you have to do and not what you're facing at the other end."

Koufax proved to be not as tough a foe as Leo Durocher. Taking over as Cubs manager in 1966, Durocher jumbled everyone's pitching roles. Rare was the pitcher who was satisfied at the way the amoral Durocher handled him. Despite his late-season success in 1965, Hendley was shuttled to the bullpen with only a few spot starts for the horrendous '66 Cubs.

"There was no consistency in what was going on with me as far as activity," Hendley said. "In sports, you get labeled. Obviously I was labeled by Leo as a loser. He was the manager, I was the player, but he called the shots. He didn't call my number too often.

"I didn't care for Leo Durocher. Of all the people I played for, he was the one person I disliked. I felt I could have done a better job with more opportunity. Once you're in the doghouse, it's tough to get out. Take Durocher and Bobby Cox. You'd be looking at opposites."

Hendley opened the 1967 season in the same mop-up bullpen role, then found himself traded to the New York Mets, just missing out on the Cubs' surprising midseason flirtation with first place. Only twenty-eight, he would not pitch another big-league game after '67.

But if an aching elbow and Durocher's mishandling had put a damper on the memories of his career, his association with Koufax was the shining light.

"I had made the statement that to get beat by class is no disgrace," he said of Koufax, a man he described as "bigger than baseball."

But not too big to reach out to Hendley. They had a special bond that will never be broken in the record books or in Hendley's heart.

An Error, a Banishment, and a Field of Dreams

Chris Krug did not have to wait almost four decades to get Sandy Koufax's opinion of his actions during Koufax's perfect game.

Still hanging his head over the throwing error that led to the Dodgers' only run, Krug ran into Koufax at a celebrity golf tournament right after the 1965 season.

"He told me, 'Chris, that [loss] wasn't your fault,'" Krug recalled.

Krug took a lot of blame in the mid-1960s. Less than a year later, Cubs manager Leo Durocher accused him of trying to start an affair with team owner Phil Wrigley's daughter-in-law, banishing him to the minor leagues as a result.

But somehow, someway, you overcome. Long before Koufax contacted Hendley, Krug had carved his own niche, literally, in American folklore. He built the famed baseball diamond, cut out of a cornfield, near Dyersville, Iowa, for the mythic 1988 movie *Field of Dreams*.

So how does a ne'er-do-well big-league catcher get to build a field on which Kevin Costner's Ray Kinsella character hosts the ghosts of the 1919 Black Sox, then spiritually connects with his late father?

That improbable tale started almost a decade earlier, when Krug was an assistant baseball coach at UCLA for his friend Gary Adams. The coaches had to work on the field after practice, and somehow Krug ended up specializing in the Bruins' grounds-keeping.

"I developed a newfound respect for groundskeepers," he said. "I remember conversations I had with the grounds crew at Wrigley Field.

"Other schools started asking who's taking care of the [UCLA] field. High schools would call, so I went out and worked on their fields a couple of times. Then I did a field from scratch: Diamond

Chris Krug and Kevin Costner at the "Field of Dreams" in 1988. Photo courtesy of Chris Krug.

Bar High School in Orange County. I'd get references to other fields. It snowballed to the point where I was making too much money to go back to coaching."

In 1984, Krug opened his own firm, Athletic Turfs, in Wildomar, California. He hasn't strayed far from his own baseball roots in Riverside, a baseball-rich area that produced the likes of Bobby Bonds, Dusty Baker, Kenny Hubbs, and Jim Shellenback. Self-taught, he asked grading and irrigation companies how they performed their craft. He built up enough of a reputation in the 1980s that when the *Field of Dreams* production company cast about for a firm to build the Iowa field, a turf company referred the producers to Krug.

"I said I'd love to [construct the field]," he said. "I worked with a turf company, got a motor home, and all expenses. It took us about ten days. I drove the truck up to the corn, where Kevin [Costner] was in the corn doing the shot where he hears voices.

"We started using earth movers. Kevin would come over and sit with us between takes. Kevin actually helped with a rake. It was bizarre. I didn't have any clue what the movie was about. It was an unbalanced field, even after we moved the dirt. It was the early summer of 1988, I remember I was there on July 4. It was a drought summer with corn just three, four feet high. They brought in prop corn, phony corn, to put in the front rows when the [ghost] players come out of the field."

Long after Costner and company departed, Krug's diamond has become a major tourist attraction.

"Almost a million people have visited that place," he said. "It's a phenomenon. They had weddings at home plate. There was a long line of people waiting to get a swing at home plate. It's brought more notoriety to me. It's helped me get other jobs."

Krug constructed the Jackie Robinson Field at UCLA and does annual work at Edison Field in Anaheim after motocross tears up the sod. Major League Baseball has contracted with him to build a $4 million to $5 million project at Compton Junior College near Los Angeles as part of an effort to boost baseball in the inner city.

"It's $150,000 bare minimum to build a field," Krug said. "I've had projects of $650,000."

He wouldn't mind getting a Wrigley Field landscaping deal. During 2003, a number of Cubs and visiting players, ranging from

Kerry Wood to Barry Bonds, said both the infield and outfield had problems in accommodating the ol' ballpark's natural drainage. The infield slopes downward into foul territory while the outfield is lumpy and uneven in some areas. In response, Cubs president Andy MacPhail said a makeover of the field to install man-made drainage had been discussed but would be expensive and require an entire off-season to complete.

Not so, claimed Krug. "I could put in man-made drainage in two months, before the winter set in," he said. "It could be done and done right. I smooth out fields for a living. It would be less than a $1 million project."

Working on fields is a far cry from Krug's early postbaseball career. He had worked in title insurance and public relations. Then he segued back into baseball, managing the Mets' farm club in the Class A New York–Penn League in 1977–1978. One of his players was future Cubs catcher Jody Davis. Then he hooked on with UCLA and his apprentice groundskeeping duties.

Krug is so busy he doesn't have all that much time to bask in the afterglow of Koufax, even if his role in the perfect game was a double negative: his error leading to the only run and his striking out as the first out in the ninth.

"It's been nothing but a positive for me," he said. "Everybody, including ballplayers, was sympathetic to me. Nobody wants to be in that position."

Krug professed to not fear Koufax when he batted against him.

"It was the first time I had seen him [in person]," he said of the night of September 9, 1965. "Left-handed pitching never intimidated me, including him. I went to the plate with great expectations.

"Jeff Torborg, who I played with through the minors, chatted a moment with me [in the ninth inning]. I asked him, 'What's this all about?' He said, 'Wait and see.' Boy, did I ever!"

And, like Hendley, Krug was happy to beat Koufax five days later in Chicago.

"It was very satisfying," he said. "We as a team wanted to beat Koufax. It was something you didn't want to live with the rest of your life. A good word was revenge, and we got it."

Krug shared yet another fate with Hendley—the bad side of Leo Durocher. Krug's place on Durocher's truck that backed up came quicker than the pitcher's. Serving as rookie Randy Hundley's backup starting the 1966 season, Krug got into just eleven games. Having finally made the majors the previous year at twenty-five but hitting just .201, he scarcely needed to rile Durocher.

Somehow, a casual conversation while he was warming up a pitcher was grossly misconstrued by Durocher. Krug had chatted with blonde Allison Wrigley, first wife of Bill Wrigley, while she sat in the box seats. Durocher was told Krug was asking for her phone number.

Both Billy Williams and Ken Holtzman claimed Durocher launched into a clubhouse tirade in which he admitted his own aggressive womanizing but also insisted he would never have sex with an owner's wife. Krug does not recall Durocher's outburst.

"If it was a clubhouse speech, I would have crawled under the bench," he said. "Leo called me into his office and tried to accuse me of hitting on this woman. I didn't know who she was. She had been there a couple of times before. The day they were talking about, she was late. Leo was looking for a reason [to get rid of me]. I had a better spring than Randy Hundley. But Leo liked Randy, so guess who played."

Krug was swiftly dispatched to Triple-A Tacoma. He washed out of the Cubs organization, resurfacing only for a short period with the expansion San Diego Padres in 1969.

But that was only a detour to Krug's true calling, a nightmare that was made up for many times over by a real field of dreams.

Gracie the "Moth"

Descriptions of Mark Grace are very basic. And now they're quite apt for his new gig.

"He likes to talk," said ol' buddy Brian McRae. "He's a natural at it. He'll do well. He has that gift of storytelling. It's kind of strange at times—his wit on baseball. But it's refreshing to have some guys with character in the [broadcast] booth and not everyone doing the same thing."

"Clearly, he was blessed with a gift of gab," said present-day partner Thom Brennaman. "There's no debate on that, along with a sense of humor and insight into the game of baseball. That's pretty good ingredients to make a broadcaster."

Yeah, anyone who knew Mark Grace from towheaded blond matinee idol as a 1988 rookie to shaven-headed, goateed veteran early in the next century can recognize these traits. Plain and simple, Grace was a "moth," a personality that was attracted to the lights of the TV cameras. He apprenticed after hours in the company of another "moth," Rick Sutcliffe, during the first four years of his Cubs tenure at first base. He got really good at it over the years, providing the sound bite, ensuring that when he was being recorded for a broadcast, nothing had to be bleeped, and was the finest politician of his time in the Wrigley Field clubhouse.

So why keep giving away a talent for which you could otherwise be paid? As soon as Grace hung up his jock for the last time, at the end of the 2003 season, he was headed straight into the Arizona Diamondbacks broadcast booth, thanks to the backing of owner Jerry Colangelo. And you don't believe him when Grace insists he hadn't been thinking a long time about teaming with Brennaman on D-Backs telecasts. Remember, they talked about Grace back in the mid-1990s as a future Cubs broadcaster. At the time, Brennaman broadcast Cubs games on radio and got to know Grace.

Employment on Chicago airwaves won't happen anytime soon. Grace is in a kind of exile from his former digs at Wrigley Field, where status as a fan favorite for thirteen seasons ended in a bitter divorce before he hooked on for his final three years in Phoenix. But you can't wipe away those baker's dozen's worth of years as a Cub, so whenever he comes to town—much more infrequently with today's baseball schedule—he's much sought-after for being, well, Gracie the Moth.

He relocated anyway in the off-season to the high-rent district of the Valley of the Sun, that Scottsdale–Paradise Valley ballplayers' redoubt, in the late 1990s, so Grace simply stays on through the searing summer months now. Just like his throwing the ball into left field all the time on reverse double plays in his rookie year, Grace is now enduring a period of adjustment on the air.

"I think it's still a work in progress," he said, retaining his boyish persona even as he passed forty. "I know the game like the back of my hand. I know the players like the back of my hand. So I'm comfortable talking about that. The things I have to learn is when I can talk, when I can't talk, when to let Tommy take over, when to just stay quiet, and when it's time we have to fill space and start jibber-jabbering."

But the Grace of the broadcast booth is no Steve Stone, crack analyst and superb "first-guesser" who won't call out mentally and physically laggard players on the air. He's, well, a former teammate of many of the D-Backs, and that will color his commentary a certain way.

"He's made it very clear that he wants to be a cheerleader up there," Brennaman said. "He knows a lot about the game, so he can be analytical at times. That's got to be a difficult thing; you just shared the locker room with a lot of these guys. Look at Matt Mantei [in early 2004]. It was very hard for Mark to criticize him. Their friendship played a factor in there.

"You have to give Mark the benefit of the doubt. If he wants to be an excellent broadcaster, there are times you have to be critical of players, situations, and manager, or all of the above. I don't know if he's yet ready to make that step."

And just because life becomes more than a little languid in the constant 105-or-more heat that settles over Phoenix from late June to early October doesn't mean the homebound fans, ducking into the air conditioning, want a languid color guy.

"They want guys who tell it like it is," Brennaman said. "I just get the feeling you have a lot of transplants come from places where they're used to people telling it like it is. I don't think there's anybody out there who doesn't want to be told the truth."

Grace himself defines his own parameters as a wet-behind-the-ears analyst.

"The only thing I'll be critical of is lack of hustle or mental mistakes, whether it's by a veteran or a young player," he said. "I can't be critical if a guy strikes out with the bases loaded or if he gives up a three-run homer with a two-run lead. Or if he makes an error. I've popped up pitches that I should have knocked four hundred feet. I've struck out with the bases loaded, and I've made errors. So I'm not going to be critical of that, because that's part of the game."

Grace could go on and on as a conversationalist. But that talent is not a virtue in the sound-bite world of baseball broadcasting— particularly on TV, where for more than half a century directors have cautioned their announcers to let the video do most of the talking.

"It helped him a lot to do the radio, doing baseball playoffs for ESPN Radio [in 1998]," Brennaman said. "Any television analyst should get started in radio first, do an entire season. They should learn how to make their point in the amount of time before the next pitch. Instead of saying things in five sentences, learn to do it in three. And you find out you do it better in three."

At least Grace has paid attention to the best in the business. Of course he'd listen to ol' night-crawler partner Sutcliffe, now a rising star at ESPN. And he always listened to Stone's analysis when he caught a Cubs game.

"I think Rick Sutcliffe does a great job," he said. "He's one of my favorite guys I like to listen to. Stoney's the guy I was brought up with, and [he was] the best in the business. I'm not going to try to be Steve Stone or Rick Sutcliffe. I've got to be me. I'm a little more screwballish than those guys. Those guys are a little more matter of fact. I'm a guy who gets a little more animated."

Grace has even more to learn. He can't dress down for his part at times. The Fox Network asked him to do color on a Saturday regional game of the week out of Pro Player Stadium near Miami.

He showed up for the telecast in a golf shirt, a stark contrast from Fox's mandated dress shirt and tie. The production crew had to scramble for anything that remotely fit Grace.

And considering that broadcasters—Lou Boudreau and Larry Dierker to name two—have been tapped to come down from the booth to manage before, Grace had to choose his words more carefully. He created a row going into the 2004 season when he stated a concurrent goal to manage in the big leagues, maybe with the Diamondbacks. But Grace did not preface the statement with "not this year or next." Such an omission did not sit well with incumbent manager Bob Brenly, who had written Grace's name in the lineup at first base throughout his Arizona years.

By midseason 2004, though, Grace did not have to worry about what his manager thought of him. The downsized D-Backs' downslide cost Brenly his job. So now Grace had nothing but a death march to announce the remainder of his rookie season in the booth.

Grace won't double as an on-field instructor for the D-Backs. He did dabble in a little uniformed advice to kids in 2004 spring training. But managing is still off in the future. He'd even consider going to the minors to get the necessary experience.

No matter what the challenges and controversies of his new job, there's no turning back. Gracie the smooth, line-drive .300 hitter is now consigned to the record books and old videos. He doesn't have the itch to play because he knows his day has passed.

"I sucked," he said of riding the bench in his final season. "I wasn't any good any more. I don't miss going 0-for-4. I don't miss having to pinch-hit off [Eric] Gagne. I don't miss being so sore and tired every day. I do miss being around the guys, being a part of that locker room, miss the rush you get going to the ballpark, love and enjoyment you get competing against the best players day in and day out."

Gracie the family man is another change in his persona since arriving in Arizona. He and wife Tonya have two sons, preschooler Jackson and toddler Preston. Growing up in a family with one brother, he must be experiencing déjà vu.

"Jackson already hits left-handed; Preston keeps me up all night," he said. "Of course it changes you. I've got two little boys; that's who I live for. That's who I'll protect with my life. Now, you don't think about baseball or your job. When you're away from them, you miss them unbelievably. You would take a bullet for them. I can't wait to get home to see them.

But while he now has to earn his livelihood in the desert, with a large audience of expatriate Cubs fans watching, Grace makes no mistake about his baseball identity. The better part of him will always be a Cub.

"Most of my personal memories are in Chicago. As far as my best years, my individual accomplishments, 95 percent are in a Cubs uniform," he said. "The best teams I played for were obviously the Diamondbacks, a world champion [in 2001], then a division champion, and in my last year were eight games over .500. That was considered a terrible year. All my accomplishments were in a Cubs uniform. When people look back and ask what I consider myself, I would say a Cub."

But other than two playoff appearances, in 1989 and 1998, Grace mostly lost as a Cub. He would have loved to have garnered that special ring in Chicago yet won't hang crepe that he had to move cross-country to earn the jewelry.

"I'm so fulfilled with my career," he said. "I had a great thirteen years here, had a great three years in Arizona, and I got my world championship. It doesn't matter what team you get it with as long as you get one.

"It was worth every 0-for-4, every error, every injury, every late night trip back in to Houston and have to bounce out to play a day game the next day. The fact that I got it with the Diamondbacks doesn't change the fact I will always go down as a world champion. I retired as a world champion."

Grace probably felt differently when he captured baseball's attention in the 1989 National League Championship Series. He tried to match the San Francisco Giants' Will Clark hit for hit, RBI for RBI. Grace hit .647 (11-for-17) with eight RBIs in the five-game series.

"I played so well, and that's where my name got put on the map," he said. "That series became almost Clark versus Grace. That's probably my best memory with the Cubs."

As the best-rated young hitter among a bumper crop of home-grown productive Cubs that season, Grace figured the future was limitless. It turned about to have a lot more barriers than he ever dreamed.

Mark Grace (left) and Thom Brennaman.
Author photo.

By 1993, many of the '89ers had been forced out of the organization, which took a turn for the worse for much of the rest of the decade. Only Grace remained.

"It would have been interesting to see what could have happened there," he said. "It was all the managements that decided to go in a different direction."

One regime, Jim Frey's general managership, tried to go in a different direction with Grace. Obsessed with home-run power from his days with the Baltimore Orioles, Frey was impatient about Grace's inability to muscle up to complement his .300-hitting stroke. Such impatience led to the trade of Rafael Palmeiro to the Texas Rangers. Frey and manager Don Zimmer tried to change Grace's hitting style early in the 1990 season to produce more power. The effort was a failure, and Grace's average plummeted. He switched back to his natural style at midseason and hit around .300 the rest of his career. But Grace never belted more than seventeen homers in any season.

He also did not reach the one-hundred-RBI plateau, coming the closest with a ninety-eight total in 1993. Although Grace was hampered by a lack of consistent leadoff men batting in front of him, he also tended to get more impatient with men on base, leaving behind his best hitting fundamentals. Popping up on a lot of first pitches with runners on second and third cost Grace some RBIs over the years.

Frey was succeeded as GM by Larry Himes, whom Grace publicly detested. Grace still holds Himes responsible for the free-agent defection of Greg Maddux after the 1992 season. He called Himes "Satan" when the GM was demoted in 1994 and still thinks the devil of him.

"He's still Satan, no question," Grace said. "I don't have anything to do with him, and I don't want him coming near me."

Despite his dissatisfaction with management and a behind-the-scenes rivalry with Sammy Sosa, Grace opted to continue to re-sign with the Cubs throughout the 1990s. He could have fled as a free agent. One time the World Series–caliber Cleveland Indians came bidding. But every time, he stayed put, drawing criticism that claimed Grace wasn't really interested in winning.

"I'm not going to apologize for that," he said. "I loved being a Cub. Whether we won or lost, I was proud to wear that patch."

Wrigley Field itself was one of the lures that kept him in blue pinstripes. Having now worked at Bank One Ballpark for more than four seasons, he can state the absolute contrasts between the old and the new.

"Wrigley Field is the old, the tradition, the mecca of the National League," Grace said. "Bank One Ballpark is change in the game; it's every accommodation you can imagine in a baseball game. Things like an exploding scoreboard, Diamond Vision. Wrigley Field doesn't have that, but that's what makes it charming. Wrigley Field was great before TVs were invented and will remain great. This is a special place. Babe Ruth was right in that same batter's box where I batted, and he called his shot."

By the end of his Cubs career, Grace almost became synonymous with Wrigley Field. Cubs fans named him to the franchise's All-Century Team in 1999. When he finished the 2000 season, he ranked fifth all-time in team annals with 2,201 hits and second in doubles with 456. Grace also ranks in the Cubs' top ten in the majority of other career batting categories. He also was one of the best defensive first basemen in team history.

But with slugging prospect Hee Seop Choi seemingly knocking

on the door at first base, team president Andy MacPhail, doubling as general manager, decided to let Grace walk as a free agent after 2000. Grace believed MacPhail did not return agent Barry Axelrod's calls about re-signing. MacPhail claimed he picked up the phone. Bad blood developed, and Grace would only cross paths with MacPhail when he came back as a broadcaster in 2004.

Choi never did claim the first base job full-time due to injuries and an eventual trade to Florida for veteran Derrek Lee. MacPhail had to trade for aging Fred McGriff, who hardly made an impact despite some decent numbers. The slick-fielding Lee finally matched Grace in fielding prowess while promising to far exceed him in power.

Long after he's gone, the Cubs finally promise to be good for a long time due to their stellar starting rotation. Grace remains close to Kerry Wood, living within a mile of the fireballer in Arizona, and even held a Wood-themed party while watching the ill-fated game 7 of the 2003 NLCS against the Marlins.

To the fans he left behind but who have never forgotten him, Grace has one simple message about handling a new, winning Cubs era: "I just say, 'Enjoy the hype while you can, and enjoy the great teams while you can.'"

Father Shawon Knows Best?

S itting in a quiet coaches' dressing room at HoHoKam Park in Mesa, Arizona, Shawon Dunston didn't have to ponder the meaning of life very long before he proclaimed, "My first advice to children is get good grades. Don't listen to me because I'm a pro athlete. I make mistakes like the next person. The person who you should listen to are a role model like your parents. Your parents aren't going to lie to you, but another person will."

On this day, as former shortstop Dunston was in the middle of his own spring break as guest instructor at the Cubs' spring-training camp, there would be no lying and nothing but the truth. That was always Dunston's style through his voluble career, ranging from the champion trash talker of the Cubs clubhouse in the 1980s to a slightly more introspective baseball elder as the twentieth century drew to a close.

Still trim and athletic, close to his playing weight and without a trace of graying, the forty-something Dunston was trying to figure out the adjustment period between longtime pro athlete and a more permanent role: professional father.

Be careful what you wish for, goes the old adage. If Dunston craved to be home with wife Tracy and their four children in the San Francisco Bay area after he took his last at bat, well, sometimes it's proved to be more of a challenge than laying off a borderline pitch or taking something off his rocket throws to first base.

Teenagers Whitney, Jasmine, and Shawon Jr., along with youngest daughter I'sha, wanted Dad at home after his eighteen years in the majors, but . . .

"I was the biggest problem around," a soft-spoken Dunston said of homelife starting after his retirement following the 2002 season.

"I was in everyone's way. Life was supposed to stop because of me, because I'm home. But you forget they have a life. They've got school; they've got friends. Here they've been saying for ten years, 'We want you home, we want you home.' Now I'm home, and nobody's home with me."

Once Dunston was touted as "the next Ernie Banks" because of his power potential and natural athleticism at shortstop. He later became just the first Shawon Dunston, a good, aggressive player with both attributes and flaws. Now he's just father Shawon, and he doesn't always know best. This might be grist for a situation comedy. Hey, doesn't ABC still have holes in its prime-time schedule?

"Right now the kids are smarter than me, and I'm the dumbest one in the family," Dunston said. "But I've enjoyed every moment. My goal in life was to be a major-league baseball player, not be a star, just be a good player. Now the goal is to be the best father I can be. I'd rather be a superstar father than a superstar player.

"It's tough. They know everything. That's going to bother me, when my daughter has a boyfriend. It's your daughter. At one time, you were a young man, and you know what you want to do with girls. You just want them to pick a respectable person.

"My wife, she's beautiful. You never know how much you appreciate your wife until you retire. I know that it was hard taking care of four kids. Travel over there, take them to school, pick them up from school, then having me call here, knowing what they're doing.

"Now that I'm home I see what she had to do, along with worrying about her fifth child, which was me. I'd call home, and I'm mad because I didn't get a hit, I made an error. She's listening to me. For me to be the player that I was, it was because I had a good wife who took the little problems away from me and just let me concentrate on baseball, just let me play.

"I need to give my wife a break. Now it's time to be the relief pitcher."

In the prime of his mouthy period, the wary would cut a wide swath around Dunston's Wrigley Field locker. Otherwise, they might get caught in the trash-talk crossfire that dimmed just a bit when slugger Andre Dawson arrived in 1987 to apply his own special guidance to the shortstop's baseball life.

But Dunston is Dunston, unashamedly. As soon as he showed up for a weeklong stint as a guest instructor at the invitation of old manager Dusty Baker, he launched into a profane mock tirade on former Cubs teammate Greg Maddux, then just arrived for his second tour of duty in Chicago. All done with a huge grin on his face to amazed media, mind you. The cleaned-up version was, "Listen to Maddux on pitching issues but nothing else."

But if you can believe it, Dunston in creeping middle age has a volume switch and a self-bleeper.

"I'm still the same," he said of trash talking. "But when you talk to females, like your daughters, you have to talk a little softer. You have to play mind games. I learned from my father [Jack Dunston] that you have to speak to your daughters different than your son. You're forty; they're fifteen. You've got twenty-five years' experience on them; they shouldn't run you. Play a little mind game on them. Every time I talk to my daughters, trying to teach them something, I keep hearing my father in my ear, when I was fifteen or sixteen."

The Dunston kids can expect Pops to hang around the house a while longer. First, he saved up his money. Second, he doesn't yet possess the mentality to coach. The spring-training visit, where he was reunited with former double-play partner / camp instructor Ryne Sandberg, was in no way a precursor to a return to uniform.

Dunston gloried in harassing Maddux from the first-base coaching box when the pitching master took his first spring at bat. After batting practice, he'd retire to the players' lunchroom and tell stories like some baseball elder. The players, some now half his age, were regaled. But after a week, he would return to Tracy and the kids to assume his chosen life and live off his baseball earnings.

"I spent feverishly [at first] because it was new to me," he said. "After you keep getting it and getting it, it becomes like nothing to you, like second nature. But I learned how to put away. I have good people around me. I still have both my parents. I had good players who were older than me who told me about a financial adviser. Now I'm very ultraconservative.

"Baseball provided me with a beautiful life where I could live comfortably. That's why I respect the game. I never had a job before. Hopefully, I never will. I really appreciate baseball."

Obviously, Dunston won't be needing to find both spring-training quarters and an in-season home anytime soon to tap into those investments. He still looks young enough to play. "It's genetics," he said. And in his mind, he's still on the field or at bat.

"I'm not there yet," he said of shifting into a coaching job anytime soon. "I still have that player's mentality. I heard someone say [it stays with you] five years. I still have that. My main objective in life is be the best father I can be. No, I'm not ready. It's still about me being this ballplayer. To be a good coach, you've got to remove yourself as a ballplayer. If someone calls me out and says you can't do it, I'll go out on the field and show you."

He doesn't have to show Baker anything. Dunston played three different times for Baker, first as a starting shortstop in 1996, then as a backup player in 1999 and 2001–2002.

Dunston's days as a shortstop regular ended at age thirty-four in 1997. That year, he returned to the Cubs for less than a full season's stay before embarking on a journey as pennant-race insurance in both the infield and outfield for various teams. Such a status prolonged his career by at least several seasons.

"It started with Dusty," Dunston said. "He made it easy. First time I did it [play different positions], I didn't like it because you just felt like you're being used. But it started a whole [second] career.

"I'd been a starter my whole career. Dusty said, 'Until you get it in your head that you'll be a good one, you'll never be one.' I got it in my head that I'd be a role player. I don't like the word 'utility.' They say 'utility.' I say 'role player.'"

Two stints on the St. Louis Cardinals with manager Tony La Russa further refined the Dunston jack-of-all-trades image.

"The way [La Russa] did it, when that guy came back, he kept me in the lineup and put me in another position. I really enjoyed it in St. Louis. Tony took care of older players. Dusty took care of older players.

"Dusty treats people like people. He played before. Tony didn't play that much [in the majors], but he understands older players. You were good at one time, but when you're older, people just want to move you away. They've been older players at one time."

Despite the late-career switch that also took him to the New York Mets, Cleveland Indians, and Pittsburgh Pirates, Dunston always will be remembered as the much-anticipated phenom who didn't live up to all the hype—but still won a center-stage role in recent Cubs history.

"I was a good player," he said. "I wasn't a superstar. There's other things come with being a superstar. That's not important as playing the game as you should play, play for the name on the front of the jersey instead of the back of the jersey. I had injuries, but I played eighteen years. Not everybody can play eighteen years. There's players now just trying to get in ten years to get a pension."

Dunston was the last number 1 June draft pick the Cubs have been able to snare, thanks to their expansion-team record in the strike-splintered 1981 season. A .790 batting average in his senior year in high school in Brooklyn wowed scouts, along with his breakneck speed and laser arm. But there was another consideration for top choice in the '82 draft—a high school pitching prodigy out of Tampa named Dwight Gooden.

Cubs player development wizard Gordon Goldsberry, always a fan of raw baseball tools, picked Dunston.

"I still think they made the wrong pick," Dunston said with a laugh. "They should have taken Doc. But I still appreciate them."

Shawon Dunston and old double-play partner Ryne Sandberg at spring training 2004. Author photo.

Dunston's signing prompted a countdown to his arrival with the Cubs, as media followed his progress around the minors. Perhaps a little prematurely, Dunston was anointed as the opening day shortstop in 1985, sparking a backstage conflict with veteran incumbent Larry Bowa.

At first Dunston flopped, earning a demotion to Triple-A Iowa. But by August 1985, he was back in Wrigley Field, pushing Bowa out and hitting .260. He ranked as the first everyday player out of the Cubs farm system to stick with the team since Don Kessinger exactly twenty years previously. Over the next three seasons, Dunston was half-potential, half-performance, with high strikeout totals, lack of patience at the plate, and low batting averages balanced out by hustle and aggressiveness.

Dunston put it together at the right time, though. When a largely homegrown collection of younger players got hot in the summer of 1989, taking over the National League East lead by August, Dunston helped lead the charge. He smoothed out much of his game, hitting more than .400 in September. The energized performance made him a folk hero with a famed "Shawon-O-Meter" sign appearing daily in the left-field bleachers to announce his batting average and attract the attention of the WGN-TV cameras.

Dunston finished with a .278 mark in 1989 with fifteen intentional walks out of the thirty overall he drew for the season. The next two seasons, he was a decent complementary hitter in the lineup, good enough to make his second All-Star team in 1990.

By then, Dunston had the guidance of a couple of special teammates.

"Hawk [Andre Dawson] was a good friend, not a father," he said. "I have a father. There's nobody in the world that compares to my father. My father's my role model, my idol.

"Hawk was a special friend who was there for me. It's how he carried himself, he and Ryno [Sandberg]. I appreciate the way they played the game. They play hard; they go about their business; they don't brag. They're stand-up people. And when they hit home runs, they don't show anybody up.

"I was very intrigued with the way they ran around the bases, came back to the dugout, sat down, didn't say a word, and didn't brag. That just impressed me. When they made a mistake, they didn't say, 'Oh, it was a bad hop.' They never said, 'Oh, I had a bad day.' They said, 'This guy was better than me.'"

Dawson's strong, silent-type personality was just the right one to play off Dunston's. Eventually it rubbed off on Dunston's game preparation.

"I talked a lot," he said. "[Dawson] didn't say no more than ten words a day in the locker room, him and Ryno. But in the clubhouse, forty-five minutes or a half hour before a game, I got quiet. I watched how they prepare. When I was on the field, I didn't talk much. I just minded my business, played hard, and played for the name in front of the jersey."

Dunston needed the support of all his teammates early in the 1992 season. He injured his back lifting Jasmine, then an infant, into a car seat. He was out the rest of the season and did not return until a cameo appearance at the end of the 1993 season.

"If I hadn't hurt my back, I would have been a much better player," he said. "After I hurt my back, I played another nine years. It was a freak injury. If I had to do it all over again, I'd hurt my back again for my daughter."

The Cubs' brass pondered a Dunston shift to the outfield upon his return. But he still considered himself a starting shortstop, albeit a high-maintenance one in the training room.

"I probably would have been the same player, a .270 hitter [if shifted to the outfield]," he said. "If we would have had an A-Rod in the minors, a [Derek] Jeter, I'd have gone to the outfield."

By 1995, Dunston was the Cubs' best clutch hitter, finishing at .296 with sixty-nine RBIs in 127 games. Inexplicably, he was let go as a free agent after the season, only to return a year later in time for the Cubs' record-breaking 0–14 start.

Most of the time the Cubs were at least a few arms short. That's why Dunston was encouraged at the makeup and leadership of the team he visited in 2004.

"Back then, we didn't have the pitching they have now," he said. "Our everyday players are better than their everyday players. We only had one Greg Maddux; they have five. It helps to have a good manager."

Although he wore many hats as a big leaguer, he still prefers blue. That's why he accepted Baker's invitation to guest-coach.

"I'm very comfortable with the Cubs, comfortable with Dusty," he said. "Maybe I would have visited the Giants or Cardinals. My kids asked me, 'Why the Cubs?' Well, I played the longest there and they treated me the nicest.

"I'm still noted as a Cub. Everywhere I go, it's 'How's the Shawn-O-Meter?' We lost, but I'm proud to be a Cub. How many people can say they can come back, laughing and joking, all the fans know you. They still think I'm playing; they want me to play. I tell them, 'Hey, we didn't win, but you people made us feel special.'

"I wasn't a superstar. I was a good player, but to the Cubs fans I was a superstar."

Managing the Change from Blue to Black and Gold

The cinder-block walls of the Wrigley Field visiting manager's office is the spartan place where Lloyd McClendon proclaims his often earthy views on baseball, managing, and life in general.

He could easily go out on the bench, hang around the batting cage, or pick anywhere else other than this cubbyhole, and he'd soak up a lot more atmosphere. But, somehow, McClendon revs up in his element in the undecorated office in front of a handful of media types. He dodges few questions.

But it was in the sunshine in 1997—not in a cinder-block office in 2004—where McClendon, just after he was named the Pittsburgh Pirates' hitting coach, revealed his goal, ambition, and dream all wrapped up into one. Growing up a Cubs fan forty miles down the Skyway and Indiana toll road in Gary, Indiana, and later playing a key role in his childhood heroes' 1989 National League East division title season, McClendon of course wanted to come home again. He wanted to manage in the big leagues, and he wanted to manage the Cubs.

By the time McClendon's time finally arrived to manage in 2001, Don Baylor seemingly was entrenched in the Cubs' job. And after Baylor failed to work out long term, management went for the home run to snare Dusty Baker to run the team late in 2002. Armed with a four-year contract, Baker wasn't going anywhere anytime soon. McClendon would manage, but emotionally and physically had to transform himself from true-blue Cubbie blue to Pirates' black and gold, colors all too familiar to longtime fans who remember Chicago's top tormentor of the late 1960s and early 1970s.

Deep down, McClendon maintains some old-time Cubs loyalties, but his heart belongs to the Pirates now. Of course you're going to return loyalty with the same when you've just been re-upped to manage through the end of 2005 and could have at least a five-year run as dugout pilot of a franchise that's done its share of 1950s-style Cubs losing.

Yet if you think in an inherently unstable job McClendon thinks he has it made because he had a guaranteed paycheck for half a decade, he says you have something else coming.

"I don't think you can be guaranteed anything," McClendon said in a soft-spoken style, sitting behind the manager's desk. "You could be fired tomorrow. I'm not trying to be facetious. That's the way I operate. I never want anything to catch up with me. I continue to try to strive to be the best and impress that personality on my players. We don't get relaxed, so to speak.

McClendon couldn't slack off at any level of baseball, anyway. It's not in the blood or the raising. He's from Gary, which has seen better days, better days he experienced when the steel mills were still going full blast, when a sense of community still pervaded the youth-baseball fields on which he excelled, fields that more recently have been empty and reek of lost hope in the inner city.

He always strived to get better as a player. As a manager, too. He insisted he could pull the strings in the dugout better than when he began in 2001, succeeding former White Sox manager (and fellow youthful Cubs fan) Gene Lamont.

"My growth as a manager, if you put the time and effort into anything you do, you should become better," McClendon said. "My dad used to say, 'No job is big unless you ignore a lot of little things along the way.'

"I tried not to ignore the little things, kept things simple, and think I've progressed. Certainly the game has slowed down. I'm a lot more relaxed. I don't bring that intensity to the game as high as I used to. That can be a little intimidating for the players. I had to back off a little bit. There's a lot of things you learn along the way."

But don't mess with McClendon if you suggest he has worked on handling pitchers, one of the two prime tasks of a manager along with keeping a lid on cracks in the psyche of the clubhouse. McClendon may have logged time at first base, third base, and the outfield over his career as a role player, but he first and foremost was a catcher by both training and mentality.

"I 'managed' fifteen years as a catcher," he said. "As a catcher, you're constantly monitoring what the pitcher is doing. The pitching aspect was the easiest part. I say that in all sincerity. That came naturally. I've been handling pitchers my entire career."

McClendon had scant experience as a manager when hired. He had worked the Fall League for the Pirates one year but had been strictly a hitting coach since his career ended after the 1995 season. If he came in with any unrealistic expectations about the job, he's now been set straight. A one-hundred-loss season will do that to you.

"It's even more [than it's cracked up to be]," McClendon said. "It's one of the most difficult jobs to perform in all of sports. It's a 162-game schedule, you're dealing with twenty-five, twenty-six different personalities. You constantly have to check the weather. It's a very difficult job."

A strong sense of family guides McClendon through the everyday rough spots as he's tried not to let the frustrations overwhelm him. He had the advantage of involved parenting growing up, and he'll provide the same for his own children. He beams with pride when he talks about daughter Schenell's attending law school and strapping son Bo's playing outfield for Merrillville High School. He will not live his career again through Bo, though.

"He's a big boy," McClendon said. "I just want him to have a successful life. It doesn't have to be in sports."

All the familial support was needed when McClendon's first Pirates team in '01 finished 62–100. Improvement has been only incremental ever since, with an ownership getting everything it ever wanted in beautiful new PNC Park in Pittsburgh but refusing to open the financial spigot. McClendon had to suffer the private humiliation of enduring one-sided, salary-dumping trades. Worst of the deals were midsummer swaps in 2003 that netted the Cubs Aramis Ramirez, Kenny Lofton, and Randall Simon, practically handing the Cubs the NL Central title, which the team clinched with a doubleheader sweep over the Buccos on September 27 at Wrigley Field.

Despite the consistent losses, few ripped the Pirates for lagging on the field under McClendon. Players may have wanted to get out of Pittsburgh or avoided the city altogether. But once they donned a Pirates uniform, they played hard for McClendon, who managed to motivate without being a martinet.

"You're dealing with a lot of different personalities, different backgrounds," he said. "I tell the players all the time, 'This is not all about hugs and kisses' and 'I love you, you love me.' Hard times will arise; we'll meet them head-on and deal with them.

"I don't try to be a tough guy. It's more important for the players to respect me. I don't want the image of being a tough guy. My philosophy is that I don't want to embarrass players, and I don't want them to embarrass me. The best way to deal with problems and confrontations is to meet them head-on. When you do that, you usually deal with the truth and meet it head-on, but usually you don't have a problem anymore. Players may not like what you say, but they certainly understand and respect what you have to say."

He blends modern research techniques with old-fashioned managing by the gut.

"I try to research; I try to plan," he said. "If I'm afraid to lose, I'll never win. I'm not afraid to take a chance.

"I try to be well rounded. I believe in the computer and what it can spit out. But to be a good manager, I have to have a pulse on my team, what they're capable of doing, and what they're not capable of. A computer printout can't tell you that—how big are their hearts, how big is their drive and determination?"

McClendon basically learned from the three managers for whom he played—Pete Rose on the Reds, Don Zimmer on the Cubs, and Jim Leyland on the Pirates. The time he logged on the bench, waiting to pinch hit or fill in for a starter, was well spent watching the managers play chess baseball-style.

"Obviously, I tried to strive to learn as much as I could," he said. "I was able to sit next to some pretty good people in the game. I certainly asked questions about why a move was made, what was the purpose? More than anything, I wasn't afraid to ask questions. I became a student of the game, so to speak."

McClendon tried not to retain the worst qualities of his former managers. Rose's shortcomings were obvious. Zimmer, never the cuddly baseball "Popeye" lifer popularly portrayed for decades, could be as brusque as they came. McClendon thought he had the

1989 Cubs made for sure on opening day. But when the team arrived at Wrigley Field, Zimmer informed McClendon he was cut.

"There was no coddling," McClendon recalled. "Just pack your bags and get out."

McClendon also benefited from the presence of Bill Virdon, a former Pirates manager, as bench coach in his rookie year. Virdon earlier had worked with McClendon as a Pirates player, so familiarity helped the two.

"He certainly was a tremendous influence," McClendon said. "Bill kept me calm, kept my feet on the ground. His demeanor and what he brought to the table put me in a more relaxed state of mind, on how I approached the game. I don't know where I would have been from the mental point if it hadn't been for him. He was a tremendous force in my stability. It was hard to put in words what he meant."

McClendon also learned it wasn't wrong to wear one's heart on his sleeve—or on the bases itself. He pulled off an old-fashioned Zimmer–Leyland–Lou Piniella–Earl Weaver tantrum on June 26, 2001 at PNC Park. Umpire Rick Reed called catcher Jason Kendall out on a close play. McClendon was ejected for protesting the call. He grabbed the first-base bag off its moorings and carried it off the field. The tactic worked, at least that night, as the Pirates edged the Milwaukee Brewers 7–6.

Appointed as manager at age forty-one, McClendon seemingly achieved his highest profile since he earned the nickname "Legendary Lloyd" in 1971. A top youth baseball star in both catching and pitching back in Gary, he led the Anderson team through a tournament minefield all the way to the Little League World Series in Williamsport, Pennsylvania. He wowed the crowds by slugging five homers in five at bats, while being walked intentionally five times, before Anderson lost the title game to Taiwan on August 28. The feat earned McClendon a visit to the White House to meet vice president Spiro Agnew.

McClendon would never forget the sense of community that produced volunteer coaches for his Little League program and busloads and planeloads of northwest Indiana fans journeying to Williamsport. Thirty years later he'd return at the All-Star break, during his first year as Pirates manager, to find the Gary field on

Lloyd McClendon. Author photo.

which Anderson had clinched a crucial game deserted and poorly maintained, with grass growing in the infield.

McClendon was at Junedale Field to conduct his annual baseball clinic, run by his McClendon Athletes against Crime (MAAC) Foundation. He had remembered how baseball was a passion of the neighborhood when he was young, how the fields were full of players all summer long, how Ernie Banks came down from Chicago to speak to his team. And now baseball has practically disappeared from the inner city, the best African American athletes being diverted to basketball and football instead.

"We are as much to blame as anyone else," he said. "We haven't done the things to market baseball to the inner city, particularly with the younger kids. We're losing them. Where are the kids? Why aren't they out here playing baseball? [In 1971] the park would be packed.

"Major League Baseball has a lot to do with it. Basketball's done a tremendous job marketing the sport. Football, too. For some reason, we're always twenty years behind."

For years the MAAC Foundation not only staged baseball clinics at the All-Star break with McClendon as chief instructor but also tried to steer campers away from gangs and drugs. In recent years, the clinics were discontinued in their old form as funding became shaky. But McClendon was able to use his high profile as manager to put the arm on the biggest area employer. He persuaded the shrunken but still prominent USX steelmaker to sponsor the foundation's reorganized efforts to refurbish northwest Indiana baseball fields and provide tuition and baseball equipment for needy families.

McClendon also established a summer-long baseball presence to help in the efforts. He owns 3 percent of the Gary–South Shore Railcats, the local independent Northern League team that plays in a stadium next to downtown. The Railcats also are involved in the MAAC efforts.

He knows all too well he can't re-create the Gary of his youth. Nor can he summon his old Cubs heroes like Jim Hickman and Willie Smith or their style of play. All he can do is keep moving forward.

That he did, throughout a long minor-league career, starting out in the Mets organization, progressing to a couple of short stints with the Reds and then the unkind cut by Zimmer after coming over to the Cubs in a trade for outfielder Rolando Roomes.

But McClendon persevered and was ready when injuries decimated the roster a month into the 1989 season. Echoing his "Legendary Lloyd" achievements, McClendon slugged a three-run homer to beat the Braves at Wrigley Field in his first game up on May 16.

He did not spend much time on the bench after his recall. McClendon filled in for an injured Mark Grace at first. Then he settled in as the right-handed half of a platoon in left field with rookie Dwight Smith. McClendon finished the '89 regular season with twelve homers, forty RBI, and a .286 average. Better yet were the teammates he met.

"I made some wonderful friendships, some that still last," he said. "[Shawon] Dunston, [Dave] Clark, [Curtis] Wilkerson, [Andre] Dawson, and you can go on and on. Some top pitchers in [Greg] Maddux, [Rick] Sutcliffe, and [Mike] Bielecki."

One friendship lasted into his Pirates tenure. Clark, a longtime pinch hitter, was McClendon's hitting coach in his first two Pirates managerial seasons.

The Cubs petered out in the 1989 NLCS against the Giants, and 1990 quickly became a disaster. The magic was gone.

"It was a nice run," he said.

McClendon couldn't hit his weight in '90, and he was let go on waivers on September 9. The move turned out to be a big break for his future career. The Pirates picked him up, with McClendon quickly becoming Leyland's top role player. Over the next three years, McClendon came close to a World Series but ended up going home to northwest Indiana each time when the Pirates were knocked out.

Already thinking about managing by the time the Pirates picked him up, McClendon ended up in the right organization. He doesn't expect to retire on his job. He knows all too well managers are hired to be fired.

Hmmm, by the time that happens, Baker may have gone fishing for good. You can be sure McClendon would rush his resume to Wrigley Field.

There Comes a Horseman

olistic Hanover begged for a sugar cube or any treat you'd give to an outwardly cuddly animal. Dan Plesac, though, wasn't going to go that sugary-sweet route. He started to emotionally work the mahogany-coated standardbred, soothing her, getting in good with the filly the way he might have worked a hitter: nibble on the corner, go inside, waste a pitch, set him up for something special on 3-and-2.

In his 3 Up, 3 Down Farms stable on thirty-eight acres outside his native Crown Point, Indiana, devoted horseman Plesac was about to take Holistic Hanover out for her paces on the property's practice track. As soon as the gear to hitch up the jogging cart would be affixed to the horse, she might turn from mellow—she nibbled on the collar of Plesac's all-blue jumpsuit—to slightly rambunctious. A set of ears bent almost straight back would be a telltale sign.

The horse has a "taste for human flesh," Plesac said. "You've got to put up with her little nasty habit of liking to bite forearms and fingers. But if she was bad and didn't have any talent, I probably wouldn't put up with her."

But as shown in the portrayal of trainer Tom Smith in *Seabiscuit*, human–equine rapport can be taken to another level. The right person can handle the right horse; no dumb animals are they. So Plesac kept Holistic Hanover relatively calm as he hitched up the jogging cart and eased her out into the dry chill of an early winter day. Still lean and lanky in creeping middle age at six feet five, Plesac and friend circled the track the requisite number of times before easing back into the barn, steam billowing off the horse as equipment came off.

How Holistic Hanover would fare when she finally broke into harness racing could not be realistically forecast at this point.

"You really don't know until you start," Plesac said. "It takes a horse about eight months [of training] for them to start racing. About the sixth month, they'll start showing signs. The faster they go, the smoother they get, their gait. Their attitude perks up.

"Some train good, but when you get them in a group of eight or ten horses in a race, it's another story. They get better or get intimidated. It's kind of like baseball players. In the minor leagues, they warm up great on the side, but when they get into the game, you don't see that same stuff. I've owned a lot of horses who did not train well; you didn't go in with much expectations, and they've done well. I've had some that fooled you."

Maybe that's the appeal of horses. Again, the baseball analogy— it's unpredictable. The joy often is in the preparation, the anticipation. But never underestimate the joy of victory.

When you're hooked, you're in it for life. The love of horses is as loyal a cult as any that exists in many parts of the world. The members range from the broken-down horseplayer in the cheap seats, to former Cubs outfielder Moises Alou studiously scanning the Daily Racing Form at his locker during his Wrigley Field tenure, to the passionate horse-rescue activists gathering for rallies to slam a horsemeat-rendering factory.

Plesac learned to love horses concurrently with the realization that he was more athletically talented than most of his friends growing up, first in industrial Gary, then further south in more rural Crown Point. The immediate family was patently urban— Dad was a steelworker in Gary's heyday; Mom was a hairdresser. But Grandpa, the first generation from the old country, had his own "green acres" itch. Just before World War II, he had acquired the Crown Point farm property, raising corn and standardbreds in a cramped stable. Frequent trips to the farm were young Dan Plesac's sugar cube.

"This obviously is a passion of mine," Plesac said. "I enjoy every morning coming out here, cleaning stalls, working with young horses. Some days they train good; some days they train bad. They make you drive home feeling like pulling your hair out.

"It's like baseball. Some days you feel great, but you don't perform well. Other days you feel lousy but pitch great."

Thus from the day Plesac made his debut with the Milwaukee Brewers in 1986 through his development as a top closer a couple of years later, to his two-year stint with the Cubs in 1993–1994, and then the rest of his career as a well-traveled lefty late-inning specialist, he carried the twin passion of horses. He exulted in all its triumphs, satisfactions, and setbacks. He could stop and visit his four-legged friends at Maywood, on the way home from Wrigley Field with the heavy daytime schedule. He also had to be creative, do a little lying, when horses and baseball clashed.

"You don't know how strong and powerful they are," Plesac said of first working with standardbreds and going to harness-racing tracks as a youth. "You don't know enough to be scared. The longer you're around them, the more in-depth you get with them.

"The first horse I bought was Technical Bounce, when I was a rookie in 1986. Driving into Balmoral one morning, I slipped and fell on my [left] arm giving her a bath. Three days after that, Technical Bounce bit me in the shoulder blade, and I had teeth marks in the back of my arm. When I got to spring training and took my physical, I told the doctor I fell backwards going out to my car when he saw the teeth marks."

But the most severe bite was inflicted on Plesac's psyche—he couldn't get enough of the business. Almost every moment not devoted to baseball, wife Leslie and daughters Madeline and Natalie were immersed in the world of the track.

"I just love everything about the horses," he said. "During the season, I always had magazines and articles and books to read. Some guys get on the plane, play cards, have a few beers. But on those two-hour plane flights, I'd catch up on my book work for my stables, then catch up with reading."

Baseball and horses became so intertwined in Plesac's reputation that Richard Balog, a close friend from the pitcher's days living in the Chicago suburb of St. Charles, wanted to name a prime young horse he had just bred after him.

"He called to ask me for an OK to put my name on the horse," he said. "I signed a release for the naming. I kind of laughed about it."

The left-hander was pitched by Balog on several occasions about partial ownership of Plesac. "At the time I had sixteen horses, and I put it off," he said. "He gave me one last chance right before his first race. I prefer to have 100 percent ownership of a horse."

But 50 percent of Plesac would have been worth 100 percent of most other horses. Balog had struck gold. Plesac became the richest standardbred ever produced in Illinois. He was a multiple stakes winner and a Breeders Cup runner-up. Only a series of injuries to the horse's legs slowed him up in 2003–2004.

Fans assumed Plesac the horse was owned by Plesac the pitcher. "Fans would come up to me after he won a race and say, 'Your horse had a great night,'" he said. "I just went along with it."

Plesac never named a horse after a teammate or manager. But remembering Harry Caray's seventh-inning admonition in his first-ever Cubs game in 1993, he tagged one horse with "Let's Get Some Runs." The standardbred ran only one race. Other horses were tagged Hawk and Wimpy, after the White Sox announcers; Pick to Click, after the Sox announcing crew's pregame player performance predictions; and the obvious Brew Cruiser.

The fact that a teammate owned and trained horses was a fascination to those who wanted to hook up for a night at the track and a chance to pose in the winner's circle. One day, two fellow Cubs cashed in their lucky ticket.

First baseman Mark Grace and catcher Steve Lake kept begging Plesac to take them out to Maywood Park. So one night, with Doomsday, the pitcher's entry, a shaky entry in a race, the trio were joined by Cardinals utility player Tracy Woodson. Doomsday had a four-length lead one hundred yards from the wire but barely hung on "by the hair on his chinny chin chin to win," Plesac recalled. The smiles in the winner's circle from Plesac, Grace, Lake, and Woodson light up one of many photos displayed in the small office in the 3 Up, 3 Down Farms stable.

Two other photos are distinctive. Plesac's most successful horse, Ball & Chain, gets top billing. A September 24, 1994, photo of the beast racking up a new track record for four-year-old pacing horses, while winning $10,000, was recorded on the same night commissioner Bud Selig, Plesac's former boss in Milwaukee, called off the World Series due to the strike.

The family horse history also is displayed. Baby Hoey is shown with all the Plesacs, including a tall eleven-year-old Dan, at Washington Park on November 28, 1973.

Of course Plesac would carry his passion to its logical conclusion. He purchased the farm from the family in the mid-1990s, then put about $500,000 into improvements, including the practice track, to upgrade it to a full-time training facility. The new stables have stalls for six horses.

But, to prove that money isn't everything to a devoted horseman, he left a $2 million contract on the table that the Philadelphia Phillies offered in the late fall of 2003. Even at forty-one, he was deemed a valuable contributor to a team building up for a World Series push in a brand-new stadium. Plesac would help newly acquired Tim Worrell set up closer Billy Wagner in the team's scenario. Yet with the stables beckoning, Plesac cut the baseball cord with some gas left in the competitive tank. He had an emotional cushion few major leaguers would possess when they decide to call it quits.

Average Joes struggling to make ends meet might be shocked. Take the $2 million, pitch your one-third of an inning, and keep running the horses on the side 'til they tear the uniform off you.

They don't know Dan Plesac all that well. He may have made millions in baseball before he could match such winnings on the track. Yet the only thing that changed about this product of a blue-collar background was his ability to properly indulge himself in training facilities for the horses. The Plesac of 1986 was much the same guy as nearly two decades later. The $50,000 offered by the St. Louis Cardinals to sign Plesac out of Crown Point High School in 1980 was still considered a considerable sum by his forty-something self in another century.

"What I've tried to do in this whole run is to treat people I come into contact with with respect and dignity," Plesac said. "I've really made an effort not to put into anyone's face what I've done, the money I've made, the people I've met. I was no different than my brother Joe, my brother Ron, the people I grew up with.

"Everybody has dreams and aspirations of doing something and being successful. You always have to be compassionate and understanding. I was lucky. I was blessed with a gift of a tremendous arm that could take a lot of beating and a tremendous willpower and drive to succeed at something.

"I've stayed away from hanging around with the wrong crowd. I was very focused and very driven. I wouldn't let anything I could control stop me from where I wanted to go. You stay away from drugs, stay away from alcohol."

Proudest of having never served time on the disabled list

through that eighteen-year run, Plesac related the one experience that convinced him to show up for work and not seek excuses. He has to go back to the very beginning of his career.

"My rookie year in 1986, we had a ten-day road trip to end the season, and we're playing in Oakland," he recalled. "I remember walking into the trainers' room. Robin Yount is on the trainers' table, getting a cortisone injection because he had turf toe. I saw the needle, and it almost got me sick to my stomach.

"Two hours later, I was running in the outfield, and I met Robin. I was in awe of him, one of the greatest players in Milwaukee Brewers history. I started up a conversation with him, and I [had] never had a one-on-one with him. I asked him, 'Boy, that shot hurt?' He said, 'Boy, does it ever.' Then I asked, 'You're not playing tonight?' Robin said, 'Yeah, I'm playing, why?'

"He said, 'Let me ask you something. When you were a kid, did you ever fake you were sick so you wouldn't have to go to school? When your mom and dad left for work, you laughed because you

Dan Plesac and friend at his stable. Author photo.

pulled one over on them.' That's the way it is in baseball. When you find out how easy it is to take a day off, you'll take them all the time. That sunk in with me for eighteen years.

"If I could breathe and I felt I could go out there and pitch, I'd pitch. Many games I'd drive home from Wrigley Field. My shoulder was throbbing. I was pitching lousy. I'd think, 'I've got to say something [about not pitching].' But the next day, driving in on Irving Park [Road], I thought, 'No, I'm not [going to beg off]. I'm going to grind this out. I'm going to get healthy somehow.'"

He did, and that's why Plesac does not look back at a Wrigley Field stint that went awry on the field with any bitterness.

Possessed of a fastball toward the high end of ninety to a hundred miles per hour, Plesac saved sixty-three games for the Brewers in 1988–1989. However, his effectiveness declined while pain in his shoulder increased the next three seasons, the Brewers even giving him fourteen starts in an attempt to straighten him out.

After the 1992 season, Plesac became available as a free agent. The Cubs were a logical destination, with Plesac having grown up forty miles southeast and also settling into a mansion in far west suburban St. Charles. Negotiations with general manager Larry Himes began in a strange off-season that resulted in the free-agent defection of Greg Maddux, the one man over the last forty years the Cubs had to keep.

Unknown to Plesac or his agent, Himes also dickered the same time with free-agent lefty closer Randy Myers. Had the Plesac camp known of the concurrent talks with Myers, he probably would not have signed with Chicago. But he inked a deal just before Myers also signed.

The acquisition of the two southpaws left the Cubs with four lefties in the bullpen, counting setup man Paul Assenmacher and young Chuck McElroy. Himes hoped to peddle Assenmacher for needed help elsewhere to thin that herd, but he outsmarted himself. Few teams wanted to pick up Assenmacher's contract; he was getting closer's money. Manager Jim Lefebvre, no deft handler of pitchers as an old hitting coach, did not have enough work for four lefties. As a result, he overworked right-hander Bob Scanlan while Plesac drew the short straw, rust adding to the aches in his shoulder. Assenmacher eventually departed to the Yankees in late July, but Plesac's fate was sealed. In sixty-two and two-thirds innings, Plesac gave up seventy-four hits, second-worst ratio of his career.

"Being with the Cubs was one of the best things to happen to me," he said. "I was able to work with Garrett Giemont and Brett Fischer, two of the finest therapists and trainers. One day I told Garrett of the problems with my shoulder. They got me on a series of exercises, but it took awhile to get me back. I went from throwing eighty-six to eighty-seven miles per hour in spring training to eighty-eight to eighty-nine in May and June. Late in '93, I thought, 'It's coming back.'

"They told me to be patient. I continued to do the program in the off-season, and I got a little better in '94 (fifty-three strikeouts in fifty-four and two-thirds innings despite a 4.61 ERA). I never did get ninety-seven miles per hour back."

In the major housecleaning during the strike after the 1994 season, Plesac, Giemont, and Fischer departed while Himes was demoted to an Arizona-based scout. But Plesac was persuaded by Giemont and Fischer to stay on the program. Signing with the Pirates, he started humping his fastball back up to ninety-three miles per hour, consistently staying in the range of eighty-eight to ninety-two miles per hour. He now established himself as a specialist against left-handed hitters in the late innings, moving from Pittsburgh to Toronto to Arizona, back to Toronto, and finally to Philadelphia, with 1,064 games, fourth all-time, on his record when he retired.

Another time, another regime, Plesac might have flourished as a Cub. The regime of Himes, team chairman Stanton Cook, player development director Al Goldis, and assistant GM Syd Thrift, on top of assorted mistakes by Himes predecessor Jim Frey, did damage to both the parent club and the farm system that took the better part of another decade to clean up.

But Plesac does not carry regrets very long. When you've coughed up games in late relief or lost on the track, you learn to file away setbacks quickly.

"The only thing I knew was the Milwaukee Brewers," he said. "I was open to whatever [the Cubs] wanted to do. This is a new team, a new organization. I just went along with it. I didn't say it was really screwed up here. I didn't know any better. Whatever they threw out on the plate, I took it and I ate it."

Nor is he damning the changes in both baseball and society since his rookie year. Horsemen take things in stride, on and off the track.

"The game has changed; society has changed," he said. "Sometimes you can look back, and try to say, 'Those were the good ol' days. The minimum salary was $60,000; now it's $300,000.'

"When I was a kid, there were no video games, no play stations. You came up with a way to amuse yourself. You played basketball all day long. You went to play a pickup baseball game at East Glen Park [Gary, Indiana] Little League. Now you've got cell phones, computers, instant messaging, so many ways to get what you want right now. I have no problem with it.

"I understand that young guy who gets called up at twenty-one with a cell phone and nice sports car, he's no different than anyone else his age. The only thing I get disappointed in is young players come up, and some guys tend to want things handed to them instead of earning it. As a pitcher, you're your own best pitching coach, your own best scout. You're the best one to prepare yourself for who you're playing, how to take care of your body, and learning what makes you tick. You can't depend on somebody to hold your hand and tell you what pitch to throw and when to throw it and what I did last week when I faced Mark Grace.

"Most guys who stay around and play ten, twelve, fifteen years, they've woken up and smelled the coffee and realized they have to help [themselves]. . . . Don't depend on scouts and their reports. You just watch the player you're going against and exploit his weaknesses."

And never second-guess yourself if you have the courage of your convictions, even if you've missed out on the baseball winner's circle of the World Series.

"I wouldn't trade eighteen years and all those things I was able to do for one World Series ring. I would rather play eighteen years the way I did it than play just five years with a World Series ring."

B-Mac the Radio Mogul

CALLER: I got a trivia question. Who was the last Cub prior to Corey Patterson to start three consecutive opening days in center field?

WHB-RADIO HOST: I betcha it's Brian McRae.

CALLER: Yeah. He did it 1995 to 1997. But let me tell you, McRae didn't get going back in 1997, just like the team . . .

WHB-RADIO HOST: Whoa, I gotta cut you off at the pass there, buddy. That's our boss you're talking about.

The above exchange is fictional. But if it ever takes place, McRae won't squelch his host's free-speech rights. He could clamp down, as part owner of a private business, all-sports WHB-Radio in Kansas City. Yet McRae, outspoken in his own baseball career when his teammates called him "B-Mac," figures common sense will prevail.

"We haven't had any problems with hosts criticizing station owners," he said. "You don't do personal attacks. State your opinions. They have the freedom to do what they have to do. But you can do it in a form that doesn't seem like you're criticizing your boss—criticize stuff on the field, not what he's doing at home."

The WHB on-air staff still have to walk a fine line. Among their owners were not only McRae but also Royals players Jeff Randa and Kevin Appier and former Royals stopper Jeff Montgomery. While most players gravitate behind the mike as color analysts or even play-by-play men after their careers, McRae's group became the powers behind those behind the mike. They are now radio moguls, or magnates, or at the very least new-wave entrepreneurs, handling millions of dollars in sale prices and advertising cash flow in running a cluster of three stations in Kansas City.

Mind you, McRae trained for an on-air role. He first majored in broadcast journalism at the University of Kansas in the years after

Hal McRae, his father, was a deadly effective designated hitter for
the Royals. He worked at NBC affiliate WDAF-TV in Kansas City
while working radio color for Kansas's baseball team and the University of Missouri–Kansas City's basketball team. More recently,
McRae hosted a twice-weekly audio-streamed talk show for MLB.
com, then handled some color analysis and pre- and postgame
show-hosting chores for Royals games on WHB after the 50,000-
watt station landed the team's broadcast rights.

But running one's own radio station, then stations, became more
fascinating to McRae in the back nine of his baseball career.

While patrolling center for the Cubs in the mid-1990s, a group
of investors from Kansas City, where McRae continued to make his
off-season home, tempted him to join their ownership group. After
thinking it over, McRae eventually jumped in. They started out
owning a smaller all-sports station, KCTE-AM, in Independence,
Missouri, a Kansas City suburb and home of the late president
Harry S Truman.

Central in the group was Montgomery, a longtime McRae teammate who had success in real estate. Eventually Appier and Randa
joined to boost the ownership rolls to more than fifteen people.
Opening their wallets, the group acquired the WHB license, moving KCTE over to take advantage of the stronger signal at 810 on
the AM dial. Soon the group added another AM station and an FM
music station.

"Jeff Montgomery and I put a lot of our money, liquid cash, into
it," McRae said. "The original group was six guys, and we put a
lot of our sweat equity into the business."

Players often complain about the content of sports-talk radio.
Now they had a chance to do something about it through ownership, an unprecedented situation.

"I never heard of players who owned stations while active or
had a stake in a flagship station for their team," McRae said.

Third baseman Randa, also a year-round Kansas City resident,
liked the idea of dabbling in radio.

"I wanted to get involved in something locally," he said. "I'm a
very low-scale owner. Brian and I have been friends for a long time.
People in the group see each other all the time. Kansas City is a
smaller town. Word travels fast.

"People have done their research. You have a lot of good people with creative ideas. Like anything else in life, you've got to take some chances."

Helping out the business was the fact that Montgomery owns the building in which the stations' studios are located. The group looked into expanding out of the market, checking out stations in Atlanta, Memphis, and Jacksonville. But the final decision was to stick to Kansas City and build up the core of three stations, especially the FM outlet.

McRae, who now owns 15 percent of the broadcast cluster, made millions in baseball. But he's surprised at the amount of money flowing in and out of the business.

The group took out some loans to buy KCTE for $8 million. They coughed up $20 million for the FM station. The payoff, though, is down the line.

"You can make some money, but your biggest return is when you sell the stations," McRae said. "We had our cluster of three stations appraised at around $45 million to $50 million. We been asked to sell three or four times, but we're having too much fun with it. We don't want to sell [now]."

In 2004, McRae and Company had a chance to really boost WHB's profile. They landed the Royals radio rights in a $10 million, four-year deal. Also coming on board was Mr. Royal, George Brett, to host a midday sports-talk program.

"We bid on the Royals three years ago but didn't get them," McRae said. "Then we bid again and got them. That's when you start to say you're a legitimate player in the industry. We expected in the first year to lose a little money. If the Royals make it to the playoffs once in the four years we have them, we'd be ecstatic."

The station owners spent money to make money with the Royals' rights—a strategy that seemingly was not practiced to the fullest during his Cubs days. McRae was a critic then of team management strategy but now understands all sides.

"At the time, Tribune Company did what they thought they needed to do to be successful," he said. "Now they're doing things in a bit different fashion [spending more on payroll]. You kind of wish it had happened that way in the mid-1990s when I was there.

"When I look at what we do at our station, if we want to be a major player, you have to spend money. You have to spend some money to make money. We feel we're a major player not only in the Kansas City market but also nationally. We have to act like it and spend accordingly.

"I think sometimes people talk a good game, but when it comes down to it, they don't want to spend the money. We're 50,000 watts, cover eight states, one of the largest sports stations in the country. To be a major player, you can't talk the game and not spend the money."

The combination of the Royals and the present and former players working in on-air roles boosted the credibility of the sports-talk operation. The gabfest format exploded in popularity in the early 1990s but usually never has been a ratings leader in most markets. And many athletes were angered by studio-bound hosts' criticism and thirdhand information, their complaints centered on the hosts not showing up at the ballparks to get to know the players.

"If you're a listener, you'll listen to guys who played or who are playing," McRae said. "If you want inside information, are you going to listen to an outsider? You're getting it from five or six reliable sources."

Brian McRae. Author photo.

Much of his group's management decisions will be driven by ratings, still an inexact science in accurately measuring listenership. McRae wants to look beyond these often-manufactured numbers in gauging the success of his stations.

"I still don't understand ratings," he said. "But ratings are just a small part of it. If you're bringing in your ad dollars, it doesn't matter. Your ratings may not be glamorous, but if you're bringing in your ad dollars, that's the bottom line. Are you generating the type of revenue you feel you want to generate?"

And based on that bottom line, McRae and his partners may have to utter the words that Donald Trump made famous: "You're fired." However, such decisions won't be made in a blind-sided manner, he vowed.

"I just treat people the way I want to be treated," McRae said. "I'm frank, up-front, and let everyone know what's going on. I don't have a problem with my employees coming to me for information. They can call me at home.

"I also try to instill in them it's part of a team, like a ball club. We can all be successful. We can all make money. We can all be happy. I hope everybody can think along the same lines. If the station's doing well, then you'll be compensated well. You're going to be taken care of. If you have one or two people who try to get on their own program, then it can hurt everyone else.

"I may be a little too blunt at times. But I think you're better off that way so people know where you stand. We're all adults here. If you can't take criticism or praise in the right manner, then maybe I don't want you working for me."

McRae was similarly blunt during his two and two-thirds seasons as a Cub. He held up his end of the bargain. The switch-hitter produced two of his best seasons after GM Ed Lynch stole him in a deal with the Royals for two minor leaguers early in 1995. But Lynch scarcely repeated such aggressiveness through much of the rest of his tenure at the helm, creating morale problems in the organization. In midsummer 1996, McRae, first baseman Mark Grace, and even manager Jim Riggleman wondered why Lynch wasn't making moves to bolster the Cubs, then marginally in contention in the National League Central.

Over the years, McRae has mellowed a bit about the teams that fell short and were shorthanded talentwise and even in payroll despite Tribune Company ownership.

"It didn't happen, and you can't look back," he said. "You can't have everything. I enjoyed the time I spent in Chicago. There's probably some things that could have gone a little better. I got here, and it wasn't the right time [for winning], but it was a good time for me. I wish we could have won more. I wish we could have gone to the postseason. But it didn't happen. To dwell on it doesn't do anybody any good.

"I still talk to [team president] Andy MacPhail quite a bit. I'm excited about the Cubs' prospects of being good for a long time. To be able to wear a Cub uniform and say I got to play at Wrigley Field was a lot of fun for me."

Although McRae did not consider himself a leadoff-type hitter, he did better than most Cubs before and since in that role. In the strike-shortened 1995 season, he scored ninety-two runs in 137 games while batting .288 with thirty-eight doubles, twelve homers, and twenty-seven stolen bases. McRae followed that up in 1996 with 111 runs scored in 157 games with thirty-two doubles, seventeen homers, sixty-six RBIs, and thirty-seven steals. A thinking man's player, McRae even batted left-handed against Braves southpaw ace Tom Glavine once to try to negate the action of his breaking pitches on a right-handed hitter.

McRae had been a decent player with the Royals but flirted with stardom as a Cub in his two peak years.

"They got me after five years in the American League and kind of feeling my way through things," he said. "The National League fit my game a lot better than the American League. I came at the right time. I was maturing and understanding myself as a ballplayer. I didn't picture I could do some of these things in Kansas City."

McRae also played alongside Sammy Sosa when the slugger gave a hint of things to come in 1996. A pitch broke Sosa's wrist, knocking him out for the season with six weeks to go and with him leading the NL with forty homers. He was on a fifty-two-homer pace. McRae could see the maturation starting to take hold in '96.

"He was getting to be a hitter and not just a home-run guy that '96 season," he said of Sosa. "Before that, he was a .240 or .260

hitter with a lot of homers and strikeouts. He was getting to be more patient and understanding himself as a hitter more.

"Sammy had a lot thrown at him early in his career. When you're on teams that are losing, you try to do a little more than you're capable of doing. As the talent got better around him, you saw him get better as a ballplayer because he knew he didn't have to do it all himself. And he relaxed a lot more."

No Cub was relaxing in the forgettable first two weeks of the 1997 season. After a spring training full of spoken dread over starting on the road against the Braves and beefed-up Florida Marlins, the Cubs fulfilled the prophecy by starting out an NL-worst 0–14. The season was over in record-quick time. McRae scuffled like most of his teammates, unable to fix the mechanics in his switch-hitting. A few days after the July 31 trading deadline, Lynch somehow worked the waiver wire. McRae and reliever Turk Wendell were dispatched to the New York Mets for center fielder Lance Johnson, starting pitcher Mark Clark, and utility infielder Manny Alexander.

Despite his comfort in Wrigley Field, McRae was pleased to go to New York.

"I was happy I got traded to a team in contention, to the wild-card race," he said. "In 1998, we missed the wild card by a game. Almost all my career, I was on teams that were in contention in September. I never got to the postseason, but I wasn't playing a lot of meaningless games in September. Nineteen ninety-two in Kansas City was the only year we were totally out of it in September. It didn't bother me going to a pennant-contending ball club."

McRae thought he thrived as a Met. He was placed in the middle of the order, producing a season-high twenty-one homers and seventy-nine RBIs in 1998.

"When I got to hit down in the order, it was more of what I could have done," he said. "But my teams before that wanted me to hit at the top of the order. Nineteen ninety-eight was the most fun, fulfilling year I had because I told people for nine years if I hit down in the order, I'd drive in a lot of runs and be more productive. The second half, I hit behind Mike Piazza. I got pitches to hit. It was fun to be able to be in that position with guys in scoring position."

But 1998 turned out to be a last hurrah for McRae. Later in the

1999 season, the Mets shipped him to the Colorado Rockies. After a seven-game stay, he moved on to the Toronto Blue Jays for thirty-one more contests. And then he walked out the door for good at age thirty-two, the art of moving money and buying radio stations neatly waiting for him.

The Shop on Calumet Avenue

The corner shop on Calumet Avenue, two blocks from the downtown—such as it is—of quaint Chesterton, Indiana, doesn't distinguish itself just by outward appearances.

But once a customer enters RSVP, run by Peg and Mickey Morandini, the senses automatically shift to a positive overdrive.

Before any pair of eyes can scan the displays in RSVP, the olfactory conduits pick up the scent of apple cinnamon. The mood is automatically soothed, and it is further relaxed by the messages offered in all the sample displays. Cards for every occasion, customized by Peg Morandini and deftly printed up in back by hubby Mickey. No problem with typos from that computer keyboard—Mickey always had good hands.

Up front by the register are a few sample gifts. Immediately to the left is a separate room devoted to weddings, with more sample cards and four white chairs surrounding a glass table. Through the rest of the store are even more samples for every happy occasion—births, anniversaries, holidays. A lavender wall backdrop completes the positive mood.

"It's a happy place, because you're dealing with happy events—weddings, new babies, parties," Mickey said.

To the best of the proprietors' research, RSVP is the only custom stationery and greeting-card shop in this part of Indiana. The alternatives are distant, probably to the west in Chicago, maybe to the east in South Bend or up in western Michigan. The Morandinis are in the right place at the right time. Folks are moving over the state line, thirty miles distant, from Illinois for Porter County's lower taxes and quieter lifestyles. A nice little population base is just a few miles to the south, beyond the Indiana toll road, in Valparaiso. The customer base is bound to grow, and word of mouth has been a strong lure for business.

Peg, animated and enthusiastic in any endeavor, is out sick today, not available to guide customers through their card designs. So Mickey has had to emerge from the back room to run the whole place solo. "I'd rather stay in the back, but it I have to do it [serve customers], I don't mind it," he said. He's at once leadoff man and cleanup hitter. Eternally boyish in appearance, clad in a pullover sweater and jeans, Morandini hasn't aged a day from a much more high-profile gig. He's a bit more than a half-decade removed from playing second base and spraying hits all over Wrigley Field, getting on base any way he could to provide more RBI grist for Sammy Sosa during the latter's starring role in the great home run chase of 1998. And here he is, a radical lineup change in his life, as a shopkeeper on Main Street, USA.

Surely there's got to be the aftereffects of a kind of mental decompression. Morandini once led a privileged life, batting second in a Cubs lineup that scraped through to a rare playoff appearance. The fans couldn't reach out to him or his teammates whenever they wanted. Yeah, look but don't touch. No more bellying up to the bar with your favorite Cub at Ray's Bleachers after games, a la 1969. They had become megamillionaire entertainers, their every whim catered to, members of the most powerful union in a country steadily shedding organized labor clout every year.

Now you can go right up to Morandini, shake his hand, ask him to serve you, and he'll gladly oblige. But you don't know Morandini that well if you think there was ever a shock to the system.

"Not really," he said when asked if there was a comedown from his late 1990s persona. "I was never a high-maintenance guy. Those things are great, but it's not something I had to have. I enjoy it now. I'd rather stay in the back, but if I have to [run the store], it doesn't bother me."

The small-but-growing-town setting has suited Morandini to a T.

"That's Mickey," Peg Morandini said a few days later, out of the sickbed. "He's more of a small-town guy. He never looks at himself as a high-profile guy. This more suits him than what he expected. He's right. He requires low maintenance."

Any trace of a big-league ego had to be checked at the shop front door. Mickey and Peg are small-business folk, and every sale counts. A woman comes into the shop, so Mickey springs to attention. The customer has a substantial holiday order. He talks with her back at a card display, then begins hunting through drawers for the right stock.

"Peg knows this store inside out," he says. He can't match her feel for her stock but hustles to catch up. That quality he knows well. Eventually he tracks down the right stock, meets the customer, completes the transaction, rings up the register, and reassures her of a solid return policy. Total bill: $243. He has not dropped the ball.

So after an aching shoulder told him baseball was past tense, after the travel and front-office politics got a little old for his tastes, with his three sons at a crucial age for two-parent nurturing, why a custom-stationery store? Surely there was a coaching or instructing job around that would keep him close to them, across that toll road from Chesterton. Or just puttering around, doing nothing, living off baseball savings and investments until the light went off some year in the future.

The answer is as basic as Morandini's personality. Peg went with him through his baseball journeys. Now it's time to follow Peg's career heart, the couple having been together since they were both students at Indiana University.

"He was really good about it," Peg said. "It's something I wanted to do. After baseball, it would be my turn. I saw the [store] location. He said, 'Let's go look.'"

"Peg always loved unique stationery," Mickey said. "Once I retired [after the 2000 season], I decided I'd take a year off to be with the kids and then go into something. Originally, I looked into a big baseball facility to do instruction. But it cost too much, and that kind of fell through.

"Then she said, 'Let's do a stationery business.'"

The couple started to investigate the market. There was none in their area. Peg and Mickey started working out of their home in October 2001. Soon they looked around for shop space in Chesterton and Valparaiso.

"This place became available, and rent was very reasonable," Morandini said. "We have our own parking lot. We went for it and finally moved into the store in March 2002."

Those years of baseball earnings paid off. Instead of having to take out a small-business loan or borrow from relatives, the Morandinis invested between $75,000 and $100,000 from their savings for the start-up costs.

"It absolutely was a big undertaking," Morandini said. "Peg started contacting companies and got her federal tax ID."

Peg would be the creative and sales end of the business, consulting with customers on design and wording of their cards, invitations, and other stationery. Did that leave Mickey as a greeter and part-time salesman when he wasn't taking their sons around to sports activities?

No way. The Morandinis are a true partnership, at home and in the shop. Mickey's role at RSVP is just as substantial as Peg's. He gives those deft hands a workout in the back office, printing the stationery and handling the financial and ordering end of the business.

"We have completely different responsibilities," Peg said. "His is all financial, inventory. He is unbelievably meticulous. Friends say, 'I wish I had a husband like that.' He makes sure everything

Mickey Morandini. Author photo.

is inventoried correctly. We're both very neat, but he's very meticulous and particular about everything. If he could take care of that, I wouldn't have to hire ten people to do that."

"Peg knows my role; I know my role," Mickey said. "We don't butt heads. That's why we get along so well, not get on each other's nerves."

The ol' ballplayer does not like to delegate.

"I always was taught if you want it done right, do it yourself," he said. "That's what we try to do here."

Morandini could get so focused he did not have to go to computer classes to learn how to print stationery. He had been tight with noted computer-jockey Curt Schilling when they were Philadelphia Phillies teammates. "Decent" on the computer, he still hadn't picked up any of the kind of sophisticated know-how needed to power a business via the keyboard.

"At the start, I just did printing," he said. "I was self-taught. It was just practicing. I went into programs, played around, figured how to rotate stuff. Some of it is high-tech. It took a month or two to really get comfortable. I've enjoyed it."

Like a deft double-play combo, the husband–wife RSVP team got the business off to as smooth a start as possible. Most businesses will expect to lose money for the first several years after opening the door. And the Morandinis opened up amid the national gloom and plummeting economy of September 11, 2001. But perhaps luck was the residue of both their design and their passion. In sad times, people had to accentuate the happy moments of their lives, so the store filled a need. Both weddings and Christmas keep going in spite of outside negatives.

"Once we put down the initial money to open up, we never had to take money from the home account," Mickey said. "It supported itself right away. It took awhile to start actually making money. By early 2004, we started to pay some bills from home from here. It's growing every year. We felt pretty fortunate."

RSVP opened its own website: www.rsvppaperie.com. The Morandinis looked to a future where customers could place orders online. And with every inch of the store crammed with displays, Peg and Mick wondered when the attorney whose office is next door might follow through on a goal of retiring, possibly opening up additional store space. "We had eleven hundred square feet, and we were crammed in here," Mickey said.

Some of their old baseball friends called on them cross-country. When Schilling was traded to the Red Sox late in 2003, Peg and Mickey concocted a Christmas card picturing Curt, wife Shonda, and their four sons along with four little red stockings on the side of the card. Mark Grace, relocated to Phoenix, commissioned a birth announcement for oldest son Jackson along with Christmas cards. Rounding out the roster of baseball customers were former Morandini teammates Steve Trachsel, Tyler Houston, and Ruben Amaro Jr., along with reliever Mike Myers and several minor leaguers.

One goal was adding more gifts—albeit not turning RSVP into a gift shop—so some time-crunched customers could do some one-stop shopping for cards and gifts. An annual trip by the Morandinis to a stationery trade show in New York may now be complemented by a visit to a similar gift show to cull ideas.

The couple do not work the typical punishing hours of retail, although Peg has found herself completing some jobs in the middle of the night at home. RSVP is open Tuesdays through Saturdays, with an employee holding forth on Saturday so the owners can spend time with Jordan, Griffin, and Braydon, their three sons.

The RSVP success story is not singular. Others may not have the same advantage in capital in starting up as the Morandinis. But fledgling business owners need not be less astute. They can make a go of it, according to the two shopkeepers on Calumet Avenue.

"Make sure it's something unique—make sure it's something people need," Mickey said. "Do some research. Make sure you're in a good area. It can be done. It's got to be the right product, and the need has to be there."

"Don't do more than you can handle," Peg said. "Even when Mickey and I started this, we wanted a couple of different locations. But the rent was higher. That [high costs] is a risk to opening a new business."

And if the hours are flexible, it will be a huge bonus. Morandini, who immediately took to Little League coaching after he left baseball, has a busy schedule of coaching his sons in both baseball and basketball dovetailing with his RSVP hours. Although the baseball training facility never materialized, Morandini conducts several baseball clinics and has done some private instruction. He also found time to perform a little baseball analysis on Fox Sports Chicago, make several trips into Wrigley Field for games, and appear at the annual Cubs Convention. The Morandinis were very active in the Les Turner (Chicago) chapter of ALS—Lou Gehrig's disease—while he played for the Cubs and still try to help out amid their busy schedule.

Morandini's devotion to family was on firm display during his two Cubs seasons. The former Peg Ohm was a native of Valparaiso. The couple had settled in the small city early in his eight-year tenure as a Phillies second baseman. But as a Cub, he had the chance to stay at home the entire season with his young sons for a price—a 120-mile round trip to Wrigley Field for each daytime home game. Morandini would stay overnight in Chicago when a day game followed a night game. Manager Jim Riggleman was mildly surprised that Morandini would endure such a long drive in the rush hour each way. Again, he didn't know Mickey as well as Peg did.

"He'd drive double the time—two hours—before [being away from his sons]," Peg said. "The drive was good for him. Going there, it was an hour of peace and quiet to think about what he would do that day. Going home, it was another hour to think about the game he had played. Surprisingly, traffic was not bad. It worked out great."

The Morandinis had enjoyed a comfortable life in Philadelphia after he had broken into the majors in 1990. Mickey played on the mullet-happy 1993 Phillies World Series team. Later, he was a model of consistency at second as the Phillies' fortunes declined through the mid-1990s. He was one of the most popular players, earning the tough Philly sportswriters' Media Good Guy Award in 1995. Morandini was not just a clubhouse moth, though. In addition to working with the ALS foundation, he and Peg annually spent $20,000 to buy tickets to Phillies games for terminally ill children, then hosted a postseason party for the kids. Children in the Easter Seals program were treated to tickets, care of Morandini, to every Sunday Veterans Stadium game.

With so much of their total energy invested in the Phillies, the Cubs weren't on the Morandinis' radar until the Christmas season of 1997.

Seeking to trim payroll, new Phillies general manager Ed Wade had his eye on Cubs outfielder Doug Glanville, who had hit .300 in his first full season in 1997. Wade had prospect Marlon Anderson coming up. On the Chicago end, Ryne Sandberg had just retired for good. The Cubs were not sold on young Miguel Cairo as his replacement. Wade sent word to counterpart Ed Lynch that if he was willing to part with Glanville, now a surplus part with veteran center fielder Lance Johnson in tow, the Phils would consider trading Morandini to the Cubs.

The deal was made two days before Christmas in 1997. Several years later, with Glanville a 204-hit, .325-hitting slick-gloved center fielder and Johnson and Morandini on their way out of Chicago, the trade netted scorn from second-guessers. But at the time, Glanville was dealt from a position of strength, while Morandini had his best-ever season—a .296 average, eight homers, fifty-three RBIs—to help Sosa amass an astounding 158 RBIs to go along with his sixty-six homers in 1998.

"We were a team that just jelled and played well together for one year," he said. "A lot of guys had career years that year. We had a lot of desire that year."

Playing at home was equal to the thrill of starting on a Cubs playoff team amid the usual packed houses at Wrigley Field.

"I think everybody would like that opportunity," Morandini said. "There's certain organizations—the Cubs, Boston, the Yankees—that fanwise take it up a step from everyone else. For two years it was convenient, part of the reason I'm pretty popular in this area. If I hadn't played for the Cubs, I don't know how popular I'd be."

Not even a downer 1999 could dim that fond memory. Morandini and Lynch could not agree on a new contract in spring training, getting the season off on a bad foot. Then the entire team collapsed in June, got swept by the White Sox at Wrigley Field, and endured their worst-ever August at 6–24. Morandini slumped to .241 and was let go as a free agent as Lynch traded for Eric Young to play second.

"I'm way past that," he said of the '99 contract squabble and inglorious end to his Wrigley Field tenure. "I'm a free spirit—what comes, comes and what goes, goes. I've got three healthy, beautiful children and a healthy wife."

Walking away from baseball at age thirty-four after splitting 2000 between the Phillies and Toronto Blue Jays was not difficult for Morandini.

"I had a bad shoulder. I couldn't throw, and that helped cut the cord a little faster. If I was healthy and still had some years left in me, it would have been harder. It happened at a good time, with the kids starting school.

"Do I miss it? I miss competition, but I don't miss the travel. Absolutely, [the travel] burns you out. More guys I talked to who are out of it say they're so glad they don't have to travel anymore. But you do miss the people.

"I don't need it right now," he said of baseball. "Someday I might like to get into coaching. Maybe a minor-league roving instructor, pick my own hours, dates. But I'm enjoying my kids too much."

If anything, Mickey and Peg are true to their own words. After Mickey was traded to the Cubs, Peg had put their lives in perspective. She accurately predicted her family's future.

"Someday we will look back on this and the life we had, remember the good things and move on," was her proclamation as 1998 dawned.

Peg knew her husband well even then. Years into the future, another customer served, a sale made, one more step toward profitability, Mickey could look around RSVP. The surroundings prevent dark thoughts, but so does the makeup of the guy in the back office.

"I can't complain," said Morandini.

Seeing the World, Thanks to Baseball

The love of baseball rewards different people in different ways.

Greg Maddux, for example, gets to pitch for a total of just two teams throughout his career, winning more than 300 games, collecting a quartet of Cy Young Awards, and ranking as the pitching guru of his generation.

But a former Maddux teammate on the Cubs had a very different fate. Lester Lancaster's scoreless streak of 30 2/3 innings in relief, bailing Maddux out of a few jams in 1989, did not cement roots for him in the game. Within three years, the right-hander Lancaster was on an odyssey that would take him from the majors to Triple A, through a slew of independent-league managing and pitching gigs ranging from New York to Mississippi, across the Pacific to Taiwan, down to Mexico and thousands of miles the other direction to Italy to pitch. Thanks to baseball, Lancaster got to see the world.

"It definitely was worth it," Lancaster said. "I still put a uniform on my back. I wouldn't have gotten to see different parts of the country, and other countries, if not for baseball. I met a lot of nice individuals."

Lately he finally stuck closer to his Athens, Alabama, home, near Huntsville. Giving the independent leagues a rest in 2004, Lancaster coached junior-high baseball while substitute teaching and completing his permanent teaching certificate.

Talk about contrasts. Here he was managing the eccentric ex-Cub Mel Hall, a 42-year-old designated hitter, in Corpus Christi, Texas, one year. And he signed his own former Cubs center-field teammate, Jerome Walton, to play, yet later could not get hold of

Walton to arrange for him to join the team. So the next season, Lancaster opted not to deal with baseball characters anymore, instead teaching seventh-graders the right way to play the game.

"I felt I'd take a break unless something falls into my life," Lancaster said. "Ultimately I'd like to coach in high school. I'm looking around."

Lancaster spent much of his thirties looking around for his next baseball job. The independent leagues, which had sprung up all over the country in the 1990's, always enabled him to find work. So would the Italian baseball league, at Bologna. Lancaster also ranked as one of the few part-owners of a team who pitched for that club at the same time.

But more about the owner-pitcher a little later. How does a workhorse reliever with a healthy rubber arm, still in his early 30's, not get called up to help fill out a bullpen during the chronic big-league pitching shortage? Perhaps it was a matter of numbers, or perception, or baseball politics or bad timing. Whatever, it started Lancaster on his journeys throughout the lower rungs of pro baseball.

After the Cubs released Lancaster in the spring of 1992, he spent the next two seasons with the Detroit Tigers and St. Louis Cardinals, respectively. In fact, Lancaster's 1993 Cardinals' line was very good: a 4-1 record and 2.93 ERA in 50 games setting up Lee Smith, another one-time Cubs teammate.

But with payrolls being slashed in advance of the strike, Lancaster found himself at Triple-A Syracuse in the Toronto Blue Jays' chain in 1994. He never got a callup. The World Series–bound Cleveland Indians were always in need of pitching, but Lancaster was stuck at their Triple-A affiliate in Buffalo for 1995.

"In 1996, I thought we had a Triple-A deal with the Astros, but John Hudek was sent down and took that spot," Lancaster recalled.

Believing his options in this country were nearly exhausted, Lancaster looked overseas for work. He hooked up with a pro team in Taipei, Taiwan, to start the 1996 season. But he left after three weeks with his body sore and his tongue hanging out.

"I thought I was in football practice," he said of the rigorous Taiwanese workouts. "They wanted pitchers to throw off the mound every day."

Lancaster quickly latched on to Oaxaca in the Mexican League.

LES LANCASTER
PREMIERE EDITION   1996

Even minor-league managers get themselves on baseball cards. Lester Lancaster was no exception as he bounced around the independent leagues. Card courtesy of Lester Lancaster.

"I enjoyed myself," he said. But at the same time, he found out about independent baseball, then just starting to sprout in the smaller cities of the United States.

"I got on the internet, looked at baseball stuff," he said. "I saw this team in Pine Bluff, Arkansas. I went ahead and called the general manager. He was excited because I went to the University of Arkansas."

Leaving Mexico in the middle of the 1996 season, Lancaster hired on as pitching coach and starting pitcher for the Big South League team. After one season, he came upon a more interesting opportunity one state over. A group was trying to put together a Big South League team in Tupelo, Mississippi, the birthplace of Elvis Presley. Native-born Texan Lancaster gravitated toward the project because his father's side of the family hailed from Mississippi.

All the while, Lancaster kept sending personal letters to big-league teams, but nothing came of the queries. He had fired his agent, who he thought wasn't serving him well.

"The only GM who took the time to talk to me was [the Astros'] Gerry Hunsicker," Lancaster said. He did not hear back from Cubs GM Ed Lynch, yet another of his ex-teammates from Chicago.

The Tupelo ownership group, running a team they christened

the Tornado, formed with Lancaster a minority investor. He put $10,000 into the team. At age 35, he also worked in the starting rotation. Lancaster was unaware of any other pitcher-owners in modern baseball history. He had additional duties as assistant general manager and sales and marketing director.

But as 1997 proceeded, the Tupelo venture was not catching on. "The GM was aggressive and cocky, and people in town were laid-back," Lancaster said. "It bit us on the backside."

Lancaster did not stick around to see the team continue to flounder in 1998. A recruiter for Bologna of the Italian League inquired about a Tupelo pitcher. "He also asked if I was interested in pitching," Lancaster said.

"The scenery was outstanding," he said. "The Italian teams played only three games a week, so I started once a week. They're allowed two imports [foreign players] each. At the time, they were still using aluminum bats. Now they're using wooden bats. I'd say there were three to four good players on each team, and they could compete on a daily basis with a Double-A team."

Later in 1998, Lancaster came home to the Northern League, the top independent baseball circuit, with the Adirondack Lumberjacks in Glen Falls, N.Y. He took over as manager for the last nine games while pitching in a handful of contests.

"I didn't think it would be something I'd get into at first," Lancaster said of managing. "But I had paid attention to the game and learned a lot. It hit home that I could help develop young talent. I could watch a pitcher's appearance on the mound, and know how he felt by the way he acted and his facial expressions."

Independent-league managers do not get wealthy. Salaries range from $20,000 to $60,000. "They still pay better than a lot of minor-league managing jobs," Lancaster said.

The Lumberjacks played well under pitcher-manager Lancaster. They reached the Northern League East playoffs in 1999. Adirondack went further, winning the league championship in 2000 as Lancaster threw a complete-game shutout in the championship series. He was named *Baseball America's* Independent League manager of the year.

But 2000 also was the year his big-league dreams were finally started to fade away.

"I had a few scouts check me out, but they all wanted me to

try out," he said. "I didn't want to do that. Nobody gave me an opportunity. Pitching up there is ridiculous. Everybody can throw a fastball down the middle."

Despite the league title, Lancaster sought a change of pace in one role only, on the mound, for the Northern League's Lincoln (Nebraska) Saltdogs in 2001. But he was soon pressed into service running the team. Manager Kash Beauchamp was arrested on a misdemeanor assault charge and suspended. Lancaster was promoted to the manager's job immediately after returning from a week's leave to see his ailing father. Lancaster continued on the job throughout 2002 as the Saltdogs made the playoffs.

However, Lancaster was on the move again after the season. "The owner and I had different theories on handling players," he said. "He didn't know anything about baseball. I wasn't going to change my theories."

Lancaster returned to his native Texas for the next season. A new team, the Coastal Bend Aviators in the Central League, had formed in Corpus Christi. Lancaster drove up to the 2002 baseball winter meetings in Nashville, landing the managing job on the spot.

He tried to help a couple of ex-Cubs. After he signed Walton, the 1989 National League rookie of the year, the vagabond center fielder did not return Lancaster's calls and disappeared into the general populace. Meanwhile, Lancaster engineered a trade for baseball greybeard Hall from the Springfield/Ozark Mountain Ducks. Hall hit well, but was released halfway through the season due to salary constraints.

Finally, Lancaster tired of playing politics with the front office. The Aviators were part of a group that owned four different teams, and the out-of-town management structure was not to his liking. He came home to Alabama, where his wife, Candice, had been transferred for her job.

With his pitching days finally at an end, Lancaster could look back with satisfaction. He was signed by the Cubs as a non-drafted free agent in 1985, had a seven-year major-league career and then another decade of pro baseball. But it's the people that made the biggest impression on him.

"I was able to play with a lot of great players," he said, citing the likes of Maddux and Rafael Palmeiro.

Maddux, Palmeiro and Lancaster were Cubs rookies together in

1987. Oddly enough, Lancaster out-pitched Maddux, the team's No. 2 draft pick in 1985, by going 8-3 in 27 games (18 starts) compared to Maddux's horrible 6-14 record and 5.61 ERA. Then he thought he might have a shot at the closer's job for 1988 when Lee Smith was traded at the 1987 winter meetings. But the Cubs signed an overripe Goose Gossage instead. Lancaster spent much of 1988 setting up for the struggling Gossage, adding five saves of his own.

Lancaster had one hole in his game. He always struggled in spring training. Such problems cost him a big-league roster spot in 1989. He was sent to Triple-A Iowa to straighten himself out as a starter. Recalled near mid-season, he thought he'd continue starting. But he pitched four innings in relief of Rick Sutcliffe in one game. Manager Don Zimmer then put Lancaster in middle relief. Soon he was promoted to setting up erratic closer Mitch "Wild Thing" Williams.

Lancaster got into the best groove of his career. As the Cubs took over first place in August, he was spotless in the seventh and eighth innings as his own scoreless streak mounted. Eventually he broke Warren Brusstar's shutout streak by $1/3$ of an inning, totaling $30^2/3$ scoreless innings.

"When I got into the mid-twenties, people started telling me about the streak, how far I had to go to break the record," he said. "I knew eventually I'd have to give up a run. I didn't want to it to be a game-winning run."

He ended up with one of the stellar lines in Cubs' relief annals: a 1.36 ERA in 44 games with a 4-2 record and just two homers allowed in $72^2/3$ innings.

Lancaster faltered a bit in the 1989 National League Championship Series against the Giants. He had an ERA of 6.00 in six innings, ranking as the losing pitcher in Game 3 on October 7 in San Francisco. Lancaster served up a game-winning two-run homer to Robby Thompson in the seventh inning that wiped out a 4-3 Cubs lead.

The positive momentum of the '89 season ended right there in the playoffs. The rest of the pitching staff took a big nosedive in the first half of 1990 as the previous year's momentum was gone. Lancaster suffered from overwork during a 9-5 campaign. Eventually, Zimmer had to rest him. "Later in the year, he told the other pitchers he didn't care if their arms fell off, I was going to get a rest," he said.

Lancaster had his share of confrontations with Zimmer, who was hardly the cuddly baseball elder of his later Yankees coaching years. Many Cubs of the era were on the receiving end of Zimmer tongue-lashings.

"Zim felt there was a certain way the game should be played," Lancaster said. "He wanted you to give everything you got. He was an in-your-face type of guy. He didn't joke around as much as he did as a coach."

Bolstering Lancaster's confidence on the mound were the presence of Andre Dawson and Ryne Sandberg behind him in right field and at second base, respectively. Dawson and Sandberg are All-Century Cubs for good reason.

"The one guy I do respect more than anyone I played with was Dawson," Lancaster said. "The preparation [for his surgery-scarred knees] he had to do before a game was unbelievable. He'd stretch, do running, take grounders, and handle fly balls. He tried to work with Walton and [Dwight] Smith on that stuff.

"There were only two times when I saw Andre get upset. The first was when he was hit in the face by Eric Show. The other time was when he got into it with [plate umpire] Joe West, when Andre threw all those bats out of the dugout."

Lancaster had a good year as a swingman between the bullpen and rotation in 1991, going 9-7. A new regime headed by GM Larry Himes and manager Jim Lefebvre came in the following season, but they were unaware of Lancaster's history of bad springs. Lancaster was sent down to Iowa, and then soon released out of the organization.

"Himes and Lefebvre didn't know me," he said. "I stayed in Arizona a week, devastated by it. Then Sparky [Anderson] called me to pitch for the Tigers. People in the Cubs organization knew I wasn't going to sit on the bench and collect a paycheck."

Many of the home-grown players who provided the Cubs hope for the future in 1989 were gone by the middle of Himes' tenure in 1994. Lancaster still regrets that team had no staying power.

"They got rid of everybody too quick," he said. "We were all young. You've got to give them a couple of seasons together."

Few of those Gordon Goldsberry–developed Cubs would go on to rack up the journey of Lester Lancaster. Baseball's a tough, unforgiving game of failure, but it can provide a variety of life experiences not seen elsewhere. And Lancaster's still soaking them up even as his travels slow down.

Gone but Not Forgotten

Vince Lloyd

Seemingly a thousand stars speckled the late-winter sky one night in 2002 above Green Valley, Arizona, a retirement community thirty miles south of Tucson. Vince Lloyd stepped outside with a visitor, looked up briefly, and pondered the symbolism.

It was as if all his old friends were looking down, blissfully elevated to a higher plane of existence yet happy that Vinnie, as he was known to countless friends, was still in corporeal form to tell all the stories, carry the torch, and keep that spark of youthful days kindling in all who grew up listening to their broadcast descriptions of Cubs baseball.

Lloyd, eighty-four, was the sole surviving member of that legendary WGN on-air crew. One by one those names left us. Jack Quinlan died too young at thirty-eight in an auto accident. Jack Brickhouse, Harry Caray, and Lou Boudreau were far luckier, living full lives and reaching their eighties. Arne Harris, the behind-the-scenes maestro of the video side of it all, was still making magic pictures when he dropped suddenly at sixty-nine at the side of Chip Caray, waiting for a dinner table just before the end of the 2001 season.

In his honored senior citizenship, Vince Lloyd, after describing a lot of heartache yet more than a fair share of on-field nobility behind the Cubs TV and radio mikes from 1950 to 1986, would never be alone. The former Myrt Giblin had come into his life as his second wife just two years earlier. Vinnie's family, first based in his native South Dakota before scattering all over the country, were always attentive and loyal. He could spend all day talking on the phone or visiting with chums if he wanted.

Yet those friends from the booth—also buddies at the card table, on the team plane, at the race track, in the gym—couldn't be replaced.

Back inside, Lloyd took some puffs on his trademark pipe at his kitchen table.

"I think about it from time to time," he said as Myrt gently squeezed his arm. "I miss those guys. I miss them terribly. But death is inevitable. We all know that. I just feel fortunate I've been around as long as I have. Twenty years ago, living to sixty-five, I thought I'd be lucky. Seventy or seventy-five was unthinkable."

The memories kept flowing. His friends spoke through Vinnie now. Their broadcast calls, the fun they had that was so easily translated to their fans at home, wouldn't soon be forgotten.

"I think about all those guys, wonderful memories we did, not just broadcasts, but things we did away from the microphone," Lloyd said. "I cherish the memories of each one of those men, and I think I'm as lucky as any can be to have worked with them and to have been friends with them.

"What more can you ask?"

You can ask to live forever, but that wish can't ever be granted. Another visit to the Lloyd household exactly a year later in 2003 provided a more disturbing image of Vinnie, still possessed of rich voice and storytelling mind yet considerably slowed and much more infirm. He would rally long enough to make the 170-mile drive with Myrt to be with Ron Santo at his Scottsdale home on the day he found out the Hall of Fame was still barred to the ol' third baseman.

And on July 4, 2003, while the Cubs and Cardinals were dueling at Wrigley Field in the type of atmosphere that used to bust Lloyd's vocal chords, the news came that he had passed away. You pushed yourself to cover the game, but you also knew that more of your childhood, of your spirits soaring as Lloyd screamed "Holy mackerel!" over a Billy Williams homer, was being purged.

But even as you aged and grayed, you would not forget. And for those whose memories weren't as firm, there was Myrt with what her husband left behind in Green Valley. Best of all, there were all of Vinnie's nephews, who waged a campaign to get their favorite uncle honored with the Ford Frick Award, the highest for a baseball announcer.

Longtime baseball executive Roland Hemond (left) with Vince and Myrt Lloyd
at a spring training game in 2002. Photo courtesy of Myrt Lloyd.

Another visit to Green Valley during spring training 2004 revealed the same tidy house without one half of the spirit inside. Myrt was there, to be sure, her love torn away by life's cycle yet bolstered by the same family and friends that enveloped her late husband.

Myrt opened Vinnie's cigar humidor. Engraved was the date "January 2, 1966" along with the initials "VLS." Remember, his given name was Vince Lloyd Skaff. But in the 1940s, a young announcer breaking into the business Anglicized any ethnic-sounding last name. Many great voices used their middle names as stage names.

Myrt had gotten to know Lloyd when she worked in the accounts receivable department for United Airlines, always closely entwined with the Cubs, in the 1960s. The airline enabled Myrt and husband Lawrence "Gib" Giblin to travel around the National League to follow the Cubs.

"We would meet Vince, Lou [Boudreau] and Jack Brickhouse in the bars after the games," Myrt said. "After awhile, they said, 'Don't buy tickets. We'll send them out for you.'"

She lost touch with Lloyd over the next few decades. "Gib" Giblin died in 1990. Four years later, Myrt called Lloyd when she heard he was filling in for an ill Harry Caray on WGN-Radio Cubs broadcasts. A few years after that, Lloyd called her, telling her his own wife, Miriam, was very ill. After Miriam died in 1999, Lloyd asked Myrt if she wanted to buy Miriam's Oldsmobile. He drove the car to her Tucson-area home.

"I was lonesome and he was lonesome," Myrt said. The two fell in love and were married on June 10, 2000.

"Vince's family said they'd never seen him so happy," she said. "Friends in Sioux Falls said he had aged because of Miriam's illness. They said, 'Don't you get old with him.' I told them, 'Don't worry, I'll get him young.' I think I did. He said it was time for bed. I told him no it wasn't.

"I think life with him was perfect from the start. I thought the world of him for years. We would laugh about Jack Brickhouse. My husband said Jack had fishhooks in his pocket. Jack would put his hands in his pockets and get his hands stuck. But Vince always picked up the tab and never took a freebie.

"He cared for people. He thought people were wonderful. I never saw him turn away an autograph. He'd stand there and talk for an hour with fans. It makes me all choked up."

The consolation, if any, was his status as beloved Uncle Vinnie. The family would come together as never before in the months after his death.

"[His nephews] idolized him, and they've been wonderful to me," Myrt said. "I cherish them. I don't have a big family. They are so openhearted and so welcoming—they're out of this world. I'm so happy they love me and accept me like they do."

The nephews did far more than just accept Myrt into their lives. In the months following their uncle's death, nephew Rich Williams, a San Francisco Bay Area resident, organized his cousins in an effort to get fans to nominate Vince Lloyd as a candidate for the 2004 Ford Frick Award. A baseball announcer is honored annually with the award at the Hall of Fame induction ceremonies in Cooperstown. But for 2004, fans had the chance to nominate a candidate via Internet voting.

Williams, cousin Vince Skaff, and others called newspapers and broadcast outlets while alerting fans on the Cubs.com website. The effort was noble but fell short. Longtime Giants announcer Lon Simmons got the Frick nod.

Williams would not have done any less after all those memories of Uncle Vinnie.

"All the times we'd meet up with him at the Sheraton and Jack Tar hotels in San Francisco when the Cubs were in town," he said. "We'd have breakfast with the team and be introduced to all the greats—Don Kessinger, Ron Santo, Billy Williams, Ferguson Jenkins, Bill Buckner, Ernie Banks, Joe Pepitone and so many others. And being able to be in the broadcast booth during their broadcast of the game. To a kid, which I was at the time, being ten to eighteen years old, it was the greatest moments which I could ever be exposed to."

The family got together again the night before Lloyd's funeral in Sioux Falls, South Dakota.

"We had dinner and I had brought a baseball that I was originally going to have my uncle sign at the upcoming family reunion," Williams said. "I had suggested that we all sign the ball, add our sentiments, and have it placed in the casket with him. So he would have something to remember us by and take with him. Everybody loved the idea and began signing the ball."

With the ball in the casket, the funeral took place with full military honors and a twenty-one-gun salute. Vince Lloyd Skaff was confident as a broadcaster but also proud to have been a U.S. Marine in World War II.

"What I will miss the most is his smile," Williams said. "His special laugh, his big warm hugs and kiss on the forehead, his gentle and peaceful ways about him, his respect and thoughtfulness towards all his fans, friends and family.

"But mostly his unconditional love."

Kenny Hubbs

Sometimes not even death can sever the bonds of brotherhood.

Kenny and Keith Hubbs were as close as siblings ever could be.

"We were brothers who hugged each other," Keith said.

Kenny Hubbs in his prime as a Cub.
Photo courtesy of Keith Hubbs.

So when Kenny Hubbs took flying lessons in 1963, overcoming an initial fear of flight, it was natural that Keith would follow suit. Keith even soloed in his brother's plane. But on a fateful day, February 13, 1964, Keith elected not to go with Kenny and friend Dennis Doyle on a flight from Provo, Utah, to their native Colton, California.

Overtaken by a snowstorm, Kenny lost his airborne bearings and crashed into an icy lake two miles short of the Provo airport in a desperate attempt to return safely. He and Doyle were killed. The Cubs lost a promising second baseman, and the Hubbs family lost their wunderkind, both as an athlete and an outstanding citizen of the world.

Or did they? Keith Hubbs, now sixty-five, has his Mormon faith that sustains him daily, teaching him that families will be happily reunited in the hereafter. And he has his own personal testimony that his brother never left in spiritual form. It's a story he only told within family circles until now.

"After Kenny was killed, we were at our parents' [Eulis and Dorothy Hubbs] house—we spent the first three nights there," he said. "Doctors had to give our parents sedatives. For three nights in a row, I had terrible nightmares of the accident. I'd wake up in a sweat.

"The fourth night, back in my own home, I went to sleep. I had a different dream. I'm standing there. All I remember is a little distance away, Kenny's walking toward me. We don't hug. He stops short of us hugging. He says to me, 'Quit worrying about me. It was quick and it was no pain.' He turns and walks away.

"I never had the [crash] nightmare again."

But if Keith's anguish was somehow relieved by a message from his brother, real or in a dream, imagine the guidance the surviving Hubbs felt when he awaited assignment on his Mormon mission in early 2003. Out of all the places in the world to which he could have been assigned after being a lifelong resident of Colton, California, near San Bernardino, Hubbs ended up in the north part of the Chicago area. Scouting for an apartment, Keith and wife Roxie found some digs just one mile north of Wrigley Field. He had come home in an important way.

His brother earned acclaim as National League Rookie of the Year in 1962, racking up 418 consecutive chances and seventy-eight straight games without an error at second base. But it was in and around the Friendly Confines where Kenny Hubbs made such an impression as an individual that he was never forgotten forty years later.

Keith would see a Wrigley Field security guard, who would tell him of Kenny's kindness in signing autographs. He would see a White Sox fan on the street, clad in his team's colors, who told him that the South Side fans, to whom anything Cubs is usually anathema, liked his brother, too. And it was at Wrigley Field in 1954, on his way back from the Little League World Series, that Kenny Hubbs fell in love with the Cubs and a rookie shortstop named Ernie Banks.

"We sat behind the Cubs dugout," Keith said. "Kenny watched Ernie in awe. He was his first major-league hero. He became a shortstop, just like Ernie."

Just the fact that Kenny Hubbs had played in the Little League World Series at age twelve was a miracle in itself. That's why the Hubbs family hasn't walked around for decades feeling cheated that Kenny lived just twenty-two years and could have contributed so many positive things beyond sports just by living through middle age.

"At six months he was lucky to live," Keith said. "He had a ruptured hernia. They couldn't operate. He wasn't expected to live.

Keith Hubbs (left) and Joey Amalfitano with Kenny Hubbs's glove from 1963. Author photo.

From the time he was in diapers 'til first or second grade, he wore a big leather ball around his waist. The doctors said, 'You will have to watch him his whole life. He never will be able to do things other kids can do.'

"Maybe in hindsight, we had him for twenty-two years when we might not have had him for any. The hernia healed itself. Don't ask me how. He did end up doing things that other kids couldn't do. He was voted on the [youth baseball] All-Stars at nine.

"Basketball was his best sport. He could take one step and dunk it with both hands. The coach from an inner-city LA school Colton played said Kenny had the fastest hands he'd seen. He had football and basketball scholarships at twenty to thirty schools. He was the starting quarterback in the all-American football game in Memphis."

But Kenny passed up all the possible collegiate glory to sign with the Cubs. He was only nineteen when he made his Wrigley Field debut at the end of the 1961 season. He showed so much promise that despite a "sophomore jinx" .235 season in his second year, his teammates saw him as an infield cornerstone for a decade to come. Ryne Sandberg later was favorably compared defensively to Hubbs.

"Billy Williams told me that if he had lived, they not only would have made the World Series in 1969 but would have won it with Kenny," Keith said.

The promise was never fulfilled. But no way were the good citizens of Colton going to forget their favorite son. Six months after Hubbs's death, a foundation in his name was formed. Doubling as a real-estate broker in Colton, Keith Hubbs served as president from the foundation's beginning until the start of his mission in 2003.

"The purpose of the foundation is to not let his memory go," Keith said.

The foundation initially had grand dreams of constructing a youth center in Colton. "But after awhile, they forget. The money stops coming in," Keith Hubbs said. Scaling back their goals, Hubbs and his colleagues began giving scholarships to graduating San Bernardino–Colton area athletes in the name of Kenny Hubbs. Eventually, the NCAA intervened, upset that athletes were double-dipping when they already were receiving athletic scholarships.

Starting in 1972, the foundation gave senior winners of the Ken Hubbs Award an engraved watch. Out of all the school winners, one was chosen Ken Hubbs Athlete of Year. Most prominent was future 49ers All-Pro safety Ronnie Lott, from Eisenhower High School in Rialto. Twenty years later, Lott's son, Ryan Nace, also won the award. Future NBA players Bryon Russell and Shawn Rooks also were similarly honored.

An even more permanent way of honoring Hubbs took place after Keith found his brother's old Cubs bag zipped up in a closet in his parents' home. "I hadn't looked at it in forty years," he said. Calling the Hall of Fame in Cooperstown, he arranged for the glove that Hubbs used to set his fielding records in 1962, along with the record-busting ball, to be displayed at the Hall. Keith Hubbs presented the glove and ball to the Hall at the FanFest that was part of the All-Star festivities at U.S. Cellular Field in 2003.

"People touched it," Keith said. "They trucked it in an air-conditioned vehicle all the way to Cooperstown. They made me a lifelong member of the Hall of Fame. It's better [for it] to be preserved for generations to come."

But some memorabilia is still in the family's hands, such as Hubbs's bat and his Little League uniform. So is his last glove, used in 1963. Keith Hubbs brought the glove to Wrigley Field on August 13, 2004, two years after the family had appeared at the ol' ballpark as part of a Kenny Hubbs rookie card replica giveaway day.

After a whole bunch of pressbox types crowded around to examine the glove, Keith showed the Rawlings-produced artifact to Cubs radio announcer Ron Santo, who in his early third-base glory years was Kenny's roommate and close confidant on the Cubs. In the back of the pressbox before the game with the Los Angeles Dodgers, Santo tried on the glove, pounded its pocket with his left fist and grinned at the reminder of his youth.

"I can't tell you how much our family admires what you've done and what you've meant to the Cubs," Keith told Santo.

Keith Hubbs and Ron Santo at Wrigley Field with Kenny Hubbs's glove from 1963. Author photo.

A few minutes later Keith went down to the field to show the glove to Joey Amalfitano, a Dodgers special consultant. Amalfitano's connection was as Kenny's successor at second base for the Cubs in 1964. Former Cubs manager-turned-Dodgers bench coach Jim Riggleman, whose own brother had sung the praises of Hubbs the second baseman way back when, also handled the glove.

Soon it was time to part, with Keith Hubbs joining a group of kids he had brought to the ballpark. The normal downtime in a ballgame was as good a chance as any to teach the kids a lesson about striving to become like his brother.

"The really great athletes are those who work like they were the worst athlete," he said.

The kid who wasn't supposed to live, who in Keith Hubbs's view will only be separated from him by mortal life, set a good example that will somehow never be purged from Wrigley Field.